PENGUIN

THE AR

Richard Du Cann was born, against the regulations, in Gray's Inn, one of the four Inns of Court. He has been interested in the law ever since. He was educated at Steyning Grammar School, Sussex, and Clare College, Cambridge.

He has reconstructed a number of trials and written plays with legal settings for the BBC. He was appointed Queen's Counsel in 1975. He has been Chairman of the Criminal Bar Association (1977–9), Chairman of the Senate and Bar Council (1980–81) and has been a Recorder of the Crown Court since 1982.

He is married with four children.

Richard Du Cann

The Art of the Advocate

REVISED EDITION

PENGUIN BOOKS

To my one and only wife

PENGUIN BOOKS

Published by the Penguin Group
Penguin Books Ltd, 27 Wrights Lane, London w8 5TZ, England
Penguin Books USA Inc., 375 Hudson Street, New York, New York 10014, USA
Penguin Books Australia Ltd, Ringwood, Victoria, Australia
Penguin Books Canada Ltd, 10 Alcorn Avenue, Toronto, Ontario, Canada M4V 3B2
Penguin Books (NZ) Ltd, 182–190 Wairau Road, Auckland 10, New Zealand

Penguin Books Ltd, Registered Offices: Harmondsworth, Middlesex, England

First published 1964
Reprinted with revisions 1980
Revised edition published 1993
014

Typeset by Datix International Limited, Bungay, Suffolk
Filmset in 10/11¼ Monophoto Baskerville
Printed in Great Britain by Clays Ltd, St Ives plc

www.greenpenguin.co.uk

Penguin Books is committed to a sustainable
future for our business, our readers and our planet.
This book is made from Forest Stewardship
Council™ certified paper.

Contents

Contents

Preface

> 'Where shall I begin, please your Majesty?'
> asked the White Rabbit.
> 'Begin at the beginning,' the King said gravely,
> 'and go on till you come to the end: then stop.'
>
> LEWIS CARROLL:
> *Alice's Adventures in Wonderland*

The King's advice should guide both an advocate and a reader. Since the subject of this book is the limited field of forensic advocacy and does not stray out of the courtroom it is tempting to begin by asking why men become advocates at all. What is it that attracts them to meddle with bits and pieces of other men's lives? It would be pleasant to think that most advocates come into practice because they wish to serve their fellow men, but the likelihood is that such social zeal influences as many grave diggers as it does advocates. There is probably no common-denominational inducement. Carson became an advocate because of parental pressure; Rufus Isaacs only after he had been hammered on the Stock Exchange; Marshall Hall originally intended to enter the Church and changed his mind solely because he wanted to have enough money to get married. No three men of the same generation (they were born within six years of each other) could have been more dissimilar, yet all three rose to the front rank of the profession.

This book tries to explain why. To do so I have drawn from cases tried during the last two hundred years of as widely differing a nature as possible, libel, assault, shipwreck, murder, and witchcraft to list a few, and involving advocates of every quality. To provide continuity throughout the book in the first edition I chose two cases, a libel, *Laski* v. *The Newark Advertiser Co. Ltd*, and a murder, *Rex* v. *Gardiner*, usually called the Peasenhall murder, the name of the Suffolk village where it occurred, the short facts of which are set out in the Prologue. These two cases are import-ant in any study of the art of the advocate, for both are widely regarded as miscarriages of justice brought about, at least in part, by the intervention of the particular advocates engaged in them, and in the Laski case additionally by the Judge who tried the case.

Warren Burger, the former Chief Justice of the United States of America, described the trial process as like a three-legged stool, with the Judge and both advocates, one for the plaintiff or prosecution, the other for the defence, each forming one of the legs. It was only, he said, if each leg was of equal length and equal strength that the stool was fit for use and the trial process would work properly. Like all pieces of homespun philosophy this has more than a grain of truth to it. Yet, although all advocates are equal before the law, in court they continuously flaunt their own inequalities. The lawyer regards this with indifference, even when the result of it is reflected in a verdict, since it is to some extent inevitable. Caught in the twin vices of tradition and precedent the advocate pursues his calling, and his prey, in a manner which has not changed basically for 200 years. He knows that if the system were to be changed merely to guard against disparities in skill in advocacy it would lose more than it would gain.

In part to show how little the system has changed and to show how other systems might operate, I have in this second edition added a third case, or series of cases, the proceedings in four different courts arising from the sinking of the ferry *Herald of Free Enterprise* outside Zeebrugge harbour in Belgium in March 1987 with the loss of 192 lives. This allows one to see how the approach of the advocate, his language and style, and the range of powers given to him can differ according to the nature of the tribunal in which he is appearing. Since this case is much more recent than Laski (1946) and Peasenhall (1903) one can also see how little his methods have changed throughout this century. Again the short facts of the *Herald* are set out in the Prologue.

Few laymen realize how extensive, indeed how dominant, are the powers given to the advocates on the two contending sides in our adversarial system. It is these powers which have given a special place to advocacy in our common law trial system in both civil and criminal courts. On the criminal side in all the Continental systems, the accusatorial approach is adopted where the Judge dominates the proceedings. The Judge decides which witnesses shall be called, often beginning the trial with questions to the accused person. The prosecutor may even sit with the Judge on the bench, playing, outwardly at least, a minor role in the proceedings. In our system the Judge presides somewhat like a referee on the football field, blowing his whistle from time to time for an infringement but not actually kicking the ball himself save in very limited or exceptional circumstances. In such a climate advocacy flourishes. In the succeeding pages the reader will find some of the most brilliant flowers which this climate has nurtured. He may find one or two weeds as well. If the system were changed these might be eradicated. But to curb the natural abilities of the advocate would at the same time rob him of his independence and freedom which are the real strengths of the English system, and it would assuredly rob him of his individuality which is one of its fascinations.

Prologue

(1) *Laski v. The Newark Advertiser Co. Ltd and Parlby*

On Saturday, 16 June 1945, at the height of the General Election, Professor Harold Laski addressed a crowd of over five hundred people from the back of a lorry in the market-place of Newark in Nottinghamshire in support of the local Labour candidate. He spoke for about three quarters of an hour. After the meeting had ended and as he was about to leave, a journalist, Mr Wentworth Day, shouted out an offensive question to Laski which included the suggestion that Laski had been guilty of cowardice by remaining in America during the war. He also asked why Laski had 'openly advocated revolution by violence' in speaking on two other occasions. Under the heading 'Reference to Violence', the *Newark Advertiser* (Mr Parlby being Editor and Managing Director) reported Laski's reply as: 'As for violence, he continued, if Labour could not obtain what it needed by general consent, "We shall have to use violence even if it means revolution".' Laski maintained that his reply was completely different in meaning, that what he had said was in support of 'revolution by consent', and that a drift to revolution by violence because the opportunity was not taken to make the great changes needed in the country would be a disaster.

In addition to being Professor of Political Science at London University, Laski was also Chairman of the National Executive Committee of the Labour Party. He had already been criticized for attempting to dictate policy to the leader of the Labour Party, so that when a report of his words in the form used by the *Newark Advertiser* reached London they were seized upon by the right-wing press as a stick with which to beat their political drum. On 20 June Laski issued writs for libel against the London newspapers, and on the 22nd against the *Newark Advertiser*.

The Statement of Claim alleged that the report was false and malicious, that, by innuendo, the report meant and was understood to mean that Laski had declared his intention to commit and to conspire with others to commit the crimes of treason, treason-felony, sedition, riot, and breach of the peace (i.e. all the crimes a man would commit if he raised a revolution), and that Laski had been thereby injured in his reputation. The defence claimed that the report was a fair and accurate one, and that the words did not mean what was alleged in the innuendo. Nine months later this defence was amended by adding the defence of justification, that is that the words set out in the report were true in substance and in fact. Particulars of the justification set out extracts from many of Laski's speeches, pamphlets, and books to support this claim that Laski had been preaching 'revolution by violence' at Newark as he had throughout his active life.

The action against the *Newark Advertiser* and Parlby was the first to be tried. It lasted five days. The jury took exactly forty minutes to decide that the report in the paper was a fair and accurate report on a matter of public concern. Because they came to this conclusion the jury did not go on to decide whether Laski had habitually advocated violence: their decision was simply a finding that he had used the words attributed to him at Newark.

The action was tried by Lord Goddard, then Lord Chief Justice of England. G.O. Slade, K.C., later Sir Gerald Slade and a Judge of the High Court, appeared for Laski. Sir Patrick Hastings, K.C., appeared for both defendants.

(2) *Rex* v. *William Gardiner*

On 1 May 1901, two youths, Wright and Skinner, saw William Gardiner and Rose Harsent go into the chapel at Peasenhall, a small village in Suffolk about twelve miles from Saxmundham. Gardiner was a married man in his late thirties, foreman of the local ironworks, and treasurer and choirmaster of the Primitive Methodist Congregation. Rose Harsent was seventeen and unmarried and worked 'living in' as a servant at Providence House about two hundred yards from the cottage Gardiner occupied with his wife and six children. The two youths claimed they heard Gardiner and the girl speaking inside in subdued voices, and the girl quoted an indecent verse from the Old Testament.

When the scandal reached the ears of the Superintendent Minister of the chapel an inquiry was held at which Gardiner and the girl denied the account given by Wright and Skinner. With two witnesses on either side no conclusion was reached by the inquiry, but Gardiner was allowed to continue in his positions in the chapel.

On the morning of 1 June 1902 the girl Rose Harsent was found dead at the foot of the stairs leading up to her room in Providence House. She had been stabbed in the heart and her throat had been cut. An attempt had been made by the murderer to burn the lower part of her body, which if it had been successful, would have hidden the fact that she was six months pregnant. Two days later Gardiner was arrested and charged with the murder.

The case against him was very strong. A letter was found in her room from someone making an arrangement to meet her at the house at midnight if she put a light in the window of her room at nine o'clock. An expert gave evidence that the handwriting was Gardiner's. The letter was inside a buff-coloured envelope of a kind used by Gardiner at the ironworks. A neighbour swore that at nine o'clock Gardiner was in the street outside his house where the window of the girl's room could be seen. A gamekeeper swore that when he passed Gardiner's house at four in the morning (the murder was committed at about one) he saw the tracks made by shoes with wide bars on the soles going from the house to Providence House and back. Gardiner owned a pair of shoes with wide bars on the soles. In his cottage was found a knife which had been recently cleaned but which bore traces of mammalian blood and which fitted the dimensions of the weapon causing death. In addition to Wright and Skinner, another witness, Rouse, claimed to have seen Gardiner and the girl continuing their association after the chapel inquiry. Beside the body were found the broken pieces of a bottle which had contained the paraffin with which the attempt to burn the body had been made. On one of the pieces was a label prescribing doses of medicine to be given to Gardiner's children. It was proved that the bottle had been given to Mrs Gardiner by the local doctor about six months previously. It was almost certain that the murderer was spattered with blood and no bloodstained clothing was found in Gardiner's cottage, but another neighbour, Stammers, swore that on the Sunday morning the body was found Gardiner had had an unusually large fire burning unusually early.

The extracts which are used here come from the report of Gardiner's second trial. The first jury to try him could not agree. Henry Dickens, K.C., later Sir Henry Dickens, Common Sergeant of London sitting at the Old Bailey, prosecuted. Ernest Wild, K.C., later Sir Ernest Wild, Recorder at the same court, defended. The second jury also failed to agree. The prosecution subsequently entered a *nolle prosequi*, and Gardiner was freed.

(3) *The Herald of Free Enterprise*

The *Herald* was one of a class of three ships, the 'Spirit' class, consisting of the *Spirit*, the *Herald* and the *Pride of Free Enterprise*, designed and built for the Townsend group of companies. Townsend owned over twenty ferries operating from English, Welsh and Scottish ports to Ireland and the Continent. The Spirit class ships were intended for the Dover–Calais crossing and the increasing lorry traffic passing through those ports. They were not beautiful ships. It was said they were no more than sophisticated 'powered pontoons on the top of which vehicles could be carried'. They were extremely efficient in operation and were ideal for the job they had to perform.

There were two through decks for vehicles, G and E, one above the other, which used with two-tier ramps permitted vehicles to be driven aboard at Dover through open doors at the stern on to both decks at the same time. All vehicles would be parked facing the bow doors, and then on docking at Calais they would be driven straight off via the ramps (adjustable to all states of the tide) on to the quay. The ships would then be loaded at Calais by the bow and the process repeated at Dover by docking at the stern. This system was called 'roll on, roll off', usually shortened to Ro-Ro. The ships were very fast and except in very bad weather could maintain a speed of 21 knots (about 25 mph) throughout the crossing. They were also very manoeuvrable: they could come to a stop from full speed ahead in no more than two and a half lengths, and to assist them in high winds experienced in the small enclosed waters of the two harbours they had propellers at both the bow and stern and 'thrusters', which by expelling air from vents at the bow allowed them to spin around their own length.

The most important doors to the bow at G deck, the deck immediately above the water line (depending on the weight of cargo about eight feet), were a clam type designed by a Scottish engineering firm. There were two pairs of double doors, the outer pair opening first in the centre then each half sliding back along the outside of the side or superstructure of the ship. When closed these doors formed the actual bow of the ship. The inner pair of doors were also of a clam type. They lay almost immediately inside the outer pair. When open the two halves pivoted back against the inside of the superstructure. The design was very effective and its operation very simple. In 60,000 crossings of the Channel undertaken by the three Spirit class vessels, major problems in closing the bow doors had been experienced on only a couple of occasions. They were believed to be very safe, much safer than the previous visor type, for with clam doors there was no danger in heavy seas.

In February 1987 the *Herald* was transferred to the Dover–Zeebrugge crossing to allow one of the other ferries regularly engaged on that run to go for an annual refit. There were some complications involved for the Spirit class vessels in doing this relief work. There was only a one-tier ramp for loading and unloading at Zeebrugge, so both operations took very much longer than ordinarily. Furthermore, at high tide and for two hours either side, the end of the loading ramp would not reach the upper loading deck, E deck, unless the ship had taken on many tons of sea-water ballast to keep the bow down, 'trimmed by the head' as it is known. The captains and crews of the Spirit class vessels were accustomed to dealing with these problems.

The *Herald* eased sternwards off the quay at 6.05 on the evening of 6 March 1987 using the bow propellers, then a touch from the port bow thruster to swing her head round in the inner harbour. On board were approximately 459 passengers, 80 crew, 81 cars, 47 freight vehicles and 3 miscellaneous vehicles. She passed the inner breakwater at about 6.20 pm and the outer mole 3 or 4 minutes later. The three main stern propellers were set at 'combination 6', which would increase her speed as she entered the Shuer Channel away from Zeebrugge to approximately 17 knots. It was a fine but bitterly cold night with a light easterly breeze. Visibility was unlimited, and there was very little sea or swell. But within minutes the *Herald* began to list to port while the ship took a course to starboard out of the channel. The helmsman reported that he had the wheel hard to port but could not control her. The list and the swerve continued until the ship settled on a sandbank on her port side facing back in the direction from which she had come with her starboard side above the waves. The capsize was complete in no more than three minutes.

At first no one other than the Assistant Bosun knew or even guessed at what had happened. Later that night as the tide fell, and in the daylight the following morning, it became plain to those at the scene and those at home watching on their television sets that somehow the *Herald* had gone to sea with the outer and inner bow doors fully open. As the shipping inquiry put it:

... thereafter, as speed built up, water entered on to the vehicle deck in large quantities and destroyed her stability. The ship then capsized rapidly.

192 people (154 passengers and 38 crew) lost their lives. It was the largest loss of life in the history of cross-Channel ferries. It caused near panic among people who were about to make a ferry crossing and the companies who ran the ferry services. Some 20 million passengers leave the United Kingdom by ferry each year.

Three days later, on 9 March, the Secretary of State for Transport used powers under the Merchant Shipping Act 1970 to order a formal investigation to be held by a Wreck Commissioner, in fact a High Court Judge from the Admiralty Division, sitting with four highly experienced and nautically qualified assessors. They sat in public for twenty-nine days starting within seven weeks of the disaster. Save when dealing with technical matters such as ship design, the atmosphere was electric. One witness called it intimidating, with intense and continuous press, radio and television coverage. The Commissioner issued the report of his findings on 24 July 1989.

Although the disaster took place in foreign waters, it involved the loss of British lives on a British-registered ship, so an inquest had to be held. It was formally opened at Dover, the home port of the *Herald*, on 10 March, before the formal inquiry had begun sitting, but no jury was panelled and no evidence was taken until after the close of the inquiry. It sat thereafter with a jury and heard evidence on twenty-three days between 7 September and 8 October 1987.

The jury returned a verdict of unlawful killing. Such a jury is not permitted to identify a person or persons who might be responsible for the unlawful killing, so the verdict clarified nothing but added fuel to comment from the press and the representatives of some of the survivors and those who had died that criminal proceedings for manslaughter should be brought against individuals and the Company.

On 9 December 1987 the Director of Public Prosecutions announced that he had ordered the Kent Police to undertake an inquiry into the loss of the *Herald*.

In July 1989 summonses for the crime of manslaughter were issued against three of the men who had been on board the *Herald* at the time: the Assistant Bosun, whose duty it was to close the bow doors, the Chief Officer, who should have supervised and/or observed the Assistant Bosun perform that task, and the Captain or Master of the *Herald* on the night of the disaster. Identical summonses were also issued against four other men: the Senior Master of the *Herald*, who had both a sea-going and shore-based role, and three who were wholly shore-based. It was said by the prosecution that these four with the Master constituted the mind of the Company, and since they too were guilty of manslaughter so also the Company was guilty, and a summons was similarly issued against the Company.

Before a trial in front of a jury on a charge of manslaughter can take place an examination of the evidence has to be made by a Magistrate in what are known as committal proceedings. These lasted for twenty-one days in December 1989 and January 1990. All the eight defendants, including the Company, were committed for trial at the Central Criminal Court, better known as the Old Bailey.

The trial itself took twenty-seven days, ending on 19 October

1990 when the High Court Judge Mr Justice Turner directed the jury to acquit all the defendants. The extracts which are used in this book are taken from the wreck inquiry, the Coroners' inquest, the committal proceedings and the eventual trial.

Chapter 1

Introduction

It would be foolish to pretend that lawyers excite nothing but respect and admiration from the public. The law troubles only those who are themselves in trouble, and it is not surprising that what Lord Simon, who rose to be Lord Chancellor of England, called a 'painful prejudice' should be created against those who appear to live on others' misfortunes. Doctors and funeral directors, against whom the same sort of unreasonable view might be taken, seem to escape from its most illogical strictures: but then they set out to please everyone, whereas the lawyer does not. In every quarrel there are at least two sides, but in every adjudication there can only be one successful party. Few men have the breadth of vision of Lynch who, after being condemned to death for treason, wrote of Carson, who had prosecuted him to conviction: 'He had done his part in condemning me to death, but these are not things that induce bad blood among men of understanding.' Fully half of those who have to resort to the courts come away dissatisfied and it is not surprising that the advocate's post should contain a good proportion of letters derogatory of his position and his powers. Professor Robson summed up the advocate's dilemma in this way:

A defeated client would abuse his own attorney for his ineptitude and his opponent's for his chicanery. His successful antagonist would resent having to pay for what he believed were his rights, and would harbour a grudge against his adversary's attorney for having subjected him to unnecessary delay and expense.

Yet in England, the right of a man to be represented in the courts, and the role of the advocate representing him, has been recognized since at least 1200. It has excited the cordial dislike of the layman ever since. In the Peasants' Revolt of 1381 more judges and lawyers were killed than any other single class of person. When the men of Kent reached London they first burnt down the house of the Lord Chancellor (the head of the English lawyers), then the Temple, the home of the advocate even then for over 200 years, and then broke into Newgate to free the prisoners. One disappointed chronicler described the escape of many lawyers from the flames:

It was marvellous to see how even the most aged and infirm of them scrambled off with the agility of rats or evil spirits.

This attitude has been faithfully represented in literature throughout the ages. Chaucer was only a little more kindly and Piers Plowman a good deal more rude. Both were subsequently supported by Montesquieu and Macaulay, Dickens and Dr Arnold, Thackeray and Trollope. Most of these criticisms of the lawyer need to be read in the context of the time at which they were written. When Jonathan Swift (1667–1745) wrote that lawyers were:

a society of men bred up from their youth in the art of proving by words multiplied for the purpose that white is black and black is white according as they are paid,

it must be remembered that honesty and decency were rarely found in those who held positions of power. Human life was then of so little value that his satire, 'A Modest Proposal', ostensibly directed to preventing the poor of Ireland using their children for food before they became a burden to them, had real point to it. It would be as misguided to judge the lawyer of today by the standards of the eighteenth century as it would be to take 'Bloody Judge Jeffreys' as representative of the present English Judiciary.

It was probably in the nineteenth century that the denigration of the lawyer reached its greatest height. The introduction of a great social legislative programme showed the country how deplorable were both the administration of the law and many of the laws themselves. As early as 1649 a member of the House of Commons had said that a man who was charged with an offence which was labelled a felony, which meant on conviction that the accused would be executed and all his property forfeited, should be allowed a lawyer to represent him on his trial in the same way

that a man accused of a lesser crime then known as a misdemeanour could be represented. He pointed out that on conviction for
the lesser crime no equally terrible penalties could be imposed,
and he said: 'A law to reform this would be just and give right to
the people.' This iniquitous rule, that a defendant accused of a
felony could not have a lawyer to cross-examine witnesses called
against him, or to make a speech to the jury, led to a series of
anomalous situations. The worst example is that of Elizabeth
Canning. In 1752, when she was eighteen years old, she disappeared in Aldermanbury Postern while walking through London
on the way home. She remained missing for a month. When she
reappeared she said she had been kidnapped by two men, taken
to a house some way out of London near the road to Hertford
where two old women had robbed her of her stays, asked her to
go 'their way' (unspecified), and kept her locked in an attic
room. After a month she had managed to escape. Mother Wells,
the owner of a house at Enfield Wash of dubious reputation, and
Mary Squires, a gipsy of unbelievable ugliness who was found in
the house, were arrested and tried at the Old Bailey for the
robbery of the stays. Robbery is a felony. Their counsel was
permitted to argue points of law but not to cross-examine, call
evidence, or make a speech on their behalf. (Neither of the
defendants was permitted to give evidence themselves.) The trial
lasted just one and a half hours. They were convicted and
sentenced to hang. The Lord Mayor of London was worried by
the verdict and ordered inquiries to be made. As a result of them
the sentence was respited and subsequently Canning was tried for
perjury. Perjury is a misdemeanour. All three of Canning's counsel made speeches to the jury, called evidence and cross-examined
the witnesses called against her. In 1695, forty-six years after the
speech already quoted, the rule was abolished in cases of treason.
But it was not until 1836, 141 years after that, by which time
England and Ireland were the only countries in the world still to
have the rule, that 'right was given to the people' and it was
abolished for all felonies.

Throughout the highly necessary reformative period of the
nineteenth century the pen of Dickens was savaging the law.
Debtors' prisons, the death penalty, the Chancery Division, and
every aspect of the criminal law, nothing passed unscathed. The

names of his lawyers – Jaggers, Stryker, Snitchey, Bounderby, Tulkinghorn and Sampson Brass – have an onomatopoeic loathing for their greed and glibness. Anthony Trollope's attorneys, Messrs Slow and Bideawhile and Round and Crook, evoke the same emotional distaste. Both authors spoke with the same powerful voice. Both reached a large and appreciative audience.

Bleak House and *Orley Farm* were published in monthly parts within ten years of one another: 1851 and 1861 respectively. In *Bleak House* Dickens comprehensively annihilated whatever respect the public had for the process of law in the Lord Chancellor's Court sitting in either Lincoln's Inn or Westminster Hall and for those who practised there. The lawyers 'play the system', refusing to take individual responsibility for it, or make any changes to it. They

do their duty, like a piece of timber, to shore up a decayed foundation that has become (for the litigant but not for them) a pitfall and a nuisance.

So the individual lawyer (in this case Mr Vholes, attorney to the bewildered and misguided Richard) looks at his client, 'as if he were making a lingering meal of him with his eyes as well as with his professional appetite', while the class of lawyer labelled barrister is

mistily engaged in one of ten thousand stages of an endless cause, tripping one another up on slippery precedents, groping knee-deep in technicalities, running their goat-hair and horse-hair warded heads against walls of words and making a pretence of equity with serious faces, as players might.

Dickens believed that he had identified the principle upon which the lawyer's capacity to mulct the public was based. He had worked for some years in an Attorney's offices in Gray's Inn and he did not hesitate to spell it out.

The one great principle of the English law is to make business for itself. There is no other principle distinctly, certainly and consistently maintained through all its narrow turnings. Viewed by this light it becomes a coherent scheme, and not the monstrous maze the laity are apt to think of it. Let them but once clearly perceive that its grand principle is to make business for itself at their expense and they will cease to grumble.

In *Orley Farm* Trollope chose a narrower target. Originally entitled *The Great Orley Farm Case*, the book's core remained the impending and then the actual trial of Lady Mason for perjury committed to hide her previous forgery of her husband's will. It allowed Trollope to concentrate on the defending lawyers, particularly the barristers, at work on the case: the dirty little Chaffenbrass, a goliath in his wig and robes at the Old Bailey, the naive, idealistic and inevitably young Felix Graham, and the mature and dishonest but outwardly respectable Furnival. Like Dickens, Trollope could be expected to display an above-average knowledge about the actual rather than assumed behaviour of the lawyer. His father was a practising barrister. Trollope wrote that his father possessed to a remarkable degree that characteristic which above all others infuriates the layman:

He was almost invariably – at least on a point of law – right. But the world differed from him in the opinion that being so gave him the right of rolling his antagonist in the dust and executing an intellectual dance of triumph on his prostrate form.

The following extract comes from Furnival's final speech to the jury on behalf of Lady Mason. It is followed by the author's comment, redolent with Victorian righteousness.

'And now I shall leave my client's case in your hands. As to the verdict which you will give, I have no apprehension. You know as well as I do that she has not been guilty of this terrible crime. That you will so pronounce I do not for a moment doubt. But I do hope that that verdict will be accompanied by some expression on your part which may show to the world at large how great has been the wickedness displayed in the accusation.'

And yet as he sat down he knew that she had been guilty! To his ear her guilt had never been confessed; but yet he knew that it was so, and, knowing that, he had been able to speak as though her innocence were a thing of course. That those witnesses had spoken truth he also knew, and yet he had been able to hold them up to the execration of all around them as though they had spoken the worst of crimes from the foulest of motives! And more than this, stranger than this, worse than this, when the legal world knew – as the legal world soon did know – that all this had been so, the legal world found no fault with Mr Furnival, conceiving that he had done his duty by his client in a manner becoming an English barrister and an English gentleman.

Trollope, like all authors before him and most authors since, ignored truth in favour of dramatic effect. No advocate since Erskine in the middle of the eighteenth century could state his own belief in his client's innocence without being immediately interrupted by the trial Judge. Further, the author's comment representing 'belief' as 'knowledge' so twists the advocate's duty to the court and his client as to be unrecognizable. (Both matters are further examined in Chapter 2.) The reader, however, carried along by the narrative in a state of elation at the subsequent acquittal of Lady Mason is left with a confirmed feeling of disgust at yet another example of the perfidy of the lawyer.

That such passages as these were and are widely believed to be accurate is largely the lawyer's own fault. His life is curiously divided between brief public appearances when he strides like a goliath treading with ill-disguised disdain on the lives of others, and long hours of lonely work on his briefs. In those hours of solitary study he learns the details of his client's case with what one lawyer called 'a minuteness and precision which passes far beyond the bounds of what is interesting or permanent'. The majority of this detailed drudgery will eventually prove to be useless. Much of it may prove to be of little importance during the trial itself, and little of it is of the slightest importance or interest once it is over. This gives rise to the justifiable complaint that: 'Lawyers' experience of human affairs is made up of an infinite number of scraps cut out of other people's lives. They learn, and do, hardly anything except through intermediaries.'

This presupposes that lawyers have no private lives of their own and are completely insulated from the realities of life. Some unfortunately are. The others pander to this belief by an everlasting questioning of the obvious. High Court Judges used to foster it by posing such questions as, 'what is a pin-up?', or by requiring proof that a number eleven bus goes past Victoria Station. Perhaps the most grotesque example occurred on the seventy-eighth day of the Tichborne case, the twentieth day of Dr Kenealy's speech to the jury. He was claiming that fat men (his client weighed twenty-six stone) were more stupid and forgetful than thin men when the Lord Chief Justice interrupted him:

L.C.J.: Is there any authority for that, that a man growing fat, his memory becomes impaired? . . .

A JUROR: There are fat men on the Jury.

L.C.J.: What do you say to Sergeant Wilkins?

KENEALY: I should have called him a large-boned man . . . I should be able to show on the whole that lean men are the cleverest men.

L.C.J.: There would be a division of opinion on that. The fat men would vote against you.

KENEALY: I have only to go to the Bench of England, and I am sure I should find that the great majority are lean rather than fat men.

L.C.J.: That is because they work so hard . . . If there are many more trials as this, we shall all become lean.

Lawyers are believed to love sycophantic scenes like this which add nothing to the proceedings except to their length, which the layman, who foots the bill, knows are long enough already. 'The law's delay' is one of the most common criticisms levelled at the lawyer. Chancery practitioners may be able to quote even more extraordinary examples than the legal battle over the will of a man who died in 1882 which was concluded in 1962, eighty years later. It involved no less than twelve major actions in the courts in that time, the legal costs of all the parties coming from the fast diminishing estate. Bentham, struggling to bring some reform to the intricacies of the procedure in the High Court, said:

The parties, unheard of and unthought of, pay their way through the offices [of the High Court] like half-starved flies crawling through a row of spiders.

Yet the law can be marvellously quick if a suitable reason is found. On a Monday in 1812 John Bellingham shot the Prime Minister of England in the lobby of the House of Commons. That night he was committed to stand trial at the Old Bailey. On the Friday he was tried (an attempt to secure an adjournment made by the defence being brushed aside by the Attorney-General as 'a contrivance to delay the administration of justice') and on the following Monday he was hanged by the neck until he was dead.

Most of the delays are seen by the layman as a means by which the lawyer lines his pockets. The Queen's Counsel who rejoiced that a claim over the sum of 35s. which went from the County Court to the Court of Appeal and then to the House of Lords, and which netted him over £200 in fees in the process, is seen as a typical example. That the lawyer is overpaid is as common a fallacy now as in the eighteenth century. Serjeant Davy's reply (in 1766) when rebuked for degrading the standards of the profession by accepting silver from a client instead of gold is thought to be typical of the lawyer's grasping nature:

I took silver because I could not get gold; but I took every farthing that he had, and I hope you do not call that disgracing the profession.

Serjeant Davy, who prosecuted Canning, and who was an ex-grocer from Exeter, was altogether too frank for the comfort of his fellow practitioners. He once told a jury:

You gentlemen who are on the outside of the curtain do not see the tricks and management within; we that are on the inside see the whole.

For this he was suitably rebuked by the Judges, who thought his remarks untrue. The public merely thought he had let the cat out of the bag, for the public, in the words of Sir John Simon, regard the lawyer

as an unprincipled wretch, who is constantly engaged in the unscrupulous distortion of the truth by methods entirely discreditable and for rewards grotesquely exaggerated.

He is expected to be a hypocrite, and if he is a successful one, he will be liberally paid for doing what was expected of him. If he is just, it is only because he has no temptation at that particular moment to be unjust. Aiming to avoid the creation of a class of men battening on the misfortunes of others in this way, the Greeks forbade the public employment of advocates. As a result even Socrates was obliged to deliver his own speech in his own defence. Almost 2,000 years later in 1690 (as David Pannick has recently pointed out) the framers of the first constitution of the State of Carolina followed the same precept when they prohibited the employment of paid advocates on the grounds that it was 'a base and vile thing to plead for money or reward'. Perhaps too they sought to shorten trials. The unhappy truth is that the lawyer incurs disapproval with every word he utters simply because he uses far too many of them. Disraeli was not far wrong when he said:

The legal mind consists in illustrating the obvious, explaining the self-evident, and expatiating on the self-evident.

Prolixity is practically the handmaid of the lawyer. It is a pity that the remedy of the Stuart Judges is not still in vogue. Then, so scandalized were they by the length of one set of pleadings (the written claim which must be submitted before a civil action can be heard in the High Court of Justice) that they ordered the offending draftsman to parade the courts with his head through the middle of them. Some Judges have made their individual protests heard. Lord Guildford, who sat during the reign of Charles II, could not tolerate speeches in his court. According to one contemporary report, when the evidence was concluded he would say: '"come make your speeches", and that looked with a sort of contempt on their talents, which gave them a distrust, and discomposed their extempore so much that for the most part they said, "No, we will leave it to Your Lordship".' Mr Commissioner Kerr (pronounced, and rightly so, 'cur') had the ledges in front of counsels' seats at the Old Bailey cut away so that they had nowhere to rest their papers. By this simple expedient, the length of speeches before him was always 'exceeding small'.

And the lawyer also courts disapproval by his frequently churlish and sometimes overbearing attitude towards those who have been forced, often much against their better inclinations, into contact with the law. Witnesses are bullied or abused, or, worse still, treated to an exhibition of the power of the cross-examiner which led Laski to write, after he had suffered at the hands of Patrick Hastings:

He performs his war dance about you like a dervish intoxicated by the sheer ecstasy of his skill in his own performance, ardent in his knowledge that, if you trip for one second, his knife is at your throat ... He moves between the lines of sarcasm and insult. It is an effort to tear off, piece by piece, the skin which he declares no more than a mask behind which any man of understanding could have grasped the foulness of your purpose. He treats you, not as a human being, but as a surgeon might treat some specimen he is demonstrating to students in a dissecting room.

Worst treated of all (though in a different manner) are those unlucky enough to be called on for jury service. They are flattered by the advocates, lectured by the Judge, and rarely given the most elementary information so as to enable them to reduce the burden which inevitably falls on those who are torn from their businesses for an unspecified time. Conditions have improved considerably since the end of the war: most jury rooms now have enough chairs for the jury to sit down while they are considering their verdict. If they are still poorly looked after it is entirely due to the bad administration of the court where they have been called on to serve, and because they have not made their opinion felt. After the Tichborne case had gone on for over a month the foreman of the jury begged some relief for himself and his companions. He asked the Lord Chief Justice if they might be excused sitting on Saturdays. Some of the jury, he said, had to do three hours' travelling to get to and from the court, others were the owners of one-man businesses. The Lord Chief Justice was horrified:

L.C.J.: Not to sit at all on Saturdays?
FOREMAN: To give us one day.
L.C.J.: You see, gentlemen, we would lose one sixth of our time.
FOREMAN: We lose five sixths of ours.

At the bottom of this welter of complaint and condemnation of the lawyer lie two immensely false impressions as to his role. Because his daily life deals with the law it is assumed that he is responsible for the state of the law. He is not. Although more reformers have come from the ranks of the law than from any other single class of persons, his duty is to see that in the courts the law is administered perfectly and not that the law itself is perfect. Secondly, because he deals in facts it is thought that he should be concerned with the discovery of truth. He is not. He is only concerned to see that the right conclusion is reached on the facts before the court. Those conclusions are reached on the evidence which is available, which sometimes has nothing to do with the truth at all.

The lawyer has done little to clear up these misunderstandings. It might even seem that the practice and profession of the law is surrounded by a mystique from which only that part has emerged which is unflattering to him. Until very recently, while privately regretting that this is so, he has taken no steps to remedy the position. Two examples may serve as illustrations. At a time when communications were very bad, the bulk of both criminal and civil work was done at the Assize towns. Four times a year the Judges set out from Westminster (where the High Court then was) on horseback to travel the seven circuits of England, the south-eastern, the western, the Oxford, the Midland, the Welsh, the north-eastern, and the north-western. Since the courts in London were closed the barristers flocked after them. To prevent them going only to those circuits where the pickings were for the moment richest, the rule was made that a barrister could only belong to and practise on one circuit. Eventually, it was realized that a client might have interests in more than one place in England, yet want one barrister to represent him in all of them. It was decided that he should be allowed free choice, provided he was willing to pay through the nose for it. If he wanted his advocate to go 'off his circuit' he had to pay him a special fee, and he had to pay another fee to another barrister from that circuit, junior to the first, who would, in all probability, sit behind the first twiddling his thumbs. Thus honour was satisfied: if the wealth was there to pay for it. Some benefits to the public were claimed on the grounds that the system encouraged the formation of 'local Bars' in cities outside London and kept down the fees of those who practised in the provinces, but the public's attention was focused on the restrictive practice mulcting them by way of excessive fees. The fact is that the system looked uncommonly like a tribal custom which should have disappeared with the coming of the railway engine instead of threatening to outlast the motor-car. Since this rule did not apply in the County Courts, which were not in existence when the circuit rules were made, many barristers admitted that the rule was illogical and the benefits illusory. Eventually, in 1965, it was abolished.

The second example is, perhaps, even more remarkable. At any time after he has been called to the Bar, a barrister is entitled to apply to the Lord Chancellor to hold the Queen's patent and dignity as one of Her Majesty's Counsel learned in the law. If granted, he may then place the letters Q.C. after his name and is obliged to wear a silk gown (hence the title 'silk' as an abbreviation: junior barristers of whatever age in years always wear stuff gowns) when appearing before Her Majesty's Judges. Probably the sole aspect of the practice of the 'silk' of which the public had general knowledge was that the silk was not permitted to appear in court without a junior, and that the junior had to be paid two-thirds of the leader's fee however substantial or insubstantial his activity during the trial. The two-thirds rule was abolished in 1964 and the rigid rule that silks must also have a junior in 1978. Until then the public were left to imagine that if the junior did not open his mouth in court he was merely busy trying to appear to be busy enough to justify his fee. They knew nothing of the ill-paid drudgery, for which the rule was some recompense in the preparation of the case, or how much more than mere presence at the trial it entails. In the eighteenth century, all the counsel briefed in a case made speeches. When Serjeant Davy prosecuted Canning for perjury he opened the case against her and so did both his juniors. Until quite recently juniors still 'opened the pleadings' in libel cases, the leaders making the full speech. At any moment in a case the leader may disappear and the junior have to carry on. Hastings is popularly, and mistakenly, supposed to have made his name when Carson, who was leading him in a libel case against Bob Sievier, was called to Ireland in the middle of cross-examining the plaintiff. As the reader will see from chapters later in the book he certainly earned his fee.

Taking silk is a mystery sometimes leading to misery. Sir John Simon said of it:

Taking silk consists of making one's head very hot in an absurdly large and heavy wig, and one's legs very cold with absurdly thin and very draughty stockings.

It can be said to be a penalty laid on ability, for it is only the advocate of considerable stature who can afford to run the risks involved. F. E. Smith and John Simon took the plunge together at the age of thirty-five. The youngest was twenty-nine. Whatever his age, his worth in the eyes of the solicitors must be such that he can command the fee of his junior as well as his own. Many juniors have bitterly regretted the promotion, finding that their solicitors have gradually deserted them and within a couple of years their income has shrunk alarmingly. But at the civil Bar the application for silk may be forced on the successful junior for it is only by escaping into silk that he can avoid the relentless and intolerable pressure of settling pleadings: work which professional rules ordain must be done by juniors. One silk described it as being 'a very simple process. You give up the practice you have got and begin again, and you run a very fair chance of incurring the risk of starvation'.

Both juniors and leaders also run the risk of starvation if their fees are not paid, for neither can sue for them. Since such a course would hardly be likely to endear him to the solicitor he sued, or prove a means of securing further employment from him it is not a step he would lightly take, even if it were practicable. The rule is a curious one and depends upon the fee being regarded as an honorarium and not evidence of a contract to secure a service. At first sight this may seem a substantial hindrance to the barrister, but as the layman instinctively knows, rules have yet to be thought of to defeat the ingenuity of the lawyer, and the other side of the coin is much more favourable to him. Since there is no contract between barrister and solicitor or between barrister and client, the barrister cannot be sued for incompetence in court. This may excite the envy of less fortunate men, but it is obvious that no advocate could be expected to perform under the peril of an action brought by any, or every, disgruntled client. Fully three quarters of all trial cases are decided on their own facts however able the intervention of the advocate. Simply because he failed to persuade a Judge or jury to adopt his client's case it would be impossible to decide that he bore a legal responsibility for the outcome of the case.

But the layman may say: the consumer deserves to be protected. The layman would be correct. In addition, it is not only the consumers in the sense of the parties to the case who deserve that protection. It is the public too who deserve that protection. It is the public who pay for the enormous edifice which is created by the civil and criminal court system. They have a direct interest in seeing that the system works properly. Section 13 of the Supply of Goods and Services Act 1982, which provides that an implied term shall be written into all contracts of service that the service will be carried out with 'reasonable care and skill', should apply. It does not. The Supply of Services (Exclusion of Implied Terms)

Order 1982 carefully excludes Section 13 from 'the services of an advocate in court or before any tribunal, inquiry or arbitrator and in carrying out preliminary work directly affecting the conduct of the hearing'. It excludes, too, 'services rendered to a company by a director of the company in his capacity as such'. The public will think of these as unusual, probably unattractive, bed-fellows.

Some clients have tried to sue their advocates. Lord Kenyon tried one of the first of such cases in 1790, with ill-disguised distaste, saying that he hoped it would be the last. It was not, he said, any contract which brought the advocate into court, but a duty (the detail of this is examined in Chapter 2)

... in the proper discharge of which not merely the client, but the Court in which the duty is to be performed, and the public at large have an interest.

Lord Kenyon's hopes were not fulfilled. A later action by a similarly disappointed client allowed Chief Baron Pollock to say:

... he is not responsible for ignorance of law, or any mistakes in fact, or for being less astute or less eloquent than he was expected to be.

Like many statements torn out of nineteenth-century judgments, this goes too far. Today all lawyers can be sued for negligence arising both from ignorance of law and mistakes of fact. All practising lawyers carry compulsory insurance to guard against mistakes which can and will occur in the best behaved families. But they cannot be sued for failures in exercising their skill or lack of it in advocacy. This is on grounds of public policy and is examined in the next chapter. In the remarkable case which finally decided this in 1963, Lord Reid said:

... where it is plain that a party seeking advice or information was trusting another to exercise such a degree of care as the circumstances required, where it was reasonable for him to do that, and where the other gave the information or advice when he knew or ought to have known that the inquirer was relying on him ...

then a duty to take care was imposed on the one giving the information or advice, and whether there was a payment made or not a breach of that duty would found an action for negligence.

In Lord Kenyon's case the client wanted damages because although he had been paid in advance his advocate did not bother to turn up at the court. A clearer breach of Lord Reid's duty to take care can hardly be imagined. If the same case were to be tried tomorrow the plaintiff would be successful. There could be no possible defence. The lawyer was not defective in his advocacy in court. He was an absent advocate, which is no advocate at all.

But if the advocate does turn up, with Kenyon and Pollock's words ringing in his ears and the words of the Exclusions of Implied Terms Order engraved if not on his heart at least on his cuff-links, does he go sailing into court and there perpetrate the most terrible blunders with impunity? The Bar, the society of barristers, believes not. It is probably right to believe so, if only because the Bar rarely attracts and even more rarely retains those whose standards are so debased that they need to rely on any immunity. Like all professions the Bar has had, and still has, its black sheep. That there are remarkably few is recognized: the denigration of the lawyer is of the class and not of the individuals composing it. Throughout the ages the individual advocate has excited admiration and respect from all sections of the community. Even Dickens dedicated *Pickwick Papers* to a barrister. During the 'Golden Age of Advocacy', from the Act of 1836 already referred to until the Administration of Justice Act of 1933, the stature of those who reached the front rank of the profession was immense: Hardinge Giffard, Edward Clarke, Charles Russell, Carson, Marshall Hall, Rufus Isaacs, Patrick Hastings, Birkett, these all became household names.

It is, however, no use ignoring the fact that the status of the advocate both in the public eye and in the courts has diminished in recent years, and that it will probably continue to do so. Few corners of any profession are now free from public inquiry, and much of the mystique of the Bar has been subjected to considerable and almost universally adverse publicity. At the same time, the rival attractions of film and television, unknown in the days of those named, have been able to fulfil for the public that craving for public idols which previously the Bar and the stage almost in equal parts used to meet. In this, the diminution in the quantity of press reports of trials has played its part, while the more factual approach of the courts to the cases coming before them has tended to discourage idiosyncrasies in the practitioner which the public found so attractive. Fact in place of fancy tends to level all men.

The greatest change has been due to a constriction in the use of juries as a means to determine fact. Since the Act of 1933, only in seven types of civil action – fraud, defamation and slander, breach of promise of marriage, false imprisonment, malicious prosecution, and seduction – can the parties insist on trial by jury. In all other actions the trial takes place before a single Judge. Jury trial may be applied for, but such applications are rare, and the Judges have an absolute discretion to refuse them. County Court Judges, who first came into existence in 1833 and whose jurisdiction is now so considerable that they try the bulk of all civil actions, always sit without a jury. In the criminal courts the extension of the jurisdiction of lay Justices and the stipendiary magistrates has led to the greater proportion of the work being tried in these inferior courts without a jury. Lord Bramwell was right when he said, 'one third of every Judge is a common juror', but it is courting failure and probably rebuke to behave as if he were twelve jurors. If all murder trials were conducted before a single Judge it is probable that few would achieve any publicity at all.

It will be realized that the 'common juror' – not a term designed to cause the public to love the lawyer – is not the same as in Bramwell's day. Until 1974 the juror from the City of London had to be a householder or the occupier of premises, or be the owner of land or personal estate valued at over £60: if he (as in all statutes, the male embraces the female) lived in the County of London he had to reside in premises of a net annual value of over £30: if he lived elsewhere the demarcation line was £20. The limitations for inclusion in the lists of 'special jurors' were even more complicated with a strange distinction between 'farm' and other premises. By these requirements juries were, as one Judge recognized, predominantly male, middle class and middle aged.

Since 1974 the general qualification for inclusion in the jury panel has been registration on the parliamentary or local government electoral lists provided the putative juror has been resident in the United Kingdom for any period of five years since he attained the age of thirteen. This has led to a dramatic change in the composition of juries. The average age has fallen. The proportion of women has increased. They are, of course, more representative of the public generally than any panel drawn from a list of rate-payers, and they demonstrate in the jury box the change of attitude and approach to the cases they hear which is to be expected. It is said as a result that they are far less susceptible to the advocate's approach, whose weapons, words, and the use he can make of them, have not changed at all.

The court too relies far less on the advocate than formerly. The felon had none to speak for him save his counsel. Now social inquiry reports must be laid before the court in all cases tried in the Crown Courts. In the Divorce Division of the High Court, no decree will be granted unless and until the court is satisfied that the welfare of the children is assured. Reports from outside independent sources can be called for by the courts. These are rocks on which an advocate can break himself before he can overcome their effect. Any advocate who is obliged to practise before some juvenile courts will feel the full blast of the change in his status. There legal principles are too often sacrificed to the new social justice which is rightly ready to jettison the millstone of strict legal etiquette, but which rarely knows what direction it ought to follow instead.

This diminution in the authority and status of the advocate is most unfortunate. It is likely to lead to a marked lowering in the quality of people coming into practice at a time when the services they can render are certainly no less important than before, and when the training they receive is at last taking account of the kind of work they will be doing. In 1900 Lord Alverstone became Lord Chief Justice of England without having taken a single examination before his call to the Bar. He had, of course, eaten his dinners in one of the four Inns of Court, and paid his dues, both of which remain essentials in the barrister's training. Dickens's Uncommercial Traveller said:

I was uncommercially prepared for the Bar, which is done, as everybody knows, by having a frayed old gown put on, and, so decorated, bolting a bad dinner in a party of four, whereof each individual mistrusts the other three.

But Lord Alverstone had spent the three years (1862–5) before his call both in the offices of a solicitor and the chambers of a barrister. He had attended every court in which he was thereafter to practise and the 'moots' or mock trials conducted by the Benchers of his Inn after the compulsory dinners. He had passed through the personal scrutiny of a profession represented by his Inn and consisting of not more than about 200 members. Such concentrated examinations over such a period meant that by the time he was called he was as well, if not better, equipped to practise law than any newly fledged barrister today.

Many, possibly most, lawyers then did not go to university. Alverstone did not. The in-house training by the four Inns of Court, Middle and Inner Temple, Lincoln's and Gray's Inn, was the university of the law. Today's entrants to the Inns have all been to university and have had their basic training in the six core legal subjects either there or at a polytechnic. The 750–1,000 who declare an intention to practise at the Bar then go through a year at the Inns School of Law in Gray's Inn at a vocation course which concentrates on the practical side: advocacy, evidence, procedure, case management, communication skills and drafting documents. The first steps in court-room techniques are taken before television cameras, and in a series of exercises the first mistakes are made and corrected.

Thereafter, the successful, if still determined to go into practice, must spend twelve months in the chambers of a practising member of the Bar. There he has the free run of all his master's papers. He can try his hand at writing opinions, drafting pleadings, or settling indictments. He has the opportunity to be with his master in court and in conference and, if the chambers are busy ones, after his first six months he may be asked to do small things in court by himself. This will be his first practical experience. It may also be his last: the first few appearances in court have ended the hopes of many embryo Marshall Halls.

The rule as to twelve months' pupillage is obligatory, but the amount he learns will depend on what use he makes of the time and what his pupil master is prepared to make of him. The old days of having six pupils at once, a system which helped to keep even Patrick Hastings (since at that time each paid fifty guineas for a six months' stay), is rapidly disappearing, but the Senate can no more recommend every barrister to be a good pupil master than a Local Education Board could recommend every one of its staff to be good teachers. The worst faults are passing. Gill, one of Her Majesty's Treasury Counsel at the Old Bailey at the turn of the century, never allowed his pupils to ask him questions. He was an immensely able advocate, but he was a deplorable pupil master. It is only if members of the Bar fulfil their duty towards their pupils properly and promptly that the standards which the public require from the advocate will be achieved. Even now, however good the pupillage may be, there are vast gaps in the barrister's training. He has none in banking procedure or book-keeping or commerce, and the rules of the profession debar him from engaging in trade.

These moves by the Bar to teach the rules of advocacy and to familiarize students with the actual application of the rules preceded the first statutory recognition of advocacy as a subject by many years. The Courts and Legal Services Act received the Royal Assent on 1 November 1990. Section 17 defines the 'statutory objective' of Part II of the Act:

... the development of legal services in England and Wales (and in particular the development of advocacy, litigation, conveyancing and probate services) by making provision for new or better ways of providing such services and a wider choice of person providing them, while maintaining the proper and efficient administration of justice.

This book inevitably draws from cases already decided. It shows advocacy as it is and as it has been in the past. Since most reported trials have taken place in the higher courts, it concentrates on the work of the barrister, the specialist advocate, who has had exclusive rights of audience as an advocate in those courts. The words in this section 'a wider choice of person providing [advocacy]', and the succeeding sections of the Act clearly envisage the barrister sharing those rights with others. Some implications of this are looked at in Chapter 12.

At present the word 'advocate' is applied to both barristers and solicitors in all courts and tribunals other than the Crown Court and the High Court. Both have the right of audience in the County Courts and in the Magistrates' Courts, before most planning tribunals and disciplinary committees, and on all interlocutory matters arising before trial in the High Court except those heard by a High Court Judge sitting in open court. Solicitors may not appear in a Crown Court (there are a few exceptions), or in any of the Divisions of the High Court. This leads to anomalies which surprise no lawyer, the law is full of them, but are inexplicable to the layman. A solicitor can appear on a bail application before a Judge of the High Court sitting in Chambers (that is, in private) but not in a Crown Court, even though it is an inferior court. Similarly, a solicitor can appear before a County Court Judge except when he is hearing divorce cases and invested with the panoply of a High Court Judge.

The division between the two professions was well recognized by the end of the sixteenth century and by the end of the seventeenth was quite firm. By the time the Law Society, the governing body of solicitors, was set up in 1870 and the Bar Council, which is not the governing body of barristers but which is the nearest equivalent, in 1895, the division had become hallowed by custom and regarded as one of the strengths of the legal system of the country. A minority argue that much of this strength is illusory in view of the right of audience of solicitors before so many tribunals. They ask: what can justify a system which decrees that a solicitor may appear before a High Court Judge in private but not in public, or present a claim in court if the sum involved is less than £20,000 but not if it is more?

All the answers to this question tend to ignore the basic differences in the roles of solicitor and barrister. The solicitor is at street level. As the general practitioner of the law his manner to the client is of greater importance than his method. For important or difficult matters there will inevitably be a class of specialists – the barrister who, dealing in one aspect of the law alone, is master of all its branches and intricacies in a way that a solicitor who has to deal in every aspect could not hope to be. Although some solicitors are very competent advocates, as some barristers are very incompetent advocates, generally speaking the barrister is also the specialist in advocacy. While the solicitor spends much of his time trying to keep his clients out of court, there inevitably comes a time when he needs the services of what the Americans call 'the trial lawyer'. In England, this is the barrister, who not only presents the case in court but also reads all the papers beforehand with an eye to the eventual arrival of the case before a court with whose customs and peculiarities he is particularly familiar.

This does not justify the system, for a class of specialists could spring up just as well from the ranks of solicitors. The real justification lies in the intimacy which exists between the barrister and the courts before whom he appears, and the gulf between the barrister and his lay client. The solicitor is so close to his client, in a small community he is often in daily personal contact with him, that he cannot give dispassionate and unprejudiced advice either to the client or to the court before whom he appears. The barrister has no such personal ties with the client at all. He only meets him through the medium of the solicitor, and he is consequently in a much better position to advise him and to advise the court in front of which the client has to appear.

The old complaint that recourse to the courts was open to all – like the Savoy Hotel – has now disappeared. Swift's additional complaint that 'Laws are like cobwebs, they may catch small flies, but let wasps and hornets break through' has not. (But see Chapter 12.) The Legal Aid and Advice Act has made the services of both solicitor and barrister available to all those whose incomes do not allow them to go to a solicitor privately. The basic idea of the scheme, that lawyers' fees should be paid by the State and not by private individuals, was first proposed in 1657. Now, over 300 years later, this is beginning to come about. It is the greatest single step towards ensuring equality before the courts ever taken in this country. But it has set a problem which has not yet been resolved. In 1866 Mr Justice Blackburn said:

It would be unprofessional for counsel to undertake the conduct of a cause giving up all discretion as to how he should conduct it . . . Few counsel, I hope, would accept a brief on the unworthy terms that he is simply to be the mouthpiece of his client.

For centuries, relying on the honouring of this obligation, the courts have acted on the certain presumption that the advocate bears full responsibility for every course adopted before them. But Mr Justice Blackburn went on:

If counsel cannot induce his client to act on his advice, the proper course is to return his brief.

What if the brief comes sanctified by the careful scrutiny of the local Legal Aid Committee, and the barrister decides that no cause of action is disclosed? To return the brief will seem to deny the client the right the Act is designed to give. Yet this must be his course of action. Once the advocate allows himself to give up his freedom of action by permitting his decisions to be influenced by one previously made by the executive he absolves himself from his responsibility to the courts and will become no more than an arm of the executive, and his status as a fearless and independent champion of the rights of the individual will disappear completely. Whatever criticisms have been made of him this title he has always held. If he is to deserve attention from the Judiciary and to command respect from the public this title he must continue to hold, for it is only by so doing that he can justify his existence.

Chapter 2

The Duty of the Advocate

Lord Macmillan, a Lord Advocate-General in Scotland and a member of the Judicial Committee of the House of Lords, declared that the duty of the advocate is fivefold: 'In the discharge of his office the advocate has a duty to his client, a duty to his opponent, a duty to the court, a duty to himself, and a duty to the State.' He could, and some say he should, have included others in this already formidable list. He thought it extensive enough to add: 'To maintain a perfect poise amidst these various and sometimes conflicting claims is no easy feat.'

In 1966, nearly forty years later, Lord Denning identified some of these duties in his own inimitable style. He said of the barrister:

As an advocate he is a minister for Justice equally with the Judge. He has a monopoly of audience in the higher courts. No one save he can address the judge, unless it be a litigant in person. This carries with it a corresponding responsibility. A barrister cannot pick and choose his clients. He is bound to accept a brief for any man who comes before the courts. No matter how great a rascal the man may be. No matter how given to complaining. No matter how undeserving or unpopular his cause. The barrister must defend him to the end. Provided only that he is paid a proper fee, or in the case of a dock brief, a nominal fee. He must accept the brief and do all he honourably can on behalf of his client. I say 'all he *honourably* can' because his duty is not only to his client. He has a duty to the court which is paramount. It is a mistake to suppose that he is the mouthpiece of his client to say what he wants: or his tool to do what he directs. He is none of these things. He owes an allegiance to a higher cause. It is the cause of justice and truth. He must not consciously mis-state the facts. He must not knowingly conceal the truth. He must not unjustly make a charge of fraud, that is, without evidence to support it. He must produce all the relevant authorities, even those that are against him. He must see that his client discloses, if ordered, the relevant documents, even those that are fatal to his case. He must disregard the most specific instructions of his client, if they conflict with his duty to the court. The code which requires a barrister to do all this is not a code of law. It is a code of honour. If he breaks it, he is offending against the rules of the profession and is subject to its discipline. But he cannot be sued in a court of law.

As this passage makes clear, some of these duties are imposed on the barrister long before he rises to his feet resplendent in his horsehair wig and stuff gown. Indeed a proper observance of them may prevent him ever rising to his feet at all, whilst a failure to follow them may result in an appearance before a disciplinary committee composed of the Judges and fellow practitioners and a layman nominated by the Lord Chancellor and the striking of his name from the list of those qualified to practise in the courts. These are duties some of which barristers are chary of acknowledging since they are really no more than trades union restrictions of a type common to all trades and most professions. As explained in Chapter 1 he must not engage in trade. In addition he must not advertise or in any way 'tout' for work. He must wait for the work to come to him. For at least one barrister who eventually rose to the House of Lords this meant waiting three years before he got his first brief. Lord Macmillan received only three in his first nine months. Although in recent years much has been done to help the young man establish himself, perhaps it is no great surprise that of the many that get called to the Bar few choose or are able to remain. In the five years 1954 to 1959 less than fifty per cent of those who passed the Bar examinations began to practise. The figures today show little change.

However, the barrister is entitled to such personal advertisement as naturally follows from his appearances in the courts, but it is improper for him 'to do, or to allow to be done, anything with the primary motive of personal advertisement, or anything calculated to suggest that it is so done'. This is cold comfort for the young and briefless barrister waiting for the opportunity to show his talents. The detailed regulations which follow from this rule will not make him any happier. He may describe himself as 'barrister-at-law' in the telephone directory for his professional address, but not for his home even though the two entries may appear next to one another. He may describe himself as 'barrister-at-law' if he stands for Parliament or in the lists of members circulated among fellow members of a Masonic Lodge or a club to which he belongs, but not on his stationery. Until recently if he wrote for the Press or took part in a broadcast he could allow his name to be given but could not also allow himself to be described as a barrister. If he allowed himself to be described as a barrister then he could not give his name. Now he may give both, and if he writes a legal textbook his name and profession may appear on the cover and title page, or if he lectures on a legal subject his name and occupation can be given to the audience.

The principle underlying rules like these is simple enough despite the apparent illogicality of these diverse regulations. His practice must be built solely on his own ability and skill. The basis of this was already well established by 1800 when Sir James Scarlett, later Lord Abinger, said:

Suppose that in every Assize town persons were employed to publish the cause in which their favourite [advocate] was engaged, and instead of fair competition of the Courts of Justice to determine who is the advocate that the public should employ, to give out fame beforehand by suppression or false representation. Would that not destroy the honour of the Bar? And would it not tend to degrade its honour still more, if among its members were to be found those capable of making favourable reports of their own exhibitions to advance their own interests, and by suppression or misstatements to injure their competitors?

This duty to obtain work by fair means and not foul does not fit into only one of the five duties of Lord Macmillan. It is a duty the barrister owes to the State, to the client and to his opponents. No single one of these claimants takes precedence. When a brief does arrive on the barrister's table tied with red tape (white if it involves representing government business or if prosecuting) then his first duty is one identified by Lord Denning: he must accept it. He is, as Lord Macmillan put it, 'on the cab rank for hire'. As already stated every man is entitled to be represented in a court of law, either by paying for it privately or through the Legal Aid and Advice Act. The barrister is bound to accept any brief which will take him into the courts in which he professes to practise. He can, if he wishes, accept every brief delivered to him, but a lawyer specializing in Admiralty matters is as unlikely to do work in the Divorce Court as a criminal barrister would dare to venture into the Chancery Division.

This then really means that he may not refuse a brief simply because he does not think much of the lay client's chances or much of the lay client, or because he thinks the facts of the case unsavoury. In 1902 Marshall Hall represented a man in Manchester who was alleged to have allowed prostitutes to congregate in and solicit in his theatre, the Comedy. A clergyman later said of him, '. . . we had a little shame that the member [of Parliament] for a religious town like Southport [Marshall Hall] should be the advocate for the man in the Comedy case which was one of the worst ever brought up in Manchester.' Marshall Hall's reply was immediate and immaculate. 'Barristers are public servants and may be called on just as a doctor may be called on to operate on a man suffering from a loathsome complaint.' This duty was recognized but not properly established when Erskine defended Tom Paine in 1792. He was widely criticized for doing so. When he addressed the jury he said:

If an advocate refuses to defend from what he may think of the charge, or of the defence, he assumes the character of a Judge; nay, he assumes it before the hour of judgment, and in proportion to his rank or reputation puts the heavy influence of perhaps a mistaken opinion into the scale against the accused in whose favour the benevolent principle of English law makes all presumptions, and which commands the very Judge to be his counsel.

Erskine held the appointment of Solicitor-General to the Queen. He was told the appointment was to be withdrawn. He replied:

From the moment that any advocate can be permitted to say that he will or will not stand between the Crown and the subject arraigned in the Court where he daily sits to practise, from that moment the liberties of England are at an end.

From that moment the toast drunk at any dinner by barristers was, 'To Erskine and Independence'. Adopted, at least in part, to assert the barrister's independence from the Crown, this remarkable rule has been applied ever since. But it applies only to barristers. It applies to no other category of advocate. It applies to no other category of lawyer. It is unique. Many rules about barristers are unique. Some are also absurd. They give much innocent pleasure to the Press and public alike, who delight in rubbing the Bar's collegiate toffee-nose in them. This rule, however, is of fundamental importance both to the profession and to the public, for it ensures that in all cases the whole of the English Bar is available to all litigants despite their personal shortcomings or the unsavoury nature of their case. In England this importance is rarely recognized outside the ranks of the profession. The Bar has failed to convince the public that it has anything to say about the conduct of its own affairs save for ostentations and unworthy attempts to cling on to its own privileges. The public believes that the rights it enjoys today including this one are inalienable and will automatically and equally be available tomorrow. Outside England, in countries where there is no such rule, it is recognized as a priceless symbol of the proper working of a truly just system of law. It is now, since 1990, identified by statute as one general principle by which an applicant shall be judged when applying for rights of audience equal to the barristers (see Chapter 12).

The rule is hedged about with innumerable qualifications. No rule devised by lawyers is ever free of them. The brief may be refused if it is not marked at a proper professional fee. The fee must be marked on the brief before he goes into court. There must be no arrangement that the payment will vary according to the result. The fee does not have to be delivered with the brief. As a result in England the barrister will often wait months or even years to be paid. In Scotland, where these things are better ordered, payment must come with the brief. There is now no minimum fee. For many years it was two guineas, retaining memories of a golden past, but it was abolished in 1971. The term 'proper professional fee' has never been defined. It depends, of course, on the length and complexity of the case, and the 'standing of the advocate' whose services are sought to be employed. The 'standing of the advocate' will forever defy definition. Happily, barristers are not often called on to calculate their own value. They are not debarred from doing so in any case where some difficulty arises, but ordinarily all negotiations over fees take place between the solicitor and the barrister's clerk.

'Special circumstances' too may justify refusal. He may have been consulted by the other side. That would certainly be a special circumstance. (It happens surprisingly frequently.) He may have some confidential information about the other side, or he may know one of the witnesses involved. In addition to these occasions there are a number of specific instances where he must refuse a brief because accepting it might lead to a clash between some office or appointment he holds and his duties as an advocate. If, for example, he is a Justice for the County of Kent he must refuse to advise on or appear in any matter, civil or criminal, which might come before his fellow-Justices or any committee on which those Justices sit.

For the barrister there are other golden rules. He must never accept instructions direct from a layman, that is, without the intervention of a solicitor. Yet even to this there are exceptions. Probably the best known was the 'dock brief', when a prisoner was allowed to choose his counsel from the dock, provided he had £2.25 (£2 to the fortunate barrister, and 25p to his less fortunate clerk) rather in the manner of a cattle breeder selecting a bull in the market: with a wary eye on the service he can expect. Most elderly barristers have their own favourite horror story of some occasion when they were chosen to represent a defendant in this manner. The most notorious led to the barrister being sued for negligence by his disappointed and convicted client, a case finally disposed of (in favour of the barrister) in the House of Lords in November 1969, exactly ten and a half years after the original criminal trial. The law reports of the case run to 187 pages because it has become the leading authority on the liability of the advocate for negligence committed in the course of a trial. The quotation from Lord Denning on page 35 is taken from his judgment in the Court of Appeal. The Court had questioned the defendant/plaintiff/appellant.

SALMON LJ: You were charged with causing grievous bodily harm. You admitted that you had caused the injuries but said you had caused them with your teeth and hands, not with a knife. That was your defence?

40

DEFENDANT: That was the basis of it – that the 'victim' was the attacker.

DANCKWERTS LJ: I understand that you admitted you bit off the lobe of the man's ear.

DEFENDANT: It sounds difficult to understand in cold blood but I can demonstrate it . . .

Lord Denning refused the offer.

The barrister may also accept instructions direct from the Registrar of the Court of Appeal (Criminal Division) or the Courts Martial Appeal Court, from a Clerk to a local authority, from the Chief Land Registrar or from the Secretary of the Church Assembly (provided he is only asked to draft rules or measures or amendments to either). He would not grow fat on the work from all these sources.

The rule that the barrister must not accept instructions from a private person is a self-denying ordinance. It does not arise from any statutory or Judge-made source. It is a rule created by the barrister and it can be dismantled by him. In recent years the process of dismantling has begun so that the barrister can now be instructed directly by the layman, provided he is only asking for advice about a problem outside the United Kingdom. This has obvious importance in relation to work in the countries of the Common Market. And the first tentative steps have been taken to allow the barrister to accept instructions from other professional men, such as accountants in tax matters, surveyors in planning and licensing. It is very likely that these exceptions to the rule will increase as solicitors obtain extended rights to act as advocates in the higher courts. Solicitors are the sole effective source of work for the barrister. Once they undertake advocacy work in those courts themselves, they will be in a position to strangle the barrister at birth. Instead of sowing the seed from which the barrister reaps the harvest in court they can become his unwilling prophylactic.

Once the advocate has searched his conscience on all these problems and accepted the brief, where does his duty lie? It is now twofold, to his client and to the court in which he is due to appear. Both are served by the first and most obvious rule: he must do the case. This is easier said than done. All advocates would like it to be said of them, as it was of Sir James Scarlett:

One of his great merits was that when he was engaged in a cause his services might always be relied on. He disdained to adopt the vicious practice of some barristers, then far too common, of wandering from court to court and taking contemporaneous briefs in all, to the damage of those whose briefs they had accepted.

So long as it remains impossible to estimate or check the garrulity of witnesses, Judges, and advocates themselves, and so long as the courts refuse to fix dates in advance for the hearing of cases it will remain impossible for any counsel to guarantee his appearance. Clearly counsel cannot wait unoccupied and therefore unpaid for one case to come into the list for trial. If he accepts another it may not finish on the day appointed for it and the date chosen for the adjourned hearing may clash with the hearing fixed for the trial of the first.

This is inevitable and very frequent. But he must not accept work which he knows he will be unable to do, and he must not hold on to a brief which he can see in advance he will not be able to do in the hope that something will happen to enable him to attend to it. His duty is to return it to the solicitor in time for him to instruct other counsel who in turn has time to master it. This may seem small comfort for the lay client who believes that his whole future rests secure in the hands of one counsel and who finds twenty-four hours (sometimes only twenty-four minutes) before the trial that he has got to make do with another of whom he has never heard. Certain priorities do exist. First come, first served is a rule-of-thumb guide. Cases in which a barrister has done the preliminary work, by settling the statement of claim or the defence, take precedence over those in which he has not. Criminal cases, since the liberty of the subject is involved, take precedence over civil cases. They are sensible, practical rules, but they do nothing to assuage the feelings of the client, who, having lost the counsel of his choice, then loses his case.

These largely unwritten ordinances may seem complicated enough by themselves. The difficulties really begin when the advocate gets into court, for all five duties may pull upon the advocate at the same time. Lord Brougham had no doubts which should take precedence. While he was defending Queen Caroline he said it was to save and protect his client without regard to all hazards and costs to others and himself. But a few years later when he repeated his words in an after-dinner speech in the Temple, Lord Cockburn, the Lord Chief Justice, rebuked him saying that the advocate owed a greater obligation to the 'eternal interests of Truth and Justice'. This idealism took more positive shape in a speech of Lord Birkenhead's who said that there was an overriding duty to the court arising from what he called 'an obligation of confidence' between counsel and the court. How does the barrister steer a safe and certain course between these conflicting doctrines?

So far as matters of law are concerned the duty on the advocate, whether in a criminal or civil court, is to bring to the attention of the court any and every relevant statute or decided case of which he has knowledge. It does not matter whether it is in his favour or not. In this instance his duty to the court dominates his duty to his client. Generally, at the criminal Bar, counsel tell their opponents of the authorities on which they intend to rely before they go into court, so that the possibilities of the court being misled by their attention being drawn to some but not all of the relevant cases is greatly reduced. This is also the custom in the High Court and in the House of Lords, but in the County Courts some advocates produce authorities from under their robes like conjurors producing rabbits from out of a hat. It may be this attitude which led one advocate to remain silent when he was not called on to argue his case in the Court of Appeal despite the fact that he had an authority before him which was directly in point and directly against him. When by chance the court learned of this the barrister concerned was publicly reprimanded. The rule is of great importance. Counsel are frequently called on to make 'ex parte' applications, that is, to present their case to a court when the other side are not present. For instance, under the old matrimonial legislation over ninety per cent of the divorces granted each year were on undefended petitions when the defendant wife or husband was rarely present or represented. The courts then rely on counsel to draw their attention to the cases which are against the proposition they may be advancing with as much care as those in favour of it. Once he has done so he is free to destroy the reasoning behind the unfavourable judgment, or to distinguish it from the facts of the case then before the court.

On matters of fact the position is quite different. The greatest discrepancies lie in the criminal courts. According to Sir Malcolm Hilbery, prosecuting counsel should be: 'An officer of Justice. He must present the case against the defendant relentlessly, but with scrupulous fairness.'

Translated, this might read: 'he must prosecute and not persecute.' In practice it means he must present all the facts to the court whether they are favourable or unfavourable to the case he is instructed to put forward. If he has in his possession statements from witnesses whom he does not intend to call but who might give relevant evidence for the defence, then the defence must be furnished with the names or addresses of those witnesses. If he knows that a witness on whom he is relying to prove his case is of bad character the defence must be given the details of his convictions. Before 1982 the rules in this area were applied in a very hit-or-miss fashion depending on the varying standards of different prosecuting authorities and prosecutors. In that year the Attorney-General issued guidelines entitled 'Information the Prosecution should make available to the defence'. This has ironed out the worst anomalies by imposing a positive duty on the prosecutor to disclose material in his possession unless in carefully defined circumstances he can justify its non-disclosure.

The rules do not mean that the prosecuting advocate must exhibit any weakness about his task. The sneering, hectoring manner which characterized those with prosecuting practices at the Old Bailey until late in the nineteenth century has given way to a school which bends itself double in trying to be fair to an accused man. In doing so the advocate often fails to ensure that every material point which could and should be made against a defendant is before the jury. Prosecuting counsel neither win victories nor suffer defeats, but weakness in presenting the case for the prosecution can lead to injustice by allowing a guilty man to escape the proper consequences of his action. One such case, tried at the Old Bailey in 1917, is referred to in the next chapter.

The position of counsel for the defence is completely different, a fact which has never ceased to irritate a large proportion of the population. How can the advocate defend someone he believes to be guilty? The question needs to be asked first: how can an advocate prosecute someone who he believes to be innocent or at least should not be convicted on the evidence which is available to be called or has been called? Before 1986 any barrister asked this question might have given two totally different answers. One was, 'My belief is irrelevant. I am instructed to prosecute and prosecute I will until the court tells me to stop. It is the job of the court to decide whether the case I am putting to the court is good or bad. It is not my decision. It is the court's decision.' The other was, 'True it is that I am instructed to prosecute and prosecute in a proper case I will. But I am not merely a mouthpiece for the police, Customs and Excise, Inland Revenue, et al. I do not jettison my judgement for any of you. My duty to you is not subservient to my duty to the court (and my conscience). It is my belief we should offer no evidence in this case and that is the course I shall adopt. If you don't like it, you must withdraw my instructions and go to another advocate.' Even when more tactfully expressed, this second course required some courage and sometimes led to a refusal by prosecuting authorities to send any more work to the barrister bold enough to stand his ground.

In 1986, at the request of the Chairman of the Bar, a Committee under the Chairmanship of Lord Justice Farquharson reported on the proper answer to this question and the related one: what does the prosecuting advocate do if he finds that not merely his instructing solicitor but also the Judge of the trial believes the case should go on? What does he do if that disagreement occurs in open court?

The report is long, almost as long as this chapter, but it is quite clear and comes down firmly on the side of the second answer. If there is time the advocate must consult those who instruct him to prosecute and allow them to seek a second opinion, if necessary by going to the Attorney-General (one can go no higher). If there is not time for a second opinion then after consulting those instructing him, even if he does not persuade them to accept his view, he must offer no evidence against the defendant and insist that a verdict of not guilty is recorded. I use the word 'insist' deliberately, for the Judge may not agree. He may say so. He probably will. The advocate must stick to his guns. In 1991 one London Crown Court Judge was outraged with what he thought was a grave error by a prosecuting counsel who said he was dropping the prosecution part way through his own case. After what the Court of Appeal politely called an 'unusually animated argument' between the Judge and prosecuting counsel, the Judge refused to allow the prosecution to discontinue the case. He called the remaining prosecution witness himself. The jury were out of court while the argument was going on, but seeing and hearing the dramatic intervention by the Judge calling the witness (sometimes called 'descending into the arena'), promptly convicted. The Court of Appeal 'could see no way in which the Judge could properly continue to call evidence for the Crown consistently with his judicial role', and the Court with one small exception approved the reasoning and conclusions of the Farquharson report.

So when prosecuting, the belief of the advocate is paramount, prevailing even over that of the Judge. No matter how strong the protests to the Judge, the Judge must give way to the judgement of his apparent inferior. Must the Judge equally give way to the judgement of the defending advocate? Certainly not. For when defending, the belief of the advocate is wholly irrelevant. It is like the first answer of the prosecuting advocate in the pre-1986 days, for the defending advocate is not Minister of Justice. He is the gladiator of the accused. He wears his garland, and like the mercenaries through the ages he has no right to ask if the cause for which he fights is just. Erskine has in part answered the question; let Dr Johnson complete it.

Sir, you do not know the cause to be good or bad until the Judge determines it ... An argument which does not convince yourself may convince the Judge to whom you argue it: and if it does convince him, why Sir, then you are wrong and he is right. It is his business to judge; and you are not to be confident in your opinion that a cause is bad but to say all that you can for your client, and then hear the Judge's opinion.

Baron Bramwell took the matter a stage further:

A man's rights are to be determined by the court, and not by his attorney or counsel. It is for want of remembering this that foolish people object to lawyers that they will advocate a cause against their own opinions. A client is entitled to say to his counsel: 'I want your advocacy, not your judgment, [in this context, judgment means decision] I prefer that of the court.'

This does not mean that the advocate is debarred from advising a client as to the eventual outcome of proceedings. 'Judgement', in the sense of sagacity and discernment, is one of the prime requisites of the advocate and an advocate must exercise his judgement if he is to advise his client well. What it does mean is that the advocate must not impose his opinion of the facts upon the client, though he may feel obliged to press it pretty strongly.

Once in court, even if his opinion is in support of his client, it is wholly immaterial. Serjeant Shee, while defending the poisoner Palmer, so far forgot this fundamental rule as to say to the jury:

SHEE: I begin Palmer's defence and say in all sincerity that I have an entire conviction of his innocence.

The Lord Chief Justice who was trying the case, Lord Campbell, told the jury:

L.C.J.: I most strongly recommend to you that you should attend to everything that Serjeant Shee said to you with the exception of his own private opinion. It is my duty to tell you that opinion ought not to be any ingredient of your verdict ... it is the duty of the advocate to press his argument on the jury, but not his opinion.

Even Erskine, carried away in defence of Tom Paine, said:

ERSKINE: I will now lay aside the role of the advocate and address you as a man,

to earn the rebuke:

JUDGE: You will do nothing of the sort. The only right and licence you have to appear in this court is as an advocate.

This passage-of-arms occurred before 1800, by which time the rule was firmly established. Hence the lawyer's irritation with passages in drama or fiction like that quoted from *Orley Farm* in Chapter 1. Authors have quite enough material with which to traduce the lawyer without inventing anything extra.

The rule that his belief, however strong, is immaterial, is not an example of the lawyer's ability to perform mental gymnastics for the position is reversed if the advocate 'knows' the defendant is guilty of the offence with which he is charged, because his client has told him so. This is no longer a matter of belief or opinion but a matter of instruction from the client. Then the advocate must decline to put forward a case which he knows to be false for that would make him a party to deceiving the court. All he is permitted to do is to allow his client to enter a plea of not guilty and challenge the prosecution to prove its case. He has full rein to test the case against his client, but he must be careful in cross-examination and in his speech not to suggest anything which he knows to be untrue. It follows from this that he must not call his client or any other witness into the witness box to swear to what is false for that would be making him a party to perjury. Sir Malcolm Hilbery explains what may seem legalistic tautology in this way:

The plea of not guilty is a formal plea, which is merely a challenge to the prosecution to prove its case. Since the prisoner is presumed innocent until proved guilty, and it is always for the prosecution to prove guilt, there is no impropriety in fighting to show that the prosecution evidence has fallen short of proof; that is entirely different from being a party to putting before the court a positive defence known to be false.

In 1840 a man named Courvoisier was tried for murder at the Old Bailey. Half-way through the trial, after some new and unanswerable evidence of his guilt had been called by the prosecution, he sent for his counsel, Phillips, and told him that he was guilty. Phillips sought the Judge's advice, and then continued in the case as if nothing had happened. He did not call Courvoisier to give evidence (this was before the Evidence Act of 1898 permitted a man charged with felony to give evidence in his own defence) or any other evidence, but he addressed the jury warning them to think long before staining their hands 'with the blood of this young man'. Courvoisier was eventually convicted, but when the facts became known to the public Phillips was savagely attacked for continuing in the case, principally by those who had fought the introduction of the 1836 Act which allowed counsel to address a jury on behalf of a defendant charged with felony. All the criticism ignored the prejudice which would have been created against Courvoisier if he had withdrawn from the case, and assumed that Phillips had said to the jury 'Courvoisier is innocent', when in fact he had been saying, 'the prosecution have not proved that he is guilty'.

The defence, unlike the prosecution, are not obliged to call any evidence however helpful they know it may be in establishing the defendant's guilt. Nor are they required to correct mistakes which a court may make in favour of the defence. It is a daily occurrence for a police officer to say of a convicted motorist that he has no convictions recorded against him while counsel for the motorist holds in his hand a long list of such convictions. It is plainly improper for him to say, 'my client has no convictions', but there is no professional impropriety if he addresses the court in mitigation of the offence to which his client has pleaded guilty or been convicted by the court provided he makes no reference to his client's character. He must not directly or indirectly refer to what he knows to be factually inaccurate. (This may seem deceit by equivocation unless the distinction between truth and evidence referred to in Chapter 1 is remembered.) These rules have grown up since the Criminal Evidence Act was passed. They give rise to one of the very few occasions that counsel can positively refuse to assist the court, for if the Judge asks the advocate about the character of his client the advocate should reply that the question is not one for him to answer.

The most difficult position of all is that faced by the defending advocate in the criminal courts to whom the client says, 'I am not guilty but I insist on pleading guilty.' The choice as to plea, guilty or not guilty, is and must be the client's. The advocate may advise, but he may not decide. He may advise in strong language, but he must never take the decision away from his client. That decision must be the client's, free and unfettered. There is a recognized discount given by the Judges in criminal cases where a plea of guilty is entered. It may lead a Judge to impose a non-custodial sentence or to suspend a sentence of imprisonment so that the client is able to walk out of court instead of being imprisoned immediately. The discount is based on a combination of factors, but dominant among them is the belief that a plea of guilty is a true acknowledgement of guilt and an indication of remorse for the conduct that caused the offence to be committed by the defendant. How then does the advocate address the court knowing that the presumptions made by the court in his client's favour are wholly misconceived? The answer is, with difficulty and a troubled conscience.

This is the only instance I know of where the advocate is not merely entitled to deceive the court but is positively required to do so. The ruling that the barrister shall continue in such circumstances to act for his client and to mitigate for him by addressing the sentencing court is one made by the Judges and is therefore binding on him. But he may not compound the deceit by, for instance, resorting to any of the more hackneyed phrases, 'the plea of guilty shows how deeply sorry the defendant is for his conduct'. If the Judge uses such language, showing that the Judge has misdirected himself into believing that by the plea of guilty the defendant is showing a degree of contrition, the advocate has no duty to correct him. The advocate may, he must, stay silent. The advocate walks a tight-rope knowing that a single question from the Judge while he is on his feet may cut the wire like a pair of well-directed bolt cutters. But walk it he must, and without displaying so much as a flicker of his own personal doubts.

The words of Dr Johnson and Baron Bramwell apply equally to civil and criminal courts. There are, however, two distinctions to be drawn between practice in the two divisions. Firstly, there is no such thing as a formal plea in the civil courts. The written documents, the writ, the statement of claim made by the plaintiff and the defence lodged in reply by the defendant, are records of the court and no barrister may go outside his instructions in drafting them. As counsel in a criminal court may not include any charge in an Indictment which is not supported by the facts set out in the depositions taken from the witnesses called in the Magistrates' Court, so counsel in a civil case is tied to the facts put before him by his client. This applies to all the documents which come into existence before the trial begins, and includes the further and better particulars, the interrogatories, affidavits or documents, and so on. Secondly, plaintiff and defendant are on an equal footing before the court. No greater duty lies on counsel on one side than on the other. Both are free as Lord Denning said:

To make every honest endeavour to succeed. He must not, of course, knowingly mislead the court, either on fact or law, but, short of that, he may put such matters in evidence or omit such others as in his discretion he thinks will be most to the advantage of his client.

He need never reveal anything to his client's discredit, but he must be careful in so doing he does not misstate anything. As Lord Macmillan said, '. . . the zeal of the advocate must not tempt him from the path of strict truthfulness'.

In 1960 a Press photographer sued an Inspector of police for assault and false imprisonment. The action arose out of disturbances in Trafalgar Square on Guy Fawkes night two years previously when the photographer had been arrested for obstructing the police in the execution of their duty. Before the action came on for trial the Inspector appeared in front of a police disciplinary board charged with offences involving the deception of a Magistrates' Court. He was found guilty and sentenced to reduction to the rank of Sergeant. This was not known to those representing the photographer. What was the duty of the advocate appearing for the Inspector in the High Court? He was not obliged to reveal anything to the discredit of his client, but he had to avoid any deception of the court. Would suppressing the truth suggest an untruth? Faced with this appalling dilemma the Inspector was permitted to give evidence in plain clothes, and nothing was said about the disciplinary proceedings. As a result both counsel for the photographer and the Judge continued to assume that the defendant was still an Inspector of police, and that the dispute lay between a Press photographer who, because of his behaviour on that night, had been convicted by a magistrate of obstructing the police and a Chief Inspector of police with twenty-two years' honourable service to his credit.

The photographer lost the action. When he learned of these facts he applied to the Court of Appeal to set the judgment aside and order a new trial. In granting the appeal Lord Justice Pearce said:

I appreciate that it is very hard at times for the advocate to see his path clearly between failure in his duty to the court and failure in his duty to his client. I accept that in the present case the decision to conceal the facts was not made lightly but after anxious consideration. In my judgment the duty to the court was unwarrantably subordinated to the duty to the client.

In one form or another this sort of problem is one which the advocate has to face almost daily. In that case the Inspector doffed his uniform. What if a man dons one when he is standing trial on a criminal charge? The rule in the Criminal Evidence Act is that no defendant may be asked any question which tends to show that he is of bad character. There are a number of exceptions. One is that if an accused person gives 'evidence' of his good character or asks questions of the witnesses which establish or suggest that he has a good character, or that the witnesses called against him have a bad character, then he may have his own bad character put before the jury. A few years ago a Sergeant of Marines stood like a ramrod in the dock in a country Crown Court, his stripes freshly blancoed and his medal ribbons freshly laundered. In fact he had a number of previous convictions. Did the uniform, stripes, and medals constitute in law a claim to good character? Even before the trial began the Judge made up his mind that it did. The members of the Bar practising at the court thought that it did not. The Sergeant had given no 'evidence', and his advocate had had no opportunity to ask a single question. Unfortunately, the matter was never satisfactorily decided because he was eventually, in plain clothes, acquitted.

Finally, what of the advocate's duty to his opponent and to himself? Here the code is unwritten but is plainer and simpler than the duties already examined. The basis of it is set out in Chapter 3. He must follow the advice of Polonius and be true to himself. If he does that then the duty he owes to his colleagues will flow from it, for he must abide by his word and never betray a confidence. (These are duties owed to the client as well.) The community of advocates is still a closely knit one, and the occasions on which it is necessary or desirable for opponents to speak to one another in confidence are frequent. It is only because counsel are able to place implicit trust in their professional brethren both when they are in practice and when they sit on the bench that the business of the courts can be so smoothly conducted, that the interests of their clients can be best served and the proceedings carried on without the mistrust which causes the rancour and ill-will which distort some foreign court proceedings. Standards of professional conduct have risen quickly since the turn of the century and scenes between advocates in court, some of which are referred to later, now rarely occur.

In the final event the determination of these difficulties must rest on the integrity of the individual advocate. In 1932 Lord Macmillan's words were regarded as the last word on this subject: 'For the solution of these daily problems no absolute code can be laid down. They are left to the advocates' honour, and I am proud to say that they are generally safely so left.' Today such statements ought to be regarded with a healthy dose of scepticism. They ignore some blatant breaches of fair play in the past: Erskine (according to Lord Campbell in his lives of the Lord Chancellors) would dress himself when out of London on circuit in a manner to attract the favourable attention of the juries he was to address, and Marshall Hall would operate his throat spray at opportune moments to drown a witness's crucial answers. Public expectation of the standards applied by the advocate have changed dramatically. 'Generally safely' will not do. The public expect a system of justice to be a really just system, available to all who need it and producing just results. A single miscarriage of justice flowing from a deficiency in the advocate fully to comply with his duties, not some attention to dead Victorian ideals of 'honour' – now a word with elastic edges – correctly incites public concern. It should also incite the profession to ensure that what is found in succeeding chapters is retained if good, and is abolished if bad.

Chapter 3

The Essentials of Advocacy

The qualities essential to the successful practice of the art of advocacy cannot be acquired like pieces of furniture. Without some natural gifts, the technical rules are useless, and without practice, precept too will be of little assistance. Roger North, later Lord Chancellor of England, wrote about his first appearance in court (in 1772) that it was 'a crisis like the loss of a maidenhead'. John Philpot Curran, cruelly hampered by a stammer, was unable to utter a word the first time he got to his feet in court. Yet he too rose to great heights, dominating the Irish courts in the same way and at the same time as Erskine in England. Between that first appearance and the extract from his speech of 1794 which follows lay twenty-five years of continuous public speaking. Here he attacks the English idea of freedom which gives liberty to its colonial subjects immediately they land on English soil but keeps them in their own subjugated territory in a state akin to slavery:

CURRAN: No matter in what language his doom may have been pronounced; no matter what complexion incompatible with English freedom an African or Indian sun may have burnt upon him; no matter in what disastrous battle his liberty may have been cloven down; no matter with what solemnities he may have been devoted upon the altar of slavery, the first moment he touches the soil of Britain, the altar and the God sink together in the dust; his soul walks abroad in his own majesty; his body swells beyond the measure of the chains that burst from round him, and he stands redeemed, regenerated, and disenthralled by the irresistible genius of universal emancipation.

This is eloquence of a very high order and of another age. There is not an advocate in practice at the Bar today who could formulate and then deliver a sentence of this kind. John Buchan recognized that eloquence is rarely found in those who practise law. He even went so far as to say that 'the successful lawyer is not often a first-class speaker'. Out of court even Erskine was not shown to be an impressive speaker. His maiden speech in the House of Commons in 1783 was a disaster. Pitt was to reply. It was reported:

Pitt sat with pen and paper in his hand, prepared to catch the arguments of this formidable adversary. He wrote a word or two. Erskine proceeded: but with every additional sentence Pitt's attention to the paper relaxed, his look became more careless, and he obviously began to think his opponent less and less worthy of his attention. At length, while every eye in the House was fixed upon him, with a contemptuous smile he dashed the pen through the paper and flung them upon the floor. Erskine never recovered from this expression of disdain; his voice faltered, he struggled through the remainder of his speech, and sank into his seat dispirited and shorn of his fame.

Allowing for the probable political bias underlying this report, it has to be recognized that the talents that made Erskine, which are essential to the forensic advocate, do not guarantee equal success in other places where he may be required to speak.

Eloquence is one of the talents. It is not enough by itself. There are other qualities of greater importance. It may have been in recognition of this that in his book *The Seven Lamps of Advocacy*, His Honour Judge Parry put eloquence fifth in the list of the seven virtues he thought all advocates should possess. The others he named were honesty, courage, industry, wit, judgement, and fellowship. It is probable that no group of lawyers would agree on a list of the qualities vital for achieving forensic success, and certain that they would never agree upon an order for them. Lord Birkett, for instance, said that 'without presence, there is nothing'. Parry does not mention it. Fellowship, which he does include in his list, is a pleasant quality, but it is by no means an essential. It can be said that a man blessed with the other six virtues is likely to have fellowship in any event and bound to possess presence. It will be said, and with greater truth, that there are few advocates who possess all of them.

Other authors on the subject have devised their own lists. David Pannick implies that one should start with Quintilian writing around A.D. 90. He might have added that a serious student of the subject should read no further, though this will seem a poor guide to a trembling advocate making his first appearance before flint-faced justices on a wet Monday morning. Quintilian wrote:

Advocacy, the highest gift of Providence to man, needs the assistance of many arts, which, although they do not reveal or intrude themselves in actual speaking, supply hidden forces and make their silent presence felt.

It is these hidden qualities which, by their existence or their absence, make or mar the advocate. Some he must have, the possession of others, pleasing adjuncts to these essentials, permits him to stand above his fellows. He must have a good command of language. Words are his tools, and without them he will be lost. They must always be to hand. While in the middle of a long and involved review of political corruption in Ireland, Curran was unnecessarily interrupted by the hostile Lord Chancellor he was addressing. Curran replied:

I am aware My Lord, that truth is to be sought only by a slow and painful process. I also know that error is, in its nature, flippant and compendious. It hops with airy and fastidious levity over proofs and arguments, and perches on assertion, which it calls conclusion.

The Lord Chancellor did not interrupt again. It was said Curran had language 'for them all'. He was as much at ease in a reproof of this nature as he was in simple and direct speech to an illiterate Irish labourer. Command of language must include the ability to choose the right word at the right moment. Wild unhesitatingly picked the right one which summed up both character and situation when he cross-examined one of the two young labourers who claimed to have seen Gardiner and the girl Rose Harsent enter the chapel at Peasenhall.

WILD: Where did you see him [the defendant] first?
WRIGHT: Against Church Lane.
WILD: So he saw you?
WRIGHT: Yes.
WILD: You were loitering about.
WRIGHT: No, I was going down the road.

But the youth was leaning against the edge of the witness-box, his hands in his pockets. 'Loitering' was what the jury were going to remember. Wild continued:

WILD: When did you see him the second time?
WRIGHT: He came down the road.
WILD: He saw you then?
WRIGHT: Yes.
WILD: And the third time too?
WRIGHT: Yes, he spoke to me.
WILD: He must have seen you all the time?
WRIGHT: Yes.
WILD: And he must have known you were about?
WRIGHT: Yes, he spoke to me.
WILD: Do you represent that, knowing you were about, he went into the chapel, and behaved in the way you state?
WRIGHT: Well, he did.

This simple example also shows how much more pointed the force of Wild's last question, and how much weaker Wright's protestation became in the face of an orderly presentation of the facts. Whether he has eloquence at his command or merely a facility with words, the advocate must not fail to use them so as to lighten the task of the Judge or jury. The easier he can make it all, the easier will the tribunal digest and retain the matters he puts before them.

Clarity and order are essential ingredients in the deployment of the words at his command. If there is some degree of gracefulness in his speech and if his voice is pleasing to the ear so much the better. But in forensic advocacy content is so much more important than complexion that neither can be said to be essentials. This should not be understood to condone what Lord Chesterfield stigmatized as 'an offensive indifference about pleasing', and in no way seeks to excuse the modern advocate who sometimes seems to believe that bands round his neck and a wig on his head permit him to lift his foot to the next seat like a dog at a lamp-post, or to appear so weary that he cannot stand without support.

He may too have the advantage of appearance and build so that he approximates to Mr Marjoribank's description of Marshall Hall:

> The Roman head on Saxon shoulders set,
> The silver hair; the tall heroic frame . . .

But this is far from essential. There is no ideal shape or size. A poor physique or unusual build is no kind of a drawback to the advocate who has all the other necessary qualities.

Honesty is certainly one of the essentials. Without it the advocate may secure a practice but he will not retain it. The need for it is obvious from an examination of the duties of the advocate in Chapter 2. The practical demonstration of it in operation sometimes takes odd turns. In the Laski case Slade contended that the plea of justification (the claim that the words printed in the newspaper were true) included the claim that Laski had been guilty of cowardice by remaining in America during the First World War since this was the suggestion made by Wentworth Day's question to Laski. If this was right it meant that Hastings also had to prove that Laski was a coward. If he did not Laski was bound to succeed. During Slade's final speech to the jury Lord Goddard interrupted to raise a matter of law, then Hastings intervened:

HASTINGS: . . . I distinctly recollect hearing Mr Slade say that he was not making a substantive claim in respect of that [i.e. that Laski was a coward] and therefore I have not even addressed my mind to it.

After further legal argument Slade left the point saying:

SLADE: I shall be very astonished to find that . . . I have allowed this case to proceed on the footing that the jury could find the whole of these words to be true, which would mean that Mr Laski had been guilty of cowardice.

Half an hour later Hastings intervened again. He had found a passage in the transcript when Sir Valentine Holmes, Slade's junior in the case, had said during an exchange with the Judge: 'We are not asking the jury as regards the part relating to cowardice to give Mr Laski damages . . .' In that one possibly ill-considered sentence, which was not vital to the argument then taking place, the whole of Slade's point, one upon which he believed he could win the whole case, was swept away in the middle of his final speech. Whatever the obligations to his client and whatever the personal feelings he had himself, Slade recognized the most important single fact of the situation: Hastings had already addressed the jury on the basis that the point was abandoned. So he told Goddard:

SLADE: . . . I am not going back on anything Sir Valentine Holmes said, any more than I should go back on anything I said myself; and I therefore prefer to err on the side of fairness, and I shall not ask the jury to deal with that part of the libel at all.

This is honest dealing of a very high order indeed. It is integrity of this kind which allows the advocate justly to claim that the code of honour among the members of his profession is probably higher than in any other. There is unfortunately another side to the coin, the use by an advocate of an argument which he knows to be improper. Henry Dickens, who led for the prosecution in the Peasenhall case, was a son of the novelist Charles Dickens. In opening the case for the prosecution he had put before the jury a number of theories which covered the gaps in his case. When Wild opened the case for the defence he reminded the jury of one of them and said:

WILD: That is mere theory – the histrionic ability my friend [Dickens] possesses from heredity and personality. It is the sort of thing which would do in a novel, but not in a murder case.

This was as unnecessary a comment as it was a despicable one. It is by an abuse of the powers which the advocate holds of this kind that juries can be led astray. It is foolish for the advocate who resorts to such tricks as this to pretend that the result of a case in which they are employed depended on the evidence available – the layman will leave firm in his belief that the advocate prefers his own plausibility to other men's truths. It is equally foolish to pretend that injustices have not resulted from an improper use of the advocate's powers. But it does not follow from that that the power itself is wrong, or that it is wrong to place it in the hands of those who wield it. It might as well be said that, because some doctors have been known to use poison improperly, the practice of medicine should be discontinued. The advocate must use his power with discretion, as 'the weapon of the warrior, and not of the assassin'.

After honesty must come judgement in the sense already referred to: sagacity and discernment. It is the judgement of the advocate and not the client which must be exercised in the conduct of a case. He is a representative and not a delegate. Mr Justice Blackburn once defined his position in these words:

The retainder of counsel to undertake the conduct of a cause does not simply imply the exercise of his discretion and eloquence. Counsel have far higher attributes, namely, the exercise of judgement and discretion on emergencies arising in the conduct of a cause, and a client is guided in his retention of counsel by his reputation for honour, skill, and discretion.

It is often difficult, and frequently unfair, to criticize the judgement of an advocate in the conduct of a case. Whatever may appear on the surface, the critic has no knowledge of the pressures upon the advocate to adopt the course which he does in court. How easy it would be, for instance, to criticize Sir Henry Curtis Bennett for calling Edith Thompson to give evidence on her own behalf in the Thompson Bywaters murder trial, when in fact he did all that he could to prevent her from entering the witness-box. In the dock brief case referred to in Chapter 2, one of the complaints of negligence made by the accused man Rondel against the barrister selected by him was that he had failed to call a witness to give evidence for him. The effect of the evidence was to support the claim by Rondel that he lawfully attended the premises where the assault alleged against him had taken place. But the witness would also have proved that Rondel's employer was Rachman, known publicly as London's worst slum landlord whose influence if not power was derived from engaging the most ruthless of convicted men to coerce the weak in order to benefit the strong. The prejudice against Rondel created by this evidence would have outweighed any advantage.

In the Mr 'A' case it was important for Lord Halsbury to establish that at a material time Mrs Robinson, the wife of the plaintiff, was a sick woman. He called a Dr Crouch:

HALSBURY: What sort of state was she in when she arrived [at the nursing home]?
DOCTOR: She was extremely ill. She told me she had not slept for some nights. She was in a state of most extreme depression and was not taking her food . . . She was in a serious condition of nerve exhaustion.

Then he was cross-examined by Sir John Simon appearing for the defendant, Midland Bank.

SIMON: Would you think it a good continuation of her cure that four days later [after leaving the nursing home] she should go off with Mrs Bevan, an immoral woman, and her husband, to Ostend and spend a lot of money? . . .

DOCTOR: No sir, it is not a good thing.
SIMON: It would not be a good way of completing her cure would it?
DOCTOR: No, certainly not.

Since it was alleged against Mrs Robinson that she was a
dishonest and immoral woman adept at hoodwinking the most
shrewd investigators, let alone a sympathetically inclined doctor,
it is easy to say that Lord Halsbury had done more harm than
good by calling the witness. But before one could do that it would
be necessary to know how Mrs Robinson had previously withstood
her own cross-examination, and the relative importance of proving the illness compared with the comment made by Sir John
Simon. And even if one knew all these things, before an accurate
assessment could be made of Halsbury's judgement on this narrow
point the fair critic would need to know what other evidence
Lord Halsbury had available. An advocate can only make bricks
with the straw supplied to him. Only too often the straw is of
poor quality and minimal quantity.

This is one of the particular challenges the advocate has to be
capable of facing. Most people can display a reasonable degree of
judgement if given plenty of time. The advocate has to use his
when he has no time at all. The trial has yet to take place where
everything can be taken for granted: the straw suddenly becomes
bricks, and bricks become straw. One Judge complained that
when he was at the Bar he never had a strong case, but now he
was on the Bench they all seemed strong on one side or the other.
It is only the advocate who can really see the yawning weaknesses
in the case he has just won with apparent ease.

He must also have courage. There must be no timidity about
his performances. Resort to the law is a form of civilized warfare,
the advocate the modern representative of the medieval champion. Courage, of course, cannot stand alone. There is a time to
stand and a time to sit for every advocate, and unless he can
solemnize some form of marriage between courage and judgement
he will never reach the first rank of the profession. It was in this
that Carson excelled. In 1892 he appeared for Lord Clanricarde
before a commission set up to inquire into the wholesale evictions
of tenants then taking place in Ireland. When he applied to cross-
examine the first witness, the President of the Court, an English

High Court Judge who should have known better, refused to allow him to do so:

PRESIDENT: I decline to hear you.

CARSON: I must press this matter. I will ask for a vote to be taken to see if every Commissioner takes your view.

PRESIDENT: I will not hear you further, and I will order you to withdraw.

CARSON: I insist upon my right till every Commissioner orders me to withdraw. I will stand up here and now for justice to be done to Lord Clanricarde as well as to everyone else.

PRESIDENT: The Commissioners have consulted and we have come to the unanimous conclusion that we will not hear you . . .

CARSON: My Lord, if I am not allowed to cross-examine I say the whole thing is a farce and a sham. I willingly withdraw from it. I will not prostitute my position by remaining longer as an advocate before an English Judge.

PRESIDENT: I am not sitting as a Judge.

CARSON (*in a loud whisper*): Any fool could see that.

And having remained on his feet throughout this exchange, Carson threw down his papers and walked out of the room. These were strong but thoroughly justified words. And Carson's judgement cannot be faulted. If he was denied the right to cross-examine there was little he could usefully do. His client lost nothing by his refusal to take any further part in the proceedings; instead the Commission lost much of the authority it expected to enjoy.

Marshall Hall possessed courage to this same high degree. But in him its display was frequently marred by petty and exacerbating faults. In the Wood (the Camden Town murder) trial at the Old Bailey the Judge put a question to one of the prosecution witnesses which was extremely detrimental to Wood's case and which had no foundation in fact. Marshall Hall interrupted:

HALL: I do not understand Your Lordship's question.

JUDGE: Are you addressing me or the Jury? If you are speaking to me I wish you would not look at them.

HALL: I am addressing Your Lordship. I said that I did not understand Your Lordship's question.

To display contempt for a Judge's rebuke and to come into open conflict with him is perilous both for the advocate and for his client. He must be as sure of his position as was Carson. The exchange continued:

JUDGE (*to Marshall Hall*): I am taking the accused's own statement. (*To the witness*) Had you any idea the defendant was living with this loose woman?

HALL: There is not a tittle of evidence . . .

JUDGE: I am addressing a witness. Counsel must not interrupt when I am putting questions on the evidence in the interests of justice.

HALL: In the interests of justice . . .

JUDGE: I must ask you not to argue with me.

HALL: My Lord . . .

JUDGE: I shall permit no argument as to the way I am putting my questions to the witness.

HALL: With great deference, I only wish, in the interests of justice, to point out that there is not a particle of evidence that the accused ever stayed with the girl or had improper relations with her.

Without courage of this kind to call on, the advocate will achieve little. Marshall Hall's was forever toppling over into rashness, or leading to situations where he was likely to lose control of his feelings.

Control of his feelings there must be, in particular of his temper. If he cannot, he will not keep control of his tongue and he will not keep control of the case. During his cross-examination of Laski, Hastings, who had been Attorney-General in the first Labour Government, broke off in the middle of a question:

HASTINGS: . . . are there any privileged in the Labour Party?

LASKI: Why, indeed, Sir Patrick, when you were a member . . .

JUDGE: No, Mr Laski.

HASTINGS: Do not be rude.

LASKI: That is the last thing I want in the world.

HASTINGS: It may be difficult for you to be courteous, but do not be rude.

LASKI: Not in the least.

HASTINGS: You are rude to everybody are you not?

LASKI: I do not think so.

Forensically simulated emotion should be one of the armaments of the advocate. Personal sensitivity is not. Hastings was clearly stung and showed it. If it amused the jury it is only because they have seen the advocate roasted on his own spit for a moment or two. It reduces him in their eyes, and it reduces the effectiveness with which he can present his client's case. He must prevent any sign emerging that anything the witness does or says has wounded him or his case.

This requires him to be alert and on guard throughout the case. He must also be alert to everything that is happening in the court. He must watch for signs from the Judge or jury that his points are going home, that he is making himself clear and that his arguments are appreciated. In the main courts in the Old Bailey and in all the Queen's Bench courts in the High Court he can take in the whole court without apparently turning his head. In many others he is required almost to be a contortionist to do so. Then the temptation to speak directly to the jury when addressing the Judge or cross-examining a witness is sometimes irresistible. Marshall Hall, as in the example quoted earlier, did it all the time. Even Sir John Simon, whose court manners were generally impeccable, committed the same error in the Mr 'A' case.

HALSBURY: I object to this, my learned friend turning to the jury and ... [putting the question to them and not to the witness]. It is done with a purpose, and it is not a question to the witness.
JUDGE: It is irregular, Sir John.
SIMON: I am sorry, My Lord.

It is always right to be seen to admit wrong. To fail to do so can do immense harm. At times, Patrick Hastings, particularly towards the end of his professional life, lost cases by failing to give way. But he made up for it by having eyes in the back of his head. He missed nothing. He once appeared for a married man of sixty-seven who was being sued for breach of promise of marriage by the youngest of three sisters, the eldest of whom had been his mistress for some years previously. (All three claimed they could give evidence of the 'Proposal'.) All three were in court on the first day of the hearing. On the second day, the eldest sister Rhoda was missing. Hastings addressed the second sister Fay:

HASTINGS: Have you seen your sister Rhoda this morning?
FAY: Yes.
HASTINGS: Is she quite well?
FAY: Quite well, thank you.
HASTINGS: I don't see her in court. Is she here?
FAY: No, she is not.

A few more questions established that she was at the Waldorf Hotel, that Fay did not know Rhoda had been writing threatening letters to the defendant as to what would happen to him if he did not pay them money before the case came on for trial. Then Hastings asked:

Is Rhoda waiting at the Waldorf Hotel to get her share if there is anything to split?

This whole line of cross-examination which helped expose an attempt to blackmail the defendant (after the case collapsed the Judge sent the papers to the Director of Public Prosecutions) would not have been possible if Hastings had not noticed that Rhoda was not in court.

Tenacity is more than an aspect of courage. Counsel must expect to cross-examine many witnesses whose evidence he will fail to destroy. He must also expect to come across a number who believe that attack is the best method of defence, and who will do all they can to embarrass him. Two such witnesses appeared in the 'Black Book' criminal libel case tried at the Old Bailey during the First World War. Noel Pemberton-Billing, independent member of Parliament for Hertford, alleged that German secret agents had compiled a list of 2,000 prominent people whose sexual proclivities and abnormalities had led to an irresolute prosecution of the war. When he criticized the dancer Maud Allen in obscene language for playing the part of Salomé in Oscar Wilde's play she prosecuted him for criminal libel. Hume Williams was briefed to prosecute. He had an extensive practice in the Divorce Division, but this did not fit him for the rougher atmosphere of the criminal courts, nor for witnesses who were prepared to stick at nothing in order to win. It allowed an unscrupulous man, with a full wave of national sentiment and war hysteria behind him, to secure his own acquittal and a travesty of justice at the same time. One of the witnesses for the defence made a reply to Hume Williams in cross-examination which led him to ask, with a note of incredulity in his voice.

WILLIAMS: People in the service of Germany are able to get British secret service agents marooned [on the Greek islands] by the orders of the British Government?
WITNESS: Yes. I think I told you that privately.

WILLIAMS: I ask you . . .

WITNESS: Do you not remember talking to me?

WILLIAMS: I? Never!

WITNESS: When I came back from Albania you met me at dinner and we had a conversation together.

WILLIAMS: I have never met you in my life.

WITNESS: I quite expected you to say that.

WILLIAMS: Because it is the truth.

WITNESS: You were never at the Clitheroes'?

JUDGE: I expect one or other of you will get marooned.

The loud laughter which greeted this sally of the Judge's disguised the defensive nature of Williams's last assertion. When one of the later witnesses made a similar claim, that she had reported a 'dangerous state of affairs' direct to Hume Williams who had advised her, 'there are too many people involved to make a personal sacrifice to expose it', he was impotent to deal with the situation. He had allowed himself to become personally involved.

In the Mr 'A' case, the facts of which are set out on page 105, Lord Halsbury had to deal with a similar situation in the High Court. A conspirator named Newton whom he was cross-examining suddenly said:

I dare say you will remember me meeting Mr Valetta [who was Halsbury's junior in the case] in your chambers Lord Halsbury.

HALSBURY: I remember your being turned out of them when you came up to them; if you want me to go into that I will. Now, I go back to the question. I want to know how many people you have blackmailed. Do you really say none?

When later Newton returned to the attack Halsbury repulsed it even more successfully.

HALSBURY: I decline to have Mr Valetta's name brought in. You came up to see him in my chambers, which he shares with me, and you were turned out.

NEWTON: That isn't true. He has lunched at my flat, and he has been to my flat on quite a few occasions.

HALSBURY: Have you anything to say against . . .

NEWTON (interrupting): I will undertake he will take my word for that

HALSBURY: I was wondering if you were going to make an attack upon the character of my junior clerk. (Laughter.) Now, what I want to know is . . .

Halsbury carefully avoids the head-on collision, the pitfall that Hume Williams fell into. Instead he 'smothers by deflection'. This is the advocate in command of the witness and not the witness in command of the advocate. It is also deftness of a very high order. It is, perhaps, only fair to record that Newton showed gifts of a similar nature in a later passage.

HALSBURY: Are you heartily ashamed of the part you played in this [conspiracy]?
NEWTON: I am rather sorry for it, yes.
HALSBURY: Are you heartily ashamed of it?
NEWTON: Naturally.
HALSBURY: When did this feeling of shame first come upon you?
NEWTON: With the likelihood of exposure. (*Laughter*.)

Witnesses like Newton are very common in every class of court. They provide a considerable test of the advocate's abilities. Two qualities are required on these occasions more than any others: tenacity and a form of question which allows no opportunity to the witness to score. Sir John Simon subsequently admitted that had Carson been against him he would not have exposed Newton to his cross-examination. (The reader will see why when he reads Carson's cross-examination of Cadbury in Chapter 8.) It is more than likely that Carson would have asked the same questions as in this last extract from the trial, but the last question would have taken a form like this: 'Did the feeling of shame first come upon you with the likelihood of exposure?' This not only prevents the witness from scoring off the advocate; it also directs the laughter against the witness.

Tenacity in cross-examination more properly belongs in the chapters on that part of advocacy. Elsewhere in the life of the advocate it is partially an aspect of courage and partially an aspect of judgement. For the advocate must never embark on a course of action unless he is ready to justify it, and when called on to do so he must defend his action until he has exhausted all the proper arguments in support of it. He is there to fight, not to capitulate. He should never allow himself to be stopped by his opponent or the Judge so that it appears he is only feebly trying to support that which he knows to be quite unsupportable. That is the quickest way to give a jury the impression he is attempting to do something dishonourable, and that he has so little faith in his own case that he needs to do something dishonourable to win it.

In the Laski case, after a prolonged cross-examination by Hastings upon some carefully selected passages from Laski's writings, Sir Valentine Holmes tried to put this question in re-examination:

HOLMES: Inasmuch as it has been suggested that this book to the ordinary reader would look like a book advocating revolution, did you read the review of it which appeared in *The Times Literary Supplement*?
JUDGE: Really, Sir Valentine.
HASTINGS: I do not want to interpose.
JUDGE: But I do because it is not regular, and it is not admissible.
HOLMES: The book was put in. If Your Lordship says that, I certainly will not.
JUDGE: The book was put in, but we cannot have the opinion of independent reviewers in this case.
HOLMES: The difficulty is that the jury cannot read the whole book. That is the difficulty in a case of this kind.
JUDGE: If you wish to submit that my ruling is wrong I will hear you.
HOLMES: No, My Lord.

The complaint was later to be made that Hastings's cross-examination of Laski on small and carefully chosen extracts, chosen for that purpose from Laski's voluminous published works, distorted the theme he was trying to present. This was the moment for the point to be made, but this was not the way to do it, particularly if Lord Goddard's undoubtedly correct ruling was going to stand without any attempt to justify the question Holmes sought to put. The difficulty Holmes complained of does not arise if the question is framed like this: 'The book was published in 1930. Sir Patrick Hastings has suggested it advocates violent revolution. Has anyone else suggested that in the last sixteen years?'

Sincerity must stand alongside command of language, judgement, honesty, courage, and tenacity as one of the qualities essential to the successful advocate. As already pointed out, if the advocate does not appear to believe in his client's cause, then he places his services at the disposal of his opponent. If he wishes to be successful, then he must wish his client to be successful. Lord Justice Wrottesley wrote that, 'earnestness is one of the most valuable attributes that an advocate can possess or display'. There are no exceptions to this statement, but it ought to be widened to read a 'sincere earnestness'. To his client a degree of insincerity may be shown. By the same token that a doctor never shows his patient his misgivings, so the advocate ought to show his client a hopeful countenance. It will be said against him that to show that same hopeful countenance to the court will be displaying in public the insincerity he has already shown in private. This is a variation on the theme song, 'how-can-you-appear-for-a-man-you-believe-to-be-guilty'.

Marshall Hall possessed this quality in its best and worst forms. He once wrote:

... if an advocate for the defence can legitimately in his advocacy, convey to the jury the impression of his belief in his client's case, he has gone a long way towards securing their verdict.

In this, as in much of his advocacy, Marshall Hall went too far. For an advocate to attempt, quite deliberately, to influence a jury not by the facts but by the intensity with which he views and presents the facts is improper. But he was faultless in emphasizing the importance of the advocate conveying sincerity in his words. He went on to describe listening to two speeches in a case:

... [one] was perfect in composition and logic, but it left one cold, whereas the speech in reply, badly as it might read in the reports, was a human speech on the level of its audience, and it won the verdict. A few days later I happened to meet one of the jury, and asked how he failed to be convinced by the other speech. 'Oh', said he, 'the speech was right enough, but he didn't believe a word of it himself; he had his tongue in his cheek all the time.'

Marshall Hall also had, probably above all advocates who have practised at the English Bar before a jury, another of the requirements: humanity. He had an understanding of human frailty which enabled him to catch the throats of all who heard him speak. When he was quite young he defended a prostitute charged with murdering one of her clients. She was forty-seven, her former attraction devoured by the life she had been forced to lead. At the end of his speech as he was about to sit down, he caught sight of her sitting hunched in the dock. On the spur of the moment he added these words:

Look at her, gentlemen of the jury. Look at her. God never gave her a chance – won't you?

But his impetuosity often led him to abuse this gift. In 1924 he was on his feet addressing a jury in a libel action brought by a woman member of Parliament against a newspaper for implying she had entered Parliament in order to gain the title of the best-dressed woman M.P. He was stopped in the middle of his speech by the two minutes' silence then observed in all the courts on Armistice Day. When the jury had sat down he said:

Members of the Jury, we have just been celebrating the anniversary of the greatest national sacrifice which the world has ever seen. We have all suffered loss in the war; you have suffered ... And now, turning from this great national ceremony, we find ourselves in this court, and have to address ourselves to the trifling grievances of this lady ...

One of those present in court later described this as a nauseating display of emotion, another simply said that it had gained the verdict which had been sought. Both opinions are correct, though it is only the second which recognizes the importance of an adaptability with which a good advocate can bend any and every circumstance arising during a case to his client's advantage.

Wit is not a vital asset, which is as well, for wits are rare, and even more rarely blessed with the other qualities vital to the acquisition of a successful practice. There are plenty of instances of witticisms in court, but they thrive only for a moment in the atmosphere of a court, and few can stand transplanting to the written page. Sir John Simon said they were like dry champagne, best when the cork is first removed and thereafter flat and stale. Most need a long preliminary statement in order to be understood. One counsel appearing before Mr Justice Day in Ireland in the eighteenth century protested when the Judge insisted on starting another case after midnight. He refused to adjourn until he received this note:

> *Try men by night? The Lord forbid.*
> *Think what the wicked world will say.*
> *Methinks I hear the rogues declare*
> *That justice is not done by Day.*

If it exists, it needs to be controlled. It is easier to rise in the legal world by a display of gravity than by undue levity. But a sense of humour is an asset. Every barrister can tell at least one story of laughing a case out of court. It cannot be described, for nothing can capture the tones and atmosphere which make of a Judge, the advocate, and the jury, not fourteen very different souls but one soul with one desire, to get rid of the case as speedily as possible. Fearnley Whittingstall did it with a single remark at a Crown Court on a hot summer afternoon. He was defending a man charged with driving under the influence of drink. The defendant was being subjected to a long and tedious cross-examination which was proving that if he had not been under the influence of drink while he was driving he was certainly a very bad witness while he was in the box. The cross-examination had lasted for well over an hour when Fearnley Whittingstall turned to his junior in the case and said in a loud voice: 'I really don't know which is the bigger fool: our client, or the chap cross-examining him.' The remark is trite, but was probably true. It may be the jury thought it was the only truth they had heard all day. Within ten minutes they had stopped the case.

There is one final necessity: industry. The advocate, as Lord Hewart said, must 'claw the facts'. If he does not, all the virtues and brilliant improvisations will not help him. They must all be retained in his memory, so long as the case lasts: dates, names, times, exhibit numbers. Then as fast as they were mastered they must be forgotten so that others in the next case he does can take their place. Memorizing facts of this kind is sheer drudgery. To do it properly the advocate must be prepared to forgo the pleasures of private life at the most inconvenient moments and for indefinite periods.

It is a heavy price to pay, but the rewards are great, financially and spiritually. There are magical moments in all advocates' lives. To sense a response in the minds and hearts of others to the words he chooses to use and the way in which he chooses to use them is the final justification for all the dull preparation which has preceded it. It wipes away all the sacrifices he has to make and the worry and responsibility he has to bear in order to follow his calling. It is particularly apposite that on qualifying as a barrister he is said to be 'called to the Bar'. Clothed with that dignity he gains an opportunity experienced by few others, which properly used can enrich both his own life and theirs.

Chapter 4

Opening the Case

The right to begin is a priceless and too often squandered asset. It was said of Sir Richard Muir, leading Treasury Counsel at the Old Bailey at the end of the nineteenth century, that the lucidity of his argument and the clarity with which he stated the facts in his openings wove a net so tightly round the prisoner in the dock that he could never afterwards escape from it. But it carries with it a liability, for the burden of proof lies on the side which begins first. This is inverting the test. The lawyer would say that it is for the side that alleges the wrong, public or private, criminal or civil, to prove its case and so gain the right to begin.

Most cases therefore begin with a single speech, in criminal cases from the prosecution, in civil cases from the plaintiff. This is so also in most of the courts and tribunals in which an advocate is employed by the parties to the case to be tried. Inevitably there are exceptions to this general rule. The *Herald* disaster showed two. The first public inquiry was conducted by a High Court Judge sitting as a Wreck Commissioner with four expert assessors. There were seven separate advocates, appearing for the Secretary of State for Transport (in effect acting as advocate for the tribunal), for the Department of Transport, for the Company who owned and operated the ferry, for the National Union of Seamen, for individual crew members and for surviving passengers and for next of kin and dependents of those who were lost in the tragedy. Each of these had separate interests to protect and different roles to play. The inquiry began with opening statements made by each of the seven advocates. The second public inquiry was conducted by the Dover Coroner. Although a number of those same persons interested in the proceedings were represented by advocates, there was no opening speech by any of them. The Coroner explained:

The office of Coroner is one of the most ancient in the country. The Coroner is a member of the judiciary and his court is a court which has a unique function: the Coroner acts both as judge and as inquisitor. In almost all other English courts the judge merely adjudicates on arguments presented to him by prosecution and defence, or plaintiff and defendant, and he does not take any active role in the investigation himself. The Coroner on the other hand has been charged ever since 1194 with investigation of breaches of the peace, sudden death and various other matters which were of interest to the Crown.

In the present day my function is much restricted . . . It is largely that of looking at sudden, unnatural or unexpected deaths and deciding who the deceased was and where, when and how he came to his death.

In this second inquiry the Coroner played a dominant role. There were no speeches from the advocates, either in opening or closing. The Coroner alone decided what witnesses were to be called and he conducted the examination of them. The advocates were permitted to cross-examine and to address argument to the Coroner, no more.

In these two exceptions to the general rule the purpose of the inquiry is not limited to the answering of a single question: in a criminal case, guilty or not guilty, in a civil case at fault or no fault. In the ordinary case, no matter what the name of the court of tribunal, the English common-law accusatorial system dominates. It determines the procedure. Whoever asserts a wrong must prove it.

In the criminal courts the onus of proof always lies on the prosecution who therefore always begin. In the seventeenth and eighteenth centuries the only important exception to this rule arose after trial if a woman, convicted of a capital offence, pleaded that she was 'quick with child'. A jury of matrons was then empanelled to try this issue which the wretched woman, denied counsel to assist her because she was a convicted felon, had to prove to their satisfaction. If she failed she was hanged with the men convicted at the same session. Today the only important exception occurs before trial if the preliminary issue of the sanity of the defendant is raised. This happened in 1959 when Gunther Podola stood trial at the Old Bailey. Before he pleaded to the Indictment charging him with the murder of a police officer a jury was sworn to try the issue, formulated by the defence, that he was unfit to plead to the Indictment (i.e. insane) because he could not instruct counsel for the defence. Since there is a presumption of law that everyone is sane, and it was the contention of the defence that he was insane, it lay upon them, on a balance of probabilities, to satisfy the jury about it. Had it been the contention of the prosecution, it would have been their duty to satisfy the jury, and their right to begin. This is not quite as academic as it sounds, for it happens fairly often.

In the civil courts, generally it is the plaintiff who begins. He asserts that a wrong has been done to him, for his is the action which bring the parties before the court, and his the claim for redress. Even so, he does not always obtain the right to start. In 1828 Bransby Cooper, surgeon at Guy's Hospital, and a nephew of the famous surgeon Sir Astley Cooper by whom he had been appointed, sued Charles Wakley for a libel published in the *Lancet*. Wakley had founded the *Lancet* only five years previously. It was then a far less respectable journal than it is today. Wakley used it to conduct campaigns against anyone or anything to whom he took a dislike. Cooper had become a favourite target since Wakley believed him to be surgeon at Guy's simply because he was Sir Astley's nephew. When it was reported that a patient, rather than face an operation for gallstones at the hands of Bransby Cooper, had decamped to St Thomas's, Wakley published this verse:

> *When Cooper's nevvy cut for stone*
> *His toils were long and heavy.*
> *His patient quicker parts has shown;*
> *He soon cut Cooper's nevvy.*

Later, reporting an operation carried out by Cooper from which the patient subsequently died, he described it as 'a melancholy exhibition, performed without proper and sufficient skill, dexterity, or self-possession'. Cooper promptly issued the writ for libel. Cooper asserted that he had performed the operation skilfully. Wakley asserted that he had performed it unskilfully. Although it was Cooper who had brought the parties to the court Lord Tenterden decided it was for Wakley to begin:

It is for the defendant to make out the truth of these allegations by evidence on his part, and until that is done the plaintiff is not called upon to give any evidence on the subject.

This ruling gave Wakley a double advantage, the ear of the jury at the outset of the proceedings, and the right to the last word as well. The rule in the civil courts is that if the defence call evidence then the 'opener' can speak last.

When the advocate has the right to begin, he should first ask himself whether he should exercise the right. In many tribunals and in some courts the procedure permits him to make only one speech. This is so, for instance, in all licensing courts: liquor, betting and gaming. Here the applicant for a licence may have little idea of the evidence which may be given in opposition until after he has called all his own evidence. Opening a case may sometimes be a 'priceless asset', but at others it can be far better to wait until all the evidence has been given.

If he does decide to open, how does the advocate begin? The procedure never varies; he introduces himself and his opponent to the court: 'I appear for the prosecution (plaintiff), my learned friend, Mr X, for the defendant.' And then? Sir James Cassels advised: 'Tell a plain story; put it in language easily understood.' W. H. Moody, in opening the case against Lizzie Borden in America, expanded on that advice:

MOODY: It is my purpose and my duty to state to you at this time so much of the history of this case and so much of the evidence which is to be introduced upon this trial as shall best enable you to understand the claim of the Government [the prosecuting authority: in England it is the Crown], and to appreciate the force and application of the testimony as it comes from the witnesses upon the stand. It is my purpose to do that in the plainest, simplest, and most direct manner.

It is not often that an advocate states his purpose before he begins, and most infrequent that he then achieves it. Moody did both. His opening is a model of clarity and conciseness. There was no over-elaboration, no unnecessary embroidery, yet save for one comment which is referred to later in this chapter, nothing was missed out from the chain of evidence he would later call before the jury. The advocate cannot afford to forget that his audience will only know as much as he remembers to put before them in his opening, and that they will only retain that knowledge if it is put in a form which they can easily assimilate. As in every aspect of advocacy, there must be order and clarity, and there must be selection of the important issues.

In the preceding paragraph the words 'his audience' are crucial. The advocate must concentrate on them and solely on them. They are the ones to decide the issues in the case he is presenting and it is his task to capture and retain their attention. Occasionally, but very rarely, he may be required to speak as if to an audience outside the court. This happens in most public inquiries, certainly all those which are concerned with major disasters. The *Herald* wreck inquiry was such a case. The counsel appointed to assist the tribunal and who would be responsible for calling most of the witnesses made the first of the seven opening speeches. He referred to the tragedy affecting the national consciousness from the first moment that the news was heard, and continued:

It was made all the more poignant by the very familiarity of the voyage, similar to one in which almost everyone in the land has undertaken at some time. It was the more immediate because our television sets, our radios and newspapers brought us the story with unbearable speed and detail. It was the more cloaked in anguish because we could all imagine ourselves and our children trying to cope with the cold, the dark and the fear.

Sir, I cannot start this Inquiry without expressing yet again the deeply felt national sense of sympathy for those who have been bereaved and for those who have been injured by this terrible incident. Now, why are we here?

Sir, the tasks are clear. First to find out what went wrong and why. The public is entitled to know how an apparently well-founded, properly manned passenger ferry can capsize in a matter of moments in good weather without any warning. The second task is to see what can be done to try and make sure that such a thing never happens again. Those who have suffered as a result of this casualty are owed nothing less than the satisfaction of these tasks and indeed so are all those who will use and continue to use the conventions of this form of transport.

Similarly, counsel for the Company needed to use the opportunity to speak to a wider audience in order to overcome a marked loss of public confidence in the ferry system:

This was on any view an appalling casualty. Sir, I would first like to make one or two observations on two aspects of the investigation: first, the cause, and secondly the future. Sir, the principal purpose of our making our remarks in relation to the cause is to make it clear that Townsend Car Ferries take responsibility for this casualty, and so far as the future is concerned, the purpose of my remarks is to underline the determination of Townsend Car Ferries that nothing like this should ever happen again.

The other counsel spoke directly and correctly to the audience in court: the presiding Judge and the four assessors. The advocate for the Captain of the *Herald* identified what was to become the central issue in the later criminal trial of manslaughter, namely whether the system of work relating to the closing of the bow doors was a safe one. She stated the reasons for the Captain believing that it was a safe system, and went on:

... his belief [was] that there was no problem with it, no danger.

Given this state of affairs, we would respectfully suggest that it would be difficult to say that he, and coincidentally all the other masters [captains of the Spirit class vessels] should be criticized for having operated a system which was presented to him because it was plainly not so dangerous to all those experienced masters that they can be said to have fallen below the standards of the reasonably prudent ferry masters.

The first days of a public inquiry like that into the loss of the *Herald* involving a massive loss of life are conducted in a highly charged and emotional atmosphere. The words used by the first advocate to speak recognize this, and by doing so to an extent diminish the intensity of that feeling. He was only partially successful. The Coroner's approach was very different. Once the jury was sworn, he told them what it was they the jury had to do and why they had to sit as an inquest jury, and what his role was in presenting the evidence to them. Then he turned to the emotional aspects of the matter:

The time for your verdict is several weeks off, as I said, and I think I should start now with the human background to the case. This has been one of the most poignant and moving tragedies of modern times. You may be forgiven for wondering why we are obliged to relive these tragic facts all over again, after so many inquiries have already taken place into the same event. The short answer is, that we are obliged by law to go through the process.

Another and perhaps more important answer is that it is widely recognized that the process of coming to terms with grief and suffering at the loss of loved ones cannot really get under way until facts about each individual demise have been brought out into the open and discussed in an objective and rational way. For this reason alone, the inquest which we are about to conduct will, I hope, have considerable value for those left behind who have to live with the memories.

Whilst others may have conducted inquiries into the causes of the capsize, we will concentrate on the human beings involved and what became of them. I have noticed in the past, in much smaller and less public inquests, how the relatives often appear much more at ease after re-hearing the facts of a fatal incident than they were at the outset, this notwithstanding the great distress which they have to go through in order to give their evidence. In this particular case we will try to bring before you oral evidence from survivors of every group on the ferry, but where those concerned have indicated that they do not feel able to go through it again in public, we have found alternative means of bringing the evidence before you. I will explain later in these introductory remarks, how I propose to achieve this.

No one reading this passage today can fail to recognize the tactful way in which the Coroner handled the opening of the inquest. Even what appears as the simplest, possibly the most trivial of cases, can generate deep and sometimes explosive feelings. They need to be grappled with either by diverting them in the sensitive manner shown by the Coroner's opening or by creating an atmosphere in which it becomes difficult for any participant or spectator to try to raise the emotional atmosphere.

In opening a criminal case to a jury the prosecuting advocate has a duty to avoid raising the emotional temperature. Lord Chesterfield told his son, 'Wherever you would persuade or prevail, address yourself to the passions; it is by them that mankind is to be taken.' This is as true today as when it was written in 1746, but prosecuting advocates must rely on evidence, not feeling. In criminal trials in particular there is much anguish and suffering which can give rise to strong reactions in the most detached and unbiased jury. He must never seek to exploit this. The flat, seemingly pedestrian opening of the manslaughter trial in the *Herald* case is as close as one can get to an ideal in this respect.

Shortly after 6 o'clock during the evening of Friday the 6th of March 1987, the cross-channel ferry, the *Herald of Free Enterprise* . . . set sail from Zeebrugge harbour in Belgium for Dover . . . She had on board, that evening, 454 passengers and 80 crew, as well as a load of vehicles. She left the harbour and was a short distance beyond the outer mole or breakwater of the harbour, as it is described, probably something of the order of three quarters of a mile, something of that sort of distance, when she capsized, and the time of capsize was about half past six, that is to say just under half an hour or so after she had left her berth in the harbour ... One hundred and fifty four passengers and 38 crew were drowned; that makes 192 people in all. Among them was a married lady in her late twenties. She was one of a number of passengers on a day trip from England, and, for the purposes of this case, the Crown has selected, for the sake of simplicity only one person who died in the capsize. You will appreciate, I am sure, that regrettably the case really concerns the deaths of all 192 people. It would have made no difference to the trial of the case however many victims had been chosen because the same considerations apply to all. I am sure you follow that, members of the jury, and effectively therefore, anyone who is guilty of the manslaughter of one person – and manslaughter is the offence charged – is, in reality, guilty of the manslaughter of all.

The most obvious reason for the capsize was that the *Herald* went to sea with her inner and outer bow loading doors open. There were other causes that did contribute to this capsize. The Crown's case is that the capsize was avoidable – it could have been avoided – and contends that this is a case of manslaughter, the unlawful although unintentional killing of another person by recklessness or gross negligence, the ingredients of which, as an offence in the criminal law, I shall return to later, although anything I say about the law is subject to my Lord's direction to you.

The Crown's case is that each of the defendants whom you are trying, the seven human defendants if I may so describe them, and the Company, is responsible in law for the deaths that occurred, because he – in the case of the human defendant – or the Company, was, by his behaviour or conduct, reckless or grossly negligent, in particular, in relation to the risk of the ship sailing in the condition in which she did on the day, the most critical feature of which was with her doors open. You do not have to be, the Crown suggests, a maritime or seafaring expert to appreciate the obvious danger and risk of sailing with the loading doors open of a roll-on/roll-off – ro-ro for short – ferry. It hardly needs to be said that once she sailed with those doors open the almost inevitable consequence was at least personal injury and, of course, in reality, death.

The Crown's case is, and the Crown suggest this, that each defendant whom you are trying, each one, contributed significantly to what happened on the day and is, therefore, responsible for the unlawful killing or manslaughter of those who died.

Now that is the briefest possible synopsis of the case, but it is necessary for me, I am afraid, to go into it in considerably more detail to explain how and why it is that the Crown makes the allegation it does against each defendant.

Lord Justice Singleton suggested that the essentials of the case should be 'summarized in a few sentences' so that the court can thereafter build on that framework of the case as the advocate advances among the detailed facts. Sir Henry Dickens followed this method when he opened the Peasenhall murder case. After telling the jury of the characters and positions of the defendant and the dead girl, and within three minutes of beginning his speech, he said:

DICKENS: ... therefore he [the defendant] was a man, both as regards his position in the church, with regard to his friends, and with regard to his wife, to whom it was imperative that no kind of suggestion of shame should be successfully imputed against him. The case we shall lay before you is that he had an immoral connexion with the girl; that his conduct raised a scandal in the church; that there was an inquiry with regard to his conduct; that having regard to the fact that he denied it and the girl denied it – there were two witnesses on each side – there was an impasse, and no real result obtainable either one way or the other; and that after this, and although he promised Mr Guy, the Minister of the church, not to have anything to do with Rose Harsent, he continued the intercourse with her, that letters passed between them until at last the girl became pregnant. She was six months pregnant at the time of her death, and our case is that he then wrote her a letter saying that he would come and see her in her room at twelve o'clock at night; that at some time that night he did visit her; that he killed her; and that he afterwards tried to burn the body. I will shortly tell you the chain of evidence we shall lay before you to support that theory.

This extract, like the whole of the opening, is largely free from comment or argument. It is often essential to comment on the facts as they are placed before the court so that the significance of them can be fully appreciated, but inessential comment, irrelevant comment, is burdensome and can be extremely dangerous. More often than not it gives an unintended opportunity to the other side to score. Even a mischosen word can give unjustified advantage to an opponent. In the extract above the very last word, 'theory', was a disastrous choice (see page 208 in Chapter 11). In fact Dickens was not advancing a theory at all. He was suggesting the jury should draw a number of irresistible inferences from facts which would be proved in evidence. Slade strayed into this error while opening the Laski case.

SLADE: The *Newark Advertiser* evidently thought that this meeting was of sufficient importance to have their own shorthand writer there to take a note of what transpired, and their own shorthand writer was Mr J. Opie. You may very well think that when you take the trouble to send your own shorthand writer there to report the meeting . . .

Notice how Slade uses the words 'own shorthand writer' three times, until the fact that it was 'their own shorthand writer' assumes a sinister significance. Hastings in his opening for the defence destroyed this suggestion (if it was intended to be a suggestion) by applying some crisp common sense:

HASTINGS: I will tell you how this ever came to be published at all. The *Newark Advertiser* in this district has a gentleman who can write shorthand, Mr Opie. Now you were told that we had sent our special correspondent or our special reporter to go there and take down every word of this monumental speech. Mr Opie is the gentleman who goes in Newark to the local flower show, the local funeral, the local wedding, anything. He is the only one we have got and he goes round with his notebook and takes notes. There was nothing more interesting in Newark, you might think, than a political meeting at the time of the General Election, and that is why he was there with his note-book . . .

If openings should be mainly recitative, to what sources may the advocate go to obtain his facts? In the same way that he may not include any matter in the pleadings or an Indictment that is not contained in his instructions, so the advocate may not open any fact to the jury that he is not in a position to prove either by the witnesses he is going to call or by the documents he can produce. At one time it was common for counsel to range at will among facts which could not possibly be proved, but by the beginning of this century the restriction placed on the discretion of the advocate set out above, was recognized and applied by the courts.

Marshall Hall fell foul of this rule as early as 1903. He appeared for the former secretary of an American lady who had brought an action against her for breach of his contract of employment and for defamation. The defamation claim was based on the lady's statement to her new secretary that the plaintiff was a disreputable person and was attempting to blackmail her. Marshall Hall had been provided with a mass of unsavoury information about the lady and her sister on which he could cross-examine her. He could prove none of it, and even if she was called to give evidence, which was extremely unlikely, the most he could do was to put the matters to her in cross-examination, for since the matters went only to the credit of the witness (a collateral issue) he would be bound by her answers. (This rule is examined in Chapter 6.) Marshall Hall was always impulsive and in the heat of forensic battle was liable to jettison all his carefully laid plans for the sake of a momentary advantage. On this occasion it was nothing more than the heat of his own rhetoric which caused him to say:

She [the defendant] cannot for one moment say that she does not know what it is to be accused of blackmail herself. I may afterwards, gentlemen, have an opportunity of asking her some questions with regard to her views on this particular subject. But be that as it may, she is a woman who knows exactly what she means by the word blackmail, and she cannot possibly have read all the American Press, dealing with her and her sister, without knowing what an accusation of blackmail really means.

Marshall Hall secured the verdict for his client; £50 for the breach of contract and £500 for the defamation. But it did his client no good, for the defendant immediately appealed, and the decision was reversed, in part on the grounds of his introduction of scandalous and irrelevant matter.

This is an extreme example. But the advocate will do well to remember that if he misstates his case he provides a heaven-sent opportunity to his opponent to berate him for his inaccuracy. It is almost the best-understood rule in the courts that 'if you haven't a case of your own, make one by attacking the other side'. Worse still, he can undermine his own witnesses, for if the facts related by the opener and then by his witness differ, it does not require very skilful cross-examination to imply that the witnesses have changed their evidence.

To recommend moderation, accuracy, and order in opening is

not to imply that the advocate should ignore the drama which lies behind the facts on which he intends to rely. No opening should be a mere catalogue of fact. The attention and interest of the court should be secured and retained. The facts should be made to do both. This American lawyer, opening Tilton's claim against Henry Ward Beecher in New York in 1875 for $100,000 damages for his 'criminal conversation' (adultery) with his wife, is too melodramatic and certainly too prolix for modern tastes.

COUNSEL: The plaintiff comes to court, and through the ordinary forms of law, says in effect that his home has been destroyed; that his wife's affections have been taken from him; that his children have been scattered; and that a once happy home is now desolate, and that the bright visions he had in this world of attaining honour and distinction and positions of honour have all been blighted; that he once had a happy family – none more so in the land – but he comes to you this morning not from that once happy family, but he comes to you from a voiceless home and a cheerless fireside, and he asks you as fathers, and as brothers and as husbands to consider his case. And against whom is this terrible charge? Is it some casual acquaintance, some casual friend? No: but he comes here and makes this charge against one of the foremost preachers in the land; against the man who, in his youth, united him in matrimony; at whose altar he received baptism. His spiritual adviser, his spiritual father, taking advantage of this sacred relation, has become, instead of his protector and comforter, his destroyer.

It needs to be recorded that this was the beginning of a trial which lasted five and a half months. It also needs to be recorded that the only thing to disturb the twenty-five days of final speeches was the interjections of the jury who thought the whole case had gone on long enough.

Although in opening the advocate must remember he is addressing an audience that knows little or nothing of the facts, he should not forget that there is a limit to everyone's patience. Moody grasped this nettle at the end of the extract quoted on page 75 by saying, 'It is not my purpose to weary you with a recital of all the details of the evidence which is to come before you.'

The vast majority of the public are not used to listening to involved argument or digesting substantial quantities of fact, for long periods at a time and, unless the advocate takes care, the discomfort of their seats will become far more apparent to them than the force of the address to which they are obliged to listen. With a professional audience, a High Court or County Court Judge, a magistrate, a planning inquiry or an industrial tribunal the advocate can afford to expand his argument provided he remembers these audiences will have heard it all before. In the Laski case Slade had to open to a special jury, which perhaps falls between the two stools. He clearly thought it necessary to explain to them why Laski believed a misuse of the residual constitutional powers in the hands of a rich and firmly entrenched minority party could force the majority of the people to violence. He also thought it necessary to define what those constitutional powers were. He had been speaking for over two hours when he said this:

SLADE: The next one [constitutional power] is something which I have never quite understood, and I do not think many lawyers have understood. It is what is known as the Royal prerogative. The Royal prerogative was considered by the House of Lords as recently as the year 1920 when a claim was solemnly put forward by the Ministers of the Crown when de Keyser's Hotel was taken over for occupation during the First World War ... So ill-defined is the Royal prerogative that so great a Judge as Lord Dunedin in the case in the House of Lords to which I have just been referring said that it had been defined by high authority as the residue of discretionary or arbitrary authority which at any given time is legally left in the hands of the Crown.

By this time the jury might be wondering, if Slade has not understood it how, or why, should they? Perhaps, too, they were wondering, what has this got to do with a remark made in the heat of the moment and at the height of an election from the back of a lorry in a Nottinghamshire market place? By the time they had heard Laski himself in the witness-box the brief, direct and down to earth approach of Patrick Hastings was all the more attractive to them.

HASTINGS: You may think Mr Laski is not a very dangerous person at all now you have seen and heard him. You may think he is more in the nature of being – I do not want to be in any way rude – troublesome, a little tiresome, but I should not think anyone could

imagine that the rather long, rather wearisome books were so dangerous that Mr Laski would be thought by a policeman or anyone else to
be guilty of high treason.

This extract and that on page 81 come from Hastings's 'opening
the defence' in the Laski case. In every case where the defence
are calling evidence in addition to the defendant or other than
the defendant they too have the right to open the evidence they
intend to call. Sometimes the right is abandoned in order to
preserve the element of surprise. Sometimes it is used to comment
on the evidence which has been called already rather than to
introduce fresh facts into the jury's mind. The rules are the same
as for the original opening, but the approach is very different. By
this stage in the case the jury have heard all the evidence on one
side. Comment on that evidence can therefore be safely made.
Any outline of evidence to come needs much less elaboration, for
the jury can slot it into the facts they have already heard for
themselves.

Hastings was never long in his openings, whether for plaintiff
or for defence, and rarely stylish. There is nothing remarkable
about the language in this last extract. In print, the words may
almost seem to have been chosen at random. Nothing could be
further from the truth. Hastings took great care over his choice of
words, and the two, 'troublesome' and 'tiresome', and the illustra-
tion of the policeman, conjuring in the jury's mind the plodding
figure in blue, were deliberately selected to bring the case within
the limits that Hastings wished to set for it.

Hastings could afford to be short when he possessed this capacity. And he could afford to be short when he was such a master
of the subject on which he had to speak that he knew exactly
what it was that he wanted to say. It is imperative for all speakers,
including the advocate, to be master of their subject to this
extent. If the advocate cannot understand the problems the jury
have to decide he will not be able to explore them sufficiently in
argument or with the witnesses to help them. A little self-
depreciation on his own incapabilities will do no harm; indeed,
since it is the last thing a layman expects to hear from a lawyer, it
might do a lot of good by arousing their sympathy. But a
confession that the subject is beyond him is to be avoided. In the

Laski case Slade made such a confession. One of the issues the jury had to consider was whether Laski had habitually advocated revolution by violence. The plea of justification filed by the defence claimed that he had, and set out extracts from his speeches and books endeavouring to show that if he had not done so at Newark he certainly had elsewhere. After an exhaustive examination of the facts and the law, including the reading of substantial and involved passages from textbooks defining the offences of treason and sedition, which was as meticulous as it was accurate, Slade began to examine Laski's political beliefs:

SLADE: Now let me come to what Mr Laski's theme is, and I want to do it as pithily as I can as a layman – because I am a complete layman in these matters; my knowledge of history is positively negligible – almost as bad as my knowledge of geography – and if I make silly mistakes, as no doubt I shall, it is merely because Professor Laski's theme is being put before you through the mouth, I am afraid, of a very imperfect medium. But I have done my best, and speaking as a layman, this is how I would, first of all – I have written it down myself – put his theme in just three lines.

This unjustified excess of honesty stamped Laski's political doctrines as so complicated that his own counsel had to write them down in order to remember them, and suggested that they went beyond the comprehension of ordinary men and women. This did less than justice to the acuteness of Slade's own mind and to the simplicity of Laski's dogma. And by alarming the jury it made them less sympathetic to Laski's subsequent attempts to explain what he meant, and more sympathetic to Hastings's swashbuckling cross-examination.

Opening not only gives the opportunity to display the attractiveness of one's own case but also the unattractiveness of the defence. Great care must be used before embarking on this course. Facts which seem to indicate that one line of defence will be employed may prove to be unreliable, and the jury may find the new and unexpected defence more agreeable simply because of its fresh appearance. Sometimes, however, it is imperative that an opening speech should knock away visible props of the defence. This is what Moody failed to do in the Borden case. Lizzie Borden was charged with the murder of her stepmother and her father. There was evidence to suggest that she hated her stepmother, and to prove that she loved her father. There was evidence to prove that she killed the stepmother first. Why then did she go on to kill her father? The jingle gives a clue to the answer:

> *Lizzie Borden took an axe*
> *Gave her mother forty whacks.*
> *When she saw what she had done*
> *She gave her father forty-one.*

The one person who would know that she had killed the stepmother would have been the father. She had to kill him to protect herself. This point was never made in the prosecution opening. By the time they came to address the jury again at the close of all the evidence it was lost to them. The idea that Lizzie loved her father had become too deeply implanted in the jury's mind. It was the linch-pin of the whole defence.

In many cases it is quite safe to anticipate subsequent events. Wakley did it in two ways. After telling the jury that he had merely published a report of the operation furnished him by an apparently competent person, he mitigated the damages that might be awarded against him by establishing his own bona fides:

WAKLEY: I shall not flinch from what I conceive to be my duty, but if it should appear, if by any possibility it should be proved, that this report is untrue, there is nothing that would give me greater regret than to have published any calamitous statement as to Mr Bransby Cooper, or any other individual.

Wakley knew that Cooper intended to call witnesses to say that the operation had been skilfully performed. He therefore sought to condition the jury's mind in advance:

WAKLEY: It is not by exposing such operations as these that we injure the profession [of medicine], it is inflicting the deepest injury on the profession when men come forward and swear that this operation was skilfully performed. I do not know what they will swear; you must infer that they were sufficiently ignorant to have performed the operation in a similar manner themselves.

'Honest' Bob Sievier had a different task, although he too opened to a special jury in the High Court, this time in 1920. He had twice been acquitted by Old Bailey juries on charges of blackmail. He had been an unsuccessful candidate for Parliament. He was a leading owner of racehorses, one of which was Sceptre, which in 1902 had won four of the five classic races. (Still a record.) He was a pugnacious and flamboyant character and the sporting British public adored him. The trainer Richard Wootton did not, and had distributed pamphlets over every racecourse in the county naming him as a swindler, cardsharper, and thief, and 'a man with whom no decent person would associate'. Sievier was forced to sue for libel. Wootton's defence (it was more like an attack) was that the contents of the pamphlets were true, and Sievier knew that directly he entered the witness box he was going to face a cross-examination which would range over every incident in his life. The jury had to be prepared for what was to come. When he was tried at the Old Bailey he had been represented by solicitor and counsel. This time he did the case himself. (Some said it was because his credit-worthiness was so bad that even the lawyers would not rely on his promise of payment.)

SIEVIER: I do not wish to pretend, however malicious and venomous the libel may be, that I come before you as a man who has led, or who professes to have led, that life of orthodoxy which some people might call respectable. I have lived a life among men in various countries. When I was seventeen I fought in the Kaffir War. I have made a book in Australia; in fact I have been to practically every country in the world, and when one has travelled in that way one doesn't come back to England to settle down and lead the aesthetic life. (*Laughter*.) Such a man belongs to Bohemia, and all my life I have lived in Bohemia ... I have lived a gay, easy, extravagant life; and a man has a right to live his own life, providing he leads it according to the standards of honour ...

It was beautifully done. He may have been a rogue, as the jury later found that he was, but he was an immensely attractive one. By the time that Carson, representing Wootton, interrupted Sievier in his opening the jury were ready to applaud Sievier's reply:

SIEVIER: Let me warn you about Sir Edward [Carson], Members of the Jury. You know what to expect from him. He can prove in argument that a black beetle is a fox-terrier. (*Laughter*.)

To prepare the jury for the weakest part of the case, in the way that Sievier prepared them for his own cross-examination, is important. To neglect to do so is to throw away one of the great advantages of having the ear of the jury before anyone else. In the Laski case the weakness for him lay right outside the facts, in his own character and the collective character of the jury. Laski was an intellectual, a political scientist, and a Socialist. As a special London jury they were likely to be Tory and unsympathetic to him. In addition Laski was in an especially vulnerable position because he had written about the very situation in which he now found himself. Within five minutes of beginning his cross-examination Hastings was exploiting Slade's failure to 'guard him against the inevitable'.

HASTINGS: Let me just read a sentence to you [from one of Laski's books] and ask you to tell me whether you agree with this: 'A London jury is fairly certain to award damages for libel to a Tory member of Parliament but it is also fairly certain to assume that a Labour sympathizer cannot be libelled.' Do you hear that?

LASKI: Yes.

HASTINGS: Would you agree with me that that is unfair, stupid, and offensive?

LASKI: No. I think this is an accurate summary of the history of political libel actions in London from some such period as the treason trials of 1794 down to some such period as 1924.

HASTINGS: Will you try and keep within a century or two, Professor Laski. What I am suggesting to you is that you write offensive, unfair, and violent things about anyone you do not like, in order to please what you think are your political supporters. What do you say to that?

LASKI: I say that is wholly and quite definitely untrue.

Two or three simple sentences from Slade would have blunted the effect of the whole of the cross-examination based on this passage.

In the *Herald* prosecution, counsel sought in opening to undermine the cross-examination of the Captains of the *Herald* and the other Spirit class vessels which he knew was bound to come on the lines forecast by counsel for the Captain at the time of the capsize at the wreck inquiry. By the time of the tragedy the ships had made thousands of crossings using the same system. Why should they, or anyone else, believe it was not a safe system? He said:

The Crown's case is that, given the system in operation, this was, regrettably, a disaster almost waiting to happen: that it had not happened sooner, despite the system rather than because of it. The fact that the system had survived without a serious incident of anything like the magnitude of what happened on the 6th of March, 1987, does not, the Crown suggest, show it was a safe system. Those previous incidents I have mentioned of the doors being left open, might be said to be trivial in comparison. Unfortunately, they are symptomatic, the Crown suggest, of a system that was unsafe. Hence it may have been and was indeed the case, that for years there was no incident involving injury or loss of life, but that, the Crown suggest for your consideration, was despite rather than because of a system inherently unsafe, that had somehow managed to operate through good fortune.

And when he has covered all the ground he thinks it expedient to deal with how does the advocate round off his opening? This is a matter of personal preference, but he ought not to have put himself in the position of the Scots advocate who thought it necessary to say, 'I think I have exhausted my subject, I fear I have exhausted your patience, I know I have exhausted myself.'

In a criminal trial the jury are frequently reminded of their duty. The way in which Dickens did this in the Peasenhall case is a model:

Gentlemen, you will have narrowly to watch the evidence, and say whether it is of such a character that you can thoroughly rely upon it, and whether the suggestions made by the prosecution are well-founded. If not, then dismiss any suggestions I have made from your minds. If there is a real doubt in the case, the point is that the accused is not merely entitled to the benefit of it. That is not a fair way of putting it. If there is a real doubt in this case, the accused is entitled to acquittal, because the Crown have to prove to your satisfaction that the accused is guilty. We not only ask for justice; we are bound to see that it is done; and it is my duty to bring home to your minds reasonable conviction. If you are reasonably convinced, taking the evidence as a whole, then according to your oaths and according to the duty you owe to society, you are bound to say that he is guilty. If we have not proved it, you also owe it, not only to the oaths you have taken, but in your duty to the accused, to acquit him upon this most grave and serious charge.

Some advocates believe that the opening should end with a short recapitulation of the facts or arguments on which the case is based. Others choose a single issue to ram home to the jury. Slade adopted this course:

One other word, and one other word only, and I have finished. As I said earlier on, whether you like Professor Laski's politics or whether you loathe them has nothing more to do with this case than with the man in the moon. All of us are agreed upon that. It does not in the least matter. It does not matter whether you have any shade of political opinion or none. You are here – as I know you will – to administer justice and to administer it impartially, and politics have not, and I hope never will have, any part in the administration of justice in this country.

No clear principle can be formulated. It is safe to say only that the advocate must at all cost avoid the tactic once indulged in by one Treasury Counsel at the Old Bailey who finished his opening with these words:

I have set the stage for you Members of the Jury. The scenery is in place. Let me ring up the curtain and the play begin.

Defending counsel, in an aside which rang round the court, asked him:

And have your actors learned their lines?

Establishing the Case

By far the largest part of the advocate's work has nothing to do with advocacy at all. Something like four fifths of the common lawyer's time is spent drafting or advising on the multifarious documents which have to come into existence before any trial can begin. Unless the advocate can master the intricacies of drafting pleadings in civil cases or charges in criminal cases he may not secure the practice of an advocate at all. If he is forever losing cases because he has pleaded inaccurately he is liable to lose his solicitors faster than any ability on his feet may gain them. In this field it is practice which makes perfect. The 'pleader' needs a hefty dose of common sense, a degree of foresight, and a knowledge of form, precedent, and law which only constant work on pleadings will bring.

The perils of pleading can be many and not at all obvious. This is particularly so in libel cases. In the Laski case the defence was amended shortly before the trial began to add the defence of justification in these words: 'Further, or alternatively, the said words are true in substance and in fact.'

This gave rise to Slade's contention that the defence were justifying Wentworth Day's implied suggestion of cowardice. His argument was that 'the said words' were without limit and included Wentworth Day's question with the implied suggestion, as well as constituting a justification of the libel (that he advocated revolution by violence) in its ordinary sense and in its innuendo sense (i.e. not only that Laski had advocated revolution by violence at Newark, but that he had habitually done so, and that in doing so he had declared his intention to commit and had conspired with others to commit, the crimes of treason, treason-felony, sedition, riot, and breach of the peace). As if this was not already complicated enough by itself, Slade told the jury that if the justification had read, 'the words in their natural and ordinary meaning are true in substance and in fact', the defence would not have been justifying the innuendo. By this stage most lawyers take a deep breath and begin all over again. It is fiendishly and unrealistically convoluted.

Compared with these, most pleadings seem almost human in their simplicity. But all of them are couched in language which is largely incomprehensible to the layman and a source of perpetual dismay to the lover of the English language. Happily the worst excesses of verbosity and rigidity were swept away by the Judicature Acts at the end of the nineteenth century and the Indictment Act of the twentieth. Prior to that time few pleadings and no Indictment could be amended; any and every error was fatal. In 1841 Lord Cardigan was charged at the Old Bailey with the murder of 'Harvey Garnett Phipps'. It was proved that he killed 'Harvey Garnett Phipps Tuckett'. The Judge had no option but to direct the jury to acquit him.

There was, however, a majesty in the language then used in most legal documents. The Indictment against Elizabeth Canning for perjury took over half an hour to read; today it would take less than two minutes. But it would not contain this:

... not having the fear of God before your eyes, but being moved and seduced by the instigation of the Devil, and having no regard for the laws and statutes of the realm, not fearing the punishments therein contained, and unlawfully, wickedly, maliciously, and deliberately advising, contriving, and intending to pervert the due course of law and justice ...

Today the majesty has disappeared. There is no pleasure to be gained from the study of similar modern documents. They have only this in common with those of the past, that they cover every eventuality. A taxi driver summoned to pick up a fare from a dance held on Army property fell over a low wall and broke his leg. The necessary particulars of negligence included in the Statement of Claim read as follows:

(a) Failed to provide any or any adequate lighting on or about the said premises.
(b) Failed to provide any or any adequate warning of the said wall which constituted an obstruction.

(c) Failed to provide any or any adequate direction as to a path which might with safety be followed to and from the premises.

(d) Failed to provide any or any adequate fencing or guard upon the said wall.

(e) Failed to take any or all reasonable care to prevent the plaintiff from being exposed to unnecessary risk and danger and/or to prevent the premises from misleading the plaintiff as to their nature and use.

(f) Knew, or ought to have known, that the said wall was, or might have been a danger, and/or unsafe, and/or a trap, to persons coming on to the said premises who were, or might have been, unacquainted with the same.

It is right that the defence should have notice of the items of negligence on which the plaintiff relies. These details however are meant to cover everything which might arise. And they do so in exhaustive minutiae. If they do not, then the likelihood is that a demand for 'Further and Better Particulars' will be made by the defence. Counsel for the plaintiff may not think the demand justified and refuse to give them. On what is known as a 'Summons for Directions' a Master of the High Court can order the delivery of the Particulars requested. Either side may appeal against the Master's order to a Judge of the High Court. If they are really determined to prove themselves in the right they can (with the leave of the Judge) appeal again to the Court of Appeal. This can go on for months. Sometimes it does. And the game can be played not only on the pleadings and the Further and Better Particulars but also with 'Discovery of Documents' and/or 'Interrogatories'. It is said that one Chancery barrister became so imbued with the spirit of such documents as these that he drafted one question in an Interrogatory:

Did you not come to the Trustees of the estate or one of them, and if so, which, with tears in your eyes, or one of them, and if so, which . . .

The system is designed to ensure that a plaintiff or a defendant to an action has the means to compel disclosure of all the facts and documents which are relevant to the action. It is as near foolproof as it could be, but it is inordinately expensive and inordinately complicated. Only a fool or a knave (or a Master of the High Court) would claim to have mastered the procedure in all its branches. There are a host of decisions on every conceivable aspect of these preliminary matters, many of them conflicting. The only really surprising thing about the system is that it is not used more than it is to delay or defeat valid claims. All the rules of the High Court are contained in one vast book: the White Book. It runs to 4,000 tightly printed pages and needs a separate volume for the index and tables. It is commonly referred to as the Bible of the High Court practitioner. This is overstating the position but it certainly contains his Ten Commandments.

But when the advocate rises to his feet and calls his first witness, it is too late for books. And who is to be his first witness? Many criminal cases are L.P.s: loser and policeman. Most civil cases depend almost entirely on the evidence of the plaintiff or the defendant. Then the choice is simple. The general rule is to call the evidence in the same sort of order as that adopted in the opening. Some order is essential. Evidence presented in disarray will not help either Judge or jury to understand it.

So much is obvious. Opinions differ, however, as to the order to be chosen when two or more witnesses have to be called to speak as to the same incident, one of whom may be a good witness and the other a bad one. Some take the view that to call the good one first will catch and retain the jury's attention; then get through the other as speedily and cursorily as possible. Others say it will only serve to diminish the court's reliance on the first witness as the subsequent ones are called, and it is better to leave the best till last. If the advocate has done his job properly in his opening it does not matter which order he chooses. Opening in a civil action for assault against four men, knowing he was calling the plaintiff and two other eye-witnesses who all gave differing accounts of what happened when the plaintiff received his injuries, one advocate said:

None of them [the witnesses] will give an exactly similar account of what happened. Of course, the human eye can only see so much, and it would be too much to expect that from their different positions, as I have described them to you, each should see every movement made by the bodies and arms of each of these four defendants. Indeed, you would think it exceedingly suspicious if they did.

So virtue was culled from necessity, and it did not matter in what order he called the witnesses.

When the examination of the witness begins, there is one rule the advocate must observe. Except upon matters which are not in dispute, he must not 'lead' the witness. That is, he must not ask questions which are so framed that the witness will understand from them the answer he is expected to give. This is more difficult than it sounds. Wakley ran into difficulties within minutes of calling his first witness, Alderman Partridge, who said he had witnessed the operation carried out by Cooper on the patient who had later died. A model of a body, tied in the way then practised to perform the operation of lithotomy, lay on the table in the well of the court. There was no objection therefore to the 'leading' nature of the first two questions.

WAKLEY (*pointing to the model*): The hands and feet were tied in this way?

PARTRIDGE: Yes.

WAKLEY: And the knees tied to the neck in this way?

PARTRIDGE: Yes.

WAKLEY: And in this position the patient remained nearly one hour?

JUDGE: You are making him assert that.

WAKLEY: How long did the patient remain in that position?

This is the form question should have taken in the first place. Despite the Judge's observation and a later protest by Scarlett who appeared for Cooper, Wakley continued to put questions which contained the evidence he wanted to establish instead of eliciting it from the witness:

WAKLEY: Did he [the patient] request to be loosened?

PARTRIDGE: He did to that effect; he desired that Mr Cooper would leave off and desist altogether.

WAKLEY: Did the operator at the same time declare he could not explain the difficulty?

PARTRIDGE: Yes.

JUDGE: You must ask what he said.

WAKLEY: What did the operator say?

PARTRIDGE: He said more than once I think, but once certainly, that he could not explain the difficulty – that he could not explain what the difficulty was – was, I think the expression.

WAKLEY: Did the operator appear hurried and confused?

JUDGE: How did the operator appear? You appear to be a man of intelligence. You know how to put your questions . . .

WAKLEY: Did he introduce his finger with great force?

JUDGE: Did he introduce his finger, and how did he introduce it? If you make it necessary for me to be constantly interrupting you, I must desire that all the questions be put through me.

This is by no means an uncommon example of an examination conducted by someone without experience. Leading questions like these do great damage; they destroy the reality of the evidence and prevent the character of the witness emerging, they destroy the reliability of the evidence by suggesting the answer the witness should give, and they stamp the partiality of the examiner. Even if they are not objected to by the Judge or the other side they substantially reduce the value of the witness's evidence. On many matters the witnesses may be led. As a case goes on and the area in conflict becomes well defined so the whole of the preliminary undisputed or unimportant evidence may be 'led' from the witnesses in order to save time.

If the witness must not be led, he must be guided. The evidence is given responsively, in answer to questions, not spontaneously, and the advocate must keep his witnesses under control. Twice during the trial of Seddon the Judge intervened to rebuke counsel for the prosecution (Rufus Isaacs) for allowing the witness to go on after he had answered the question he had been asked He told one witness:

JUDGE: These people are being tried on a capital charge. It might possibly be, if you do more than answer the question or make any remark, you might be doing or saying something which would not be evidence, and then the trial might have to be begun all over again.

This objection has greater importance in a criminal trial before a jury than before a single Judge sitting alone. The lawyer, by the time he becomes a Judge, has considerable experience of putting out of his mind irrelevant or prejudicial matter. A jury has none at all, and will sometimes discover in facts which ought not to be before them (e.g. the character of a defendant) good reason for deciding what verdict to return.

The witnesses must not be kept so tightly reined that their evidence is robbed of character, or they are unable to show their own characters. Abraham Lincoln declared that Henry Ward Beecher was the greatest living American. By 1875, the year of

Tilton's action against him, he had made the Congregationalist Church in Brooklyn one of the best known in the English-speaking world. He was an accomplished actor and mimic. Of the power of the human voice he said:

The voice is the bell of the soul, or the iron and crashing of the anvil. It is a magician's wand, full of incantation and witchery; it is the sceptre in a King's hand and sways men with imperial authority.

To have kept such a witness on too tight a rein would have wasted his finest assets. One of the things said against him, after Mrs Tilton had confessed to her husband her adulterous union with Beecher, was that he had entered her room alone where she was lying prostrate with nervous exhaustion and had wrung a written retraction out of her. His attorney, Evarts, in examining him on this part of the case, led him, then guided him, and then unleashed him.

EVARTS: You came through the door that went immediately into the room where the bed was?
BEECHER: I did.
EVARTS: Were the folding doors closed at that time?
BEECHER: No sir, they were open.
EVARTS: Did they remain open?
BEECHER: They remained open, I think, all the time . . .
EVARTS: Describe the scene, as you saw it, as you entered the room.
BEECHER: The bed was dressed in pure white, Mrs Tilton was dressed in pure white, and her face was as white as the bed, lying a little above a level, reclined on pillows (*arching himself back in demonstration*), her hands in that form (*placing his hands palm to palm*), in a very natural way on her breast. I drew a chair, or there was a chair by the bedside. I sat down on it. I said to her . . .

At this point there was a long interruption as to whether the conversation was admissible. The Judge ruled that it was and Evarts, who had clearly decided on this course of action in advance, asked only one question to get Beecher started again:

EVARTS: Mr Beecher proceed now . . .
BEECHER: I said to her, 'Elizabeth, I have just seen your husband, and had a long interview with him. He has been making many statements to me, and charges, and has sent me to you in respect of some of them that you should verify them.' I then said: 'He has charged me that I

have corrupted your simplicity and your truthfulness. He has also charged me with attempting improprieties ...' It is a hard thing (*starting to weep*) for a man to speak to a woman that he reveres such things, and I could not express myself very clearly. 'Are these things so Elizabeth?' She – there was the faintest quiver, and tears trickled down her cheeks, but no answer. I said to her ...

This went on for over ten minutes. Newspaper reports of the trial claimed that no one breathed throughout this narrative, so close was the attention given to it. This showed no lack of control on Evarts's part, rather the complete harmony existing between the witness and himself. Once the narrative was ended, Evarts was there to drive home the point he wanted to make:

EVARTS: During the writing [of the retraction by Mrs Tilton] did you in any manner dictate or suggest any of the language used?
BEECHER: No, sir.
EVARTS: Did you in any manner indicate any form of expression or substance in it?
BEECHER: I did not.

Ideally an examination should be a form of 'spontaneous conversation' between examiner and examined. This cannot be done if the advocate's head is buried in his brief. The order in which he wants the witness to give his evidence and the main lines of that evidence should be memorized. And it cannot be done with most witnesses, the vast majority of whom are incapable of spontaneous conversation even outside the strange and worrying atmosphere of a court room. They may be timid or garrulous, ebullient or simply stupid, and the advocate will have precious little time in which to decide which category to place them in before he begins the examination. He must never forget that the first few minutes in a witness-box can be terrifying. It is the loneliest place on earth. If the examiner does not then appear as a friend, it is unlikely he will ever be able to get everything he wants from the witness or give him the opportunity to appear in his best light. If misunderstandings occur they are difficult to clear away. It is of the utmost importance therefore that the examiner does not let his patience desert him. Nothing of his own personal feelings, which may direct the jury's attention unfavourably on the witness, must be allowed to escape.

There is no magic formula to be learned and then used for these purposes. Common sense and practice will show only that the best questions are short questions, the best language plain and simple: the ordinary and the unambiguous should be chosen in preference to anything else. In the *Herald* case a few witnesses were called three times, at the wreck inquiry, at the Coroner's inquest and at the manslaughter trial at the Old Bailey. One of these was the Third Officer. One part of his evidence was directed to showing that at the time 'Harbour Stations', the announcement to the officers and crew to prepare to cast off moorings and go to sea, was called on the ferry, the Chief Officer was on G deck, the main car deck. The inner and outer clam bow doors, the ones which were left open, were on this deck. It was the duty of the Chief Officer to ensure at least that the Assistant Bosun was in position to shut these doors before proceeding to sea. At the wreck inquiry he was asked these questions:

COUNSEL: When you arrived on the loading deck, as I understand it, there had been loading on G deck, attention had turned to E deck [the second and higher vehicle loading deck] . . . and you continued loading E deck?

WITNESS: Correct.

COUNSEL: Shortly after arriving the Chief Officer went?

WITNESS: Correct.

COUNSEL: So, as I understand it, you were the officer on the car decks responsible for loading.

WITNESS: Yes.

COUNSEL: Now at some stage the Chief Officer in fact returned to the loading decks, is that right?

WITNESS: That is correct.

COUNSEL: What stage had the loading reached?

WITNESS: I blocked the ship in between the casings up as far as the fore end of the alleyways on G deck.

. . . . .

COUNSEL: When the Chief Officer came down did you meet him?

WITNESS: Not face to face.

COUNSEL: How did you realize he was there?

WITNESS: Because he took over supervision of the deck.

COUNSEL: How did he do that if you did not meet him face to face?

WITNESS: Because he took over direction of traffic and communication by radio (of which I also have one) with the shore.

COUNSEL: But did you have a discussion with him as to who was taking over the job of being responsible for loading?

WITNESS: No, but I was aware of the situation.

. . . . .

COUNSEL: When you left the area at the forward end of G deck, who did you leave behind in that area?

WITNESS: Chief Officer.

The statement made by the witness on which this examination was conducted was very brief and gave little detail. To obtain the detail he wanted, the advocate had to ask a number of questions where he did not know what the witness's answer was going to be. In such circumstances it is very easy to get diverted from the course that the examiner really wishes to pursue. Between the last two questions there were over fifty others covering other aspects of the witness's recollection. Such questions tend to become less precise and to employ more words than are necessary.

Six months later the same witness was called by the Coroner to speak on the same matter.

CORONER: Can we have a look at the loading of E and G decks? We have heard from several other witnesses that there were vehicles, 'drops' they called them, loaded on to G deck to make it partly loaded, and then people turned their attention to E deck, which was fully loaded and the bow door of E deck was closed. Would you have had any part in any of that stage of the operation?

WITNESS: I did not have any part in the loading of drops on G deck. I took over from the Chief Officer on E deck. Early on in the loading there, we were both down there, and then he left, and left it for me to get on with it.

CORONER: Yes. Did you later on meet the Chief Officer on G deck?

WITNESS: After we had fully loaded E deck, and then, yes I did.

CORONER: Yes. Was there any kind of argument between you?

WITNESS: No.

CORONER: Was there any discussion?

WITNESS: No.

CORONER: *No argument and no discussion?* Was there a time when he suggested you should go aft?

WITNESS: Yes.

CORONER: Could you tell me why he suggested you should go aft.

WITNESS: Because harbour stations had been called.

CORONER: *Harbour stations had been called.* What would you do aft at harbour stations?

WITNESS: Seek permission from the bridge to single up.

CORONER: That's the ropes holding the stern of the ship . . .

WITNESS: Reduce the number of ropes holding the ship alongside. When that was done we, you would just wait until you got the order to let go.

Apart from the first question, which is no more than a scene-setter, the questions are much more to the point and much shorter. They would have been shorter still but for the unfortunate repetition of the answers by the questioner (italicized for emphasis). Many examiners develop this unnecessary and immensely irritating habit. It can drive the hearer into a frenzy since it gives the impression the examiner is not capable of hearing the answers himself. Repeating a single significant answer with loving attention to the exact words used, as if savouring the devastating effect of them on one's opponent's case, can be very effective. Doing it like this is not.

Exactly three years later, the witness was called for the third time.

COUNSEL: Were you the loading officer at some stage?

WITNESS: Yes.

COUNSEL: For the whole time?

WITNESS: Yes

COUNSEL: Who else was the loading officer at any time?

WITNESS: Chief Officer.

. . . . .

COUNSEL: Do you remember – I do not think there is any dispute about this – some sort of problem with the shore side loading personnel about some vehicle, or something of that sort?

WITNESS: Yes.

COUNSEL: How did that affect who the loading officer was, this problem, if in any way?

WITNESS: Well, the Chief Officer arrived on the vehicle deck.

COUNSEL: Which deck are we talking about please?

WITNESS: G deck.

COUNSEL: What did he do?

WITNESS: He took over the loading from me.

COUNSEL: Once he had taken over, where did you go?

WITNESS: Nowhere at first.

COUNSEL: Are you still on G deck for the time being?

WITNESS: Yes.

COUNSEL: Can I approach it in this way: harbour stations must have been called?

WITNESS: Yes.

COUNSEL: Do you remember who gave the instruction to call harbour stations?

WITNESS: No.

COUNSEL: Who normally gave it?

WITNESS: Well, the person who was loading the deck.

COUNSEL: I suppose it could have been you or the Chief Officer, could it?

WITNESS: Yes.

COUNSEL: Is that the correct position?

WITNESS: I can't remember.

COUNSEL: But in any case, did the time come when you left G deck?

WITNESS: Yes.

COUNSEL: Is that before or after harbour stations was called, do you remember?

WITNESS: After, as best I remember. Well, yes after.

This is as close to an ideal examination as could be achieved. The questions are clear, short, and to the point. This is an examiner who is singing the first line of the old song 'I know where I'm going' with a confidence that is as reassuringly plain to the witness as it is to the court. He must avoid, at all costs, getting on to the second line: 'But God knows who's going with me'.

Alas, despite possessing and exhibiting all the skills, no examiner and, as we shall see later, no cross-examiner can know when he is going to come unstuck. The same examiner referred to in the preceding paragraph came spectacularly unstuck only three weeks later. The wreck inquiry decided, '... by the autumn of 1986 (about six months before the disaster) the shore staff of the company were well aware of the possibility that one of their ships would sail with her stern or bow doors open'. If this could be established in the criminal trial then the 'unsafe system' could be proved against those shore staff and the company and the charge of manslaughter proved. The wreck inquiry justified their finding by reference to four memoranda written by Masters of the Spirit class ships as a result of occasions when the doors were left open at sailing. The prosecution relied on the same memoranda and the same occasions. One had been written by the Master of the sister ship the *Pride of Free Enterprise* in October 1984. This read:

Twice since going on the Zeebrugge run, this ship has sailed with the stern or bow doors open. No doubt this is caused by job/rank changes from the Calais run, however all those named persons must see that the system is worked to make sure this dangerous situation does not occur. Give it your utmost attention.

The Master had not been called to give evidence at the wreck inquiry. That court acted on the basis that the document correctly represented the facts. No criminal court, at least in England, could afford to make such a presumption, so the Master had to be called to give evidence. This is the relevant part of the examination. The Master was asked to look at the document.

COUNSEL: Do you recognize your signature to that memorandum?
WITNESS: Yes.
COUNSEL: Just refresh your memory, we've had it read many times, just refresh your memory.
WITNESS: Yes, fine.
COUNSEL: Do you recall what caused you to pose that memorandum to the deck officers, Bosun and Assistant Bosuns aboard the *Pride*?
WITNESS: Well, in the context as I said in my statement that it is now some six years since I wrote that memo, so the complete details I won't be sure on but the overriding situation, yes.
COUNSEL: Is there anything more than appears from what is in that memo that you could help us about at this time gap?
WITNESS: Well, yes. Would you like me to go through what I remember of the incidents of that time?
COUNSEL: First of all, were you serving onboard during any incident to which this memo, as a result of which this memo was published?
WITNESS: I don't particularly remember being onboard at either incident. As I've said in this statement this time on, I cannot remember whether I was onboard for one of those incidents or both, in fact, but I don't believe so.

The advocate correctly abandoned the topic. If he had gone on asking about the contents of the document he would have been attempting to obtain evidence of the incidents at second hand, based on what others had told him. It would be 'hear-say' evidence and not admissible in a criminal trial. The witness could be asked about such evidence in cross-examination. Later he was. He said the incidents had occurred before the ferry had 'sailed', and that the memorandum did not correctly state what had happened. He had 'beefed it up' to add importance to the message he was sending the crew, for the document had never, in any event, gone to the shore staff.

It is a mistake to assume that witnesses help the advocate with his examination. Even a man on trial for his life like Robert Wood made his own examination by Marshall Hall as difficult as possible. Marshall Hall asked at the outset:

HALL: Did you kill Phyllis Dimmock? (*No reply. The witness 'cast his eyes to Heaven'*.)
Did you kill Phyllis Dimmock?
WOOD: Ridiculous. (*Arms spread wide.*)
HALL: You must answer straight. I will only ask you perfectly straight questions. Once again, did you kill Phyllis Dimmock?
WOOD: No, I most certainly did not.

It was a disastrous start. But with patience and tenacity it can be overcome. (Wood was acquitted.)

The good examination does more than simply elicit the evidence the witness can give. In the same way that one of the tasks in opening is to anticipate the weaknesses, the advocate must do the same in examination-in-chief. It not only reduces the area open to the cross-examiner but also allows the witness to present the best possible face on awkward facts. In 1924 Sir John Simon appeared for the Midland Bank in the Mr 'A' case. They were being sued for the return of £130,000 by a Mr and Mrs Robinson. The money had been obtained from Mr 'A', in fact an Indian prince, by blackmail. Mrs Robinson had allowed herself to be 'seduced' by the prince and carried off to a hotel in Paris. As the result of a conspiracy between the prince's A.D.C., a solicitor named Hobbs and another man named Newton, Newton, posing as Mr Robinson (Mr Robinson was not presentable enough to play the part of the husband of a society lady) burst into the bedroom while the prince and Mrs Robinson were in bed together and obtained a cheque for £150,000 to assuage the outraged feelings of the 'husband', and to prevent divorce proceedings, naming the prince as co-respondent, being brought. The cheque was drawn in the name of Robinson, but to keep the amount obtained secret from the real Robinson, it was paid into the Midland Bank by Hobbs in the name of Robinson. Then paying the Robinsons a mere £20,000, Hobbs successfully double-crossed them by drawing out the remainder and absconding. Some years later when he learned the truth, the real Robinson sued the Midland Bank for negligence in allowing Hobbs to get away with the balance. It could hardly be described as a meritorious action and the Bank fought it tooth and nail. Their defence was that since the money had been obtained by fraud, Robinson was not entitled to it. To prove the fraud and that the Robinsons were parties to it the bank called Newton, an admitted member of the conspiracy.

Newton had not been prosecuted for his part in the adventure. Following its successful conclusion he had taken the precaution of living in France. To come to England was tantamount to putting his head in a noose. To enter a witness-box and tell the story of the conspiracy was to help tighten the noose. Simon knew Newton would be cross-examined on the inducement which had overcome his natural caution. So at the end of his opening he said this:

SIMON: We are a Bank you must remember, and if you believe me, the Midland Bank and the solicitors who appear for them are deeply concerned in this matter that they may do what is their duty here to this court and the Judge; and that is all. We conceived it to be our duty, and I think we were quite right, to see whether there was any means of getting Newton here; it was not a question of getting his statement, his statement we had got; it was not a question of getting his evidence, his evidence we had got. The question was, could we get him here? Well, Mr Newton, after some reflection, with which we had nothing to do, decided that he was prepared to run the risk – and it is a very serious risk – of coming from abroad to this country, if he was promised a certain payment. We promised him that payment. We promised him £3,000. There [*pointing*] is Mr Newton. I call him into the witness-box.

Whatever cross-examination came on this subsequently, the effect of it was now blunted by this full and frank, and highly dramatic, ending to his opening. But Simon had not finished there. He knew Newton had a conviction for forgery. If that were sprung on the witness during the cross-examination, not only would it unsettle him, it would also upset the jury. Simon put it before the jury himself. He was examining Newton about the time after the cheque had been obtained.

NEWTON: During lunch Hobbs said, 'you must take the cheque and go and open an account in the name of Robinson with it', which I refused to do.

SIMON: So he wanted you to do it?

NEWTON: Yes.

SIMON: And you refused to do that?

NEWTON: Yes.

SIMON: I am sorry to have to ask you Mr Newton, but I had better ask you here; have you been convicted of forgery?

NEWTON: Yes I have, Sir John. If I hadn't been, I probably should not be here now for £3,000 or £30,000.

SIMON: I think that was in 1907, or 1908 perhaps; and you served a sentence in respect of it?

NEWTON: I did, yes.

SIMON: So the invitation to pay the money in yourself did not attract you . . .

JUDGE: I think we may take it: once bit, twice shy. (*Laughter.*)

The Judge's intervention (it was Darling, whose weakness for witticisms contributed to the travesty in the 'Black Book' case) rounded the episode off perfectly although it may have obscured the date Simon had been so careful to put in, since there were seventeen years between Newton's conviction and the Mr 'A' trial.

It is obviously the duty of the advocate to present his witnesses so that they may appear in as favourable a light as possible. He is not there to highlight their faults. That is the task of the other side. Simon's, 'I'm sorry to have to ask you', in circumstances such as these implying how distasteful and regrettable it was to have to rake over the past, was ideal. In many cases, certainly in all sexual cases, it is only by great deftness, by communicable tact and sympathy, that an advocate can induce women witnesses to give evidence. It requires much more than the plain guidance already referred to. There the advocate is steering the witness through his evidence keeping to the relevant portions and keeping him from straying into the irrelevancies. Here the difficulty is to get the witness started at all. It was said of Hume Williams, who had a large practice in the Divorce Division, that his voice and manner soothed and comforted women petitioners stumbling through the miserable task of relating in public the crude and cruel wounds they had received in private. To put them at their ease he always began with half a dozen seemingly irrelevant questions. He listened to the answers with deep attention. By the time he reached the important matters he had established such trust between himself and the witness that they could answer all his questions as simply and directly as they were put.

Properly examined, women and children are by far the best witnesses. But women, in addition to the normal disadvantages from which witnesses suffer, are suddenly thrust into an aggressively male world, and they tend to don a protective armour. Some become blatantly flirtatious, others unnecessarily shy; all are unnatural to a greater or lesser extent because they are suspicious. By the time Mrs Gardiner came to give evidence at the second trial of her husband she was free from any such effects. A very sick woman, and under immense strain, the effect of this alibi evidence she gave, covering the time the murder was committed, can only have been very powerful:

WILD: When you got into bed could you sleep?
GARDINER: No. As soon as I got into bed my little boy Bertie woke up.
WILD: What happened then?
GARDINER: I went to him.
WILD: How long were you with him?
GARDINER: Five minutes or more because he cried very much.
WILD: After you came back from Bertie, did you go back to the bedroom?
GARDINER: Yes.
WILD: Was your husband there?
GARDINER: He was in bed.
WILD: Then what did you do after?
GARDINER: I got out of bed again, because I had got a pain in my body, and I said to my husband, 'I shall go and get some brandy, as I have such pains in my body', and I did so.
WILD: What did your husband say?
GARDINER: He said he would go and get some for me, and I said, as I was out of bed I would get it.

Wild then established the time with her and went on:

WILD: Did your husband go to sleep?
GARDINER: Yes, he did, but I didn't.
WILD: Did you sleep after that?
GARDINER: I did not sleep till after the clock struck five.
WILD: Did anything else happen in the night to any of the other children?

GARDINER: Yes, the twins woke up. I put one in bed with my husband and me, and one with the eldest girl.

WILD: Did the twin remain in bed with you?

GARDINER: Yes, till we got up in the morning.

WILD: When you went to sleep was your husband by your side?

GARDINER: Yes, with the little girl in his arms.

WILD: Could he possibly have left the room from the time you went to bed and went to sleep?

GARDINER: He could not.

A simple tale, simply told. There are no histrionics, no effects, no high and vibrant tones. There is only a quiet narration, little above a whisper, about a man who is alleged to be a murderer, sleeping beside his wife with one of their children in his arms. It could not have been done more effectively.

It will be noticed that there is nothing remarkable about Wild's questions to Mrs Gardiner. In print, robbed of the atmosphere of their delivery, they seem pedestrian in the extreme. It is this which gives them their virtue. They do not intrude. This is almost the best test of an examination-in-chief. To achieve this state, as Lord Justice Wrottesley said, 'will often tax the advocate to the utmost of his skill and sagacity'. It is cross-examination which receives all the attention, but more cases are won by a proper examination-in-chief than by the most brilliant cross-examination.

It was said that Scarlett always examined his witnesses himself, not trusting them to anyone else. This is not true, but it points the importance he attached to it. His particular ability was said to lie in his capacity to get the witness to tell his story as if for the first time. His manner was contented and his tone conversational. He was never, or at least he never appeared to be, discomforted by the replies he received. If the advocate gives any sign that he finds difficulty in believing the witness, how can he expect the jury to do so?

Finally, when he has finished, he must sit down. This is much more of a problem than it sounds. The temptation to improve on an answer already given, allied to a fear that the subject has not been sufficiently covered, all too often leads an advocate to ask one last question. It is nearly always fatal. Examination-in-chief is no time for exploration. Sir Valentine Holmes may have seemed to fall into this trap when he examined one of Laski's witnesses who had been present at Newark.

HOLMES: Could you hear Professor Laski's reply [to Wentworth Day's question]?

WITNESS: Mainly, yes.

HOLMES: Did you hear him at any time say, 'As for violence, if Labour could not obtain what it needed by general consent, we shall have to use violence, even if it means revolution'?

WITNESS: No.

HOLMES: Or anything like it?

WITNESS: Similar, but the words 'Labour Party' were never used in it at all.

In his final speech to the jury Hastings chided Holmes for that last question: 'Perhaps Sir Valentine Holmes said that a little rashly.' Then he went on to say:

HASTINGS: He [Laski] did not mention the Labour Party, but who else was going to start it? There it is; it is admitted by Mr Poole that in substance that is what Professor Laski said. I think Mr Poole was one of the first witnesses called; he was released quite quickly and went back to this town where, no doubt, he was suitably reproved for having given away something which was not entirely desired.

This was not very accurate, but it was immensely attractive. Hastings was not an advocate to whom entries could be given with impunity. If he fails in all his other objectives, no advocate should end his examination-in-chief knowing that he has smoothed the task of his opponent.

Experts, without exception, provide the advocate with his most painful experience. Some are 'witness-trained', in the sense that although their reports are written in the incomprehensible jargon of their particular field, they have the capacity in court to translate complex language and ideas into simple, straightforward words which they use at a pace which those who have to listen and make a final decision can master. Most experts are not so trained and have no or little understanding of the inability of the layman to understand what on earth they are talking about. In these cases the advocate must act as an interpreter. This means he must know the language and he must have a full grasp of the subject. The right evidence will only be given if the right questions are asked. All too frequently, both in evidence-in-chief and in cross-examination, the right questions are not asked.

In the wreck inquiry into the loss of the *Herald* the Judge and the four assessors had considerable experience and expertise in the areas covered by the experts' evidence. They had copies of the reports and by agreement a short cut was taken, with the advocate reading the report and only asking occasional questions. If this had not been the case, all passages like this would have been double Dutch to most people:

QUESTION: Can we go back to page 2 and can we just first of all pick up your comment about the bow wave and squat calculations? You say: 'The non-linear calculation method,' and you refer to references 3 and 4, 'usually predicts the wave profile along a ship's side, and its bow and stern sinkage, with fair accuracy. In this method the shape of the underwater part of the hull at rest is defined by a table of lateral and vertical offsets at a number of axial linear stations. The same definition of hull shape can be used in an alternative linear theory evaluation of the wave profile. Results obtained by these two methods for the *Herald of Free Enterprise* at 6m draft in the speed range 15–20 knots are shown in Fig. 5 as solid lines.' We will come back to that in a moment. 'It can be seen that the two theories give roughly similar results, with the apparent rise of water at the hull side, equal to bow sinkage plus wave height relative to far upstream, in all cases less than one metre at the FP.' What does that stand for? A. Forward Perpendicular.

Such a course could not be adopted in front of a lay tribunal. Before the witness was allowed to launch into his calculations, the basic terms 'bow wave' and 'squat' would need to be explained. If they were not then the audience would be unable to follow and absorb the evidence.

Generally, laymen are fascinated by expert evidence. If it is lucidly presented, their powers of concentration are remarkable whatever their outward symbols of intellectual status. But if the evidence is not so presented, that same audience will switch off. Once that is done it will take a great deal to make them switch on again. In a City fraud trial a witness was called to explain to the jury a hedging operation to guard against sudden falls in the market price of a particular share traded on the Stock Exchange. A document which was an exhibit in the case was read to the witness which contained the terms 'put option', 'FTSE [pronounced Footsie] option' and 'hedging the residual amount'. The witness was American and spoke English with a strong accent. He also spoke very fast.

COUNSEL: I want to ask you, having gone through that, to explain to us in the simplest terms if you can, what that was all about and what the strategy was, because the concept of the put options and hedging is something that I have been waiting for you to explain if you will.

WITNESS: Oh dear.

COUNSEL: So if you can help us in the simplest way.

The reply of the witness does not suggest that he had been warned before he came into court what his role was to be. It was not a good start. The likelihood of obtaining an answer which was going to assist the lay audience to understand was reduced by asking the witness to answer four separate questions at the same time:

1 What the document was 'all about'.
2 What the 'strategy' was.
3 The 'concept of put options'.
4 The 'concept of hedging'.

The reply did not help.

WITNESS: Right. The situation with the rights issue was, of course, uncertain in terms of the residual position that the Bank would be left with, if any at all. I mean, the – that is something which we could not – we could not judge with any particular certainty at that time. Consequently, it was not – it would have been quite risky to have hedged in any other way than the, the FTSE option which involved paying a premium and the worst situation was you would have lost your investment in the premium. If—

COUNSEL: I am going to slow you down because it is obviously a matter in which you deal every day, and you are an expert in it. When you say 'paying a premium', what are you actually buying or hiring when you take out FTSE options?

Counsel was obviously right to attempt to slow the witness down. He had not yet answered any one of the four questions. In such a position it can be seen that an examining advocate must insist that his expert clearly and concisely defines the terms he finds it necessary to use. Unless he does so the lay audience is not going to follow the evidence. They will not understand it, still less remember it. This witness was allowed to blunder on.

WITNESS: Well, the puts – puts option was that we would – you would pay a premium and in the event that the stock, the index, the FTSE index, went below a certain level which would be set on the, the, the options once a month. We bought a series of these. We would be able to exercise that option at our choice, at our timing, and would be able to obtain from the writer of the option the difference between where the index stood and that index level that we'd guaranteed. So, effectively we were, we were guaranteeing to the Bank the – that a worse-case scenario, and for a known sum of money which was the premium that we had paid.

This reads very badly. It probably sounded just as bad. It is almost incomprehensible. The advocate must now do one of two things. He can abandon ship by sitting down or passing on to a totally different topic. If he does this, he is implicitly admitting that the evidence is of little importance, and possibly that the witness should not have been called at all. Or, if the evidence is of importance, he must persevere. He takes a deep breath, he hides his inner fury, and with a warm and encouraging smile to the witness and in a voice as soft as silk he says:

I am so sorry. I must interrupt you. The fault is entirely mine and not yours. I must ask you to start at the beginning.

And he starts all over again.

Meanwhile, his opponent sits smirking at his discomfiture. If he has any sense he will smirk behind his hand, because he knows that next day or next week he will probably stumble in much the same sort of way.

Chapter 6

Cross-Examination: Aims, Duties, Dangers

The aims of cross-examination are two-fold: to weaken the case for the other side, and to establish facts which are favourable to the case for the cross-examiner. It is possible to subdivide these headings almost indefinitely, but since the two aims so frequently overlap it is both exhausting and unrewarding. Even more frequently the second merges completely into the first, for it is obvious that if the defending advocate can demolish the case presented by the plaintiff or the prosecution, then he will win the action without being called upon to establish anything at all. He will have established a negative: that there is no case against his client.

It is probably for this reason that most authorities are content with making a statement as to what cross-examination is without attempting a definition as to its aims. That given by Lord Hanworth, Master of the Rolls, is typical:

Cross-examination is a powerful and valuable weapon for the purpose of testing the veracity of a witness and the accuracy and completeness of his story.

However incomplete this statement may be as a definition, all the authorities are careful to add to it an important proviso as to the manner which the advocate should adopt in cross-examination. Lord Hanworth continued in this way:

It [the right to cross-examine] is entrusted to the hands of counsel in the confidence that it will be used with discretion and with due regard to the assistance to be rendered by it to the court, not forgetting at the same time the burden that is imposed on the witness.

Lord Macmillan had no doubt that 'properly used' cross-examination in an English court constituted the finest method of eliciting and establishing the truth yet devised. The tragedy of the English courts is that, even today, the right to cross-examine is too often abused. In the case in which Lord Hanworth was delivering judgment his view was that the cross-examination failed to conform to the standards he had laid down. He described it as failing

to display that measure of courtesy to the witness which is by no means inconsistent with a skilful, yet powerful, cross-examination.

The change in the manner and methods of the courts has already been referred to in Chapter 1. It is inconceivable that a witness today would be reduced to the state of fear of one who appeared before Judge Jeffreys who cried out.

My Lord, I am so baulked, I do not know what to say myself. I am cluttered out of my senses; tell me what you would have me say.

By the end of the nineteenth century conditions had improved to a marked degree. At the Old Bailey in particular Sir Richard Muir had been responsible for introducing an atmosphere of fairness and impartiality which had never been seen before. Archbishop Whately, however, rightly believed that he was justified in writing:

I think that the kind of skill by which the cross-examiner succeeds in alarming, misleading, or bewildering an honest witness may be characterized as the most, or one of the most, base and depraved of all possible employments of intellectual power.

Conditions are continually improving. But Lord Hanworth's judgment was not as the result of an appeal from some out-of-the-way court where the new enlightened views have not yet penetrated, but in a civil case tried by a High Court Judge in 1934. When the case reached the House of Lords (it was a case worth taking further; the Court of Appeal reduced the damages awarded to the plaintiff by the trial Judge from £35,000 to 40s.) the Lord Chancellor was even more outspoken. He described the cross-examination of the plaintiff as 'indefensible', and conducted

... without restraint, and without the courtesy and consideration which a witness is entitled to expect in a court of law.

The Lord Chancellor restored to the plaintiff the £35,000 damages originally awarded, which was the primary object of the appeal, but even this sum and these words could not be expected to erase the feeling aroused in a man subjected to a cross-examination deserving such forthright criticism. Since the criticism applied also to the cross-examination of the unfortunate defendant who had to pay the damages, he was left with the mere words as recompense.

The right which an advocate has to cross-examine witnesses as to their credit (their general trustworthiness as individuals) and their credibility (the trustworthiness of the evidence they give) is restricted in many important particulars. But within these limits he is free to adopt any tactic which he believes will secure from the witnesses answers favourable to his client. And it is for him to decide how he will go about this task. As a result it is possible to see in the work of one advocate an approach quite different from that of another. With some it is even possible to recognize a style of cross-examination which can easily be differentiated from that acquired or created by another. But whether the advocate wishes to develop such distinction as a style of his own, or whether he simply wishes to conduct his cases as well as his capabilities allow, he ought never to display a lack of consideration towards witnesses or misuse his position to browbeat them.

To do so is extremely easy. Sir Edward Clarke recognized that there is bred from engagement in any trial

an instinct of antagonism which the strongest determination to be absolutely impartial and fair cannot be trusted to clear him [the advocate] from prejudice or passion.

And if he is not he not only abuses the right which he has, he may bring about a miscarriage of justice, for cases can be, and sometimes are, won or lost not on the evidence, but on the methods adopted by the advocate.

Patrick Hastings was the finest cross-examiner seen in the courts this century, yet all too frequently he was guilty of ruthless and gross discourtesy. It was unfair to the witness, and it led the courts to draw wrong conclusions. Wherever he practised his methods went unrebuked. In the Laski case, one of Laski's witnesses was Air Vice-Marshal Sir Hugh Vivian de Crespigny. At the time of the trial he was one of the Military Governors in Germany. At the time of the election he had been Labour candidate at Newark, and in that role had been present at the meeting at which Laski had spoken. This is the whole of his cross-examination.

HASTINGS: Do you recognize this expression: 'It did not lie in the mouth of any member of the Tory party, who helped to organize mutiny in the British Army over Home Rule in 1914, to discuss the question of violence'? Do you remember anything like that being said by anyone?

SIR HUGH: No, I do not. That does not mean to say that it was not said.

HASTINGS: Many things may have been said that you did not hear?

SIR HUGH: Sir Patrick . . .

L.C.J.: Will you try and answer the question Yes or No. We really must try and get on with this case.

SIR HUGH: There was nothing vital that I would not have heard.

HASTINGS: If you did not hear it, how do you know whether it was vital or not?

SIR HUGH: I must ask your permission to elucidate this so as not to give the wrong impression . . .

HASTINGS: No, thank you (*sitting down*).

SLADE: I have no questions in re-examination.

A regular attender at the courts will quickly realize that lawyers, who are themselves constitutionally incapable of answering any questions with a straight Yes or No, are always demanding of laymen that they should do so. To such an observer the Lord Chief Justice's intervention would come as no surprise. Following so close upon it, and perhaps deriving justification from it, Hastings's refusal to allow the witness to give the evidence he wanted to give might seem to be warranted. But should an advocate decline to permit a jury to hear an explanation a witness wishes to give? More important, should any advocate, however eminent or powerful, be allowed to do so? The reader might think the most remarkable thing about this passage is that it brought no protest from Slade or the Judge. To the jury it might have seemed that Slade had decided to abandon the witness.

This does not mean that an advocate is obliged to accept the answers he receives in his cross-examination, only that he must allow a witness a fair opportunity to answer in the way he wishes. If it becomes apparent that he is incapable of answering a straight question with a straight reply, or he is deliberately trying to avoid answering, then the advocate is entitled to interrupt and to insist that the witness answer what he is being asked. With evasive and dishonest witnesses it is only by forcing them to answer the questions asked that the advocate can expose their worth. Sir Charles Russell once defended a man sued for libel by Sir George Chetwynd, an ex-steward of the Jockey Club. Russell's client had said of Chetwynd that he ran his stables dishonestly by continuing to employ a jockey named Wood long after he knew that Wood had been pulling his horses. Early in his cross-examination of Sir George Chetwynd Russell asked:

RUSSELL: Do you know a betting man named Walton?

CHETWYND: Yes.

RUSSELL: Did you hear that Walton had paid large sums to Wood for information about his mounts?

CHETWYND: No.

RUSSELL: Do you say that you never heard that Walton had paid large sums to Wood?

CHETWYND: Well, I heard something mentioned about a race in which Wood rode.

RUSSELL: Do you say that you never heard that Walton had paid large sums to Wood?

CHETWYND: I only heard of one instance.

Russell does not interrupt. He does not bully. He is not discourteous in any way. This is a direct and perfectly fair insistence that the witness answer the question truthfully.

Thus there is a duty on the advocate to be courteous and to be fair. In conforming to that duty how far can he go when he attempts the destruction of the case for the other side by cross-examination? No problem arises while he seeks to establish new facts, nor while he tries to undermine the evidence the opposing witnesses give. He may ask any question that seems to him to be relevant, whether he is instructed upon it or not. But if he is seeking to undermine the evidence by undermining the witness – by assaulting his bona fides, or his credit, or his bias – then there are a number of rules which bind his behaviour.

These are concrete and immensely complex. Many of the intricacies spring from the piecemeal growth of the rules of evidence, some of which may seem designed to keep from the jury facts which the layman will think they ought to know. In a criminal trial prosecuting counsel may not ask a defendant about his character. If, however, a defendant gives evidence that he has a good character then he may not only be cross-examined to show that he has in fact got a bad character but evidence may be called to prove it, should he deny what is put to him. Similarly if he attacks, through his advocate, the character of the witnesses for the prosecution when he goes into the witness-box he too can be cross-examined upon his bad record. If he does not go into the witness-box he cannot be cross-examined. It is only if upon cross-examination he denies his record that positive evidence can be called to prove it. By the simple expedient of not going into the witness-box at all the jury will not learn of his convictions. (This anomaly is due to bad draftsmanship in the Criminal Evidence Act and not any lawyer's guile.)

In civil cases evidence may be called to establish a witness's 'general reputation' for untruthfulness. Although the witness whose reputation is attacked may be cross-examined on the particular incidents which have gained for him that reputation, the witnesses subsequently called to speak about it are confined to stating their general belief without reference to the separate incidents. Yet a witness's bias may be proved by calling evidence of such particular incidents: for instance, evidence may be called to prove that a woman witness is the mistress of the party calling her. But if, in a criminal case, a woman alleges she has been raped, although she may be cross-examined (only with the permission of the Judge) about acts of intercourse voluntarily indulged in by her with other men, the cross-examiner is 'bound by her answer' and may not call evidence to substantiate the suggestions he makes to her. This is because the questions go to the credit of the witness, which is irrelevant to the issue before the court (the rape), whereas to show the witness's bias or general reputation for untruthfulness is said to be material whatever the issue before the court. The distinction has been hallowed by at least two centuries of use. The layman may find it difficult to understand, and impossible to justify.

Above all others, rape trials have highlighted the difficulties which have to be faced if issues of the kind that inevitably arise in such trials are to be disposed of fairly. Public interest has been led to focus on the plight of the woman complainant: the care, or lack of it, shown to her after her ordeal by the police and the medical profession, and the care, or lack of it, shown to her at trial by the advocates and Judges. Substantial steps have been taken to ease the complainant's path through what for the genuine complainant must be a prolonged nightmare. The advocate must show that he is aware of this even though his duty may be to test as firmly in such cases as in any other whether the complainant is a genuine victim. He must show it, of course, to the victim and the jury in front of whom the examination is to take place, and he must show it to the Judge to whom the advocate must apply for leave to cross-examine about other acts of intercourse, for the Judge has a balancing act to perform. Some prefer to call it judicial juggling.

The Judge must balance the competing interests, the complainant, the defendant and the public, in order to arrive at a conclusion which is as just as the circumstances permit. It is on this that the lawyer would wish to focus, recognizing that while he is retained as an advocate in a case he is not required to show balance at all. That is exclusively for the Judge. The advocate must show judgement in deciding what his course of action should be. Once he has taken his decision he must go hell-for-leather in putting it into effect. So in the rape case, although the cross-examiner is 'bound by the answer' of the witness denying previous acts of intercourse, he is not so bound if evidence available to him to be called later shows that she has acted as a prostitute.

This, it is said, is because such evidence is relevant to the issue of consent. What if the number of acts of intercourse and the number of men involved suggests that the woman complainant is happily promiscuous? The Court of Appeal has said:

... in any age of changing standards of sexual morality it may be harder to say where promiscuity ends and prostitution begins and it may be unnecessary to decide on which side of the dividing line the particular conduct falls which a man charged with rape may wish to prove.

Evidence which proves that a woman is in the habit of submitting her body to different men without discrimination, whether for pay or not, would seem to be admissible . . .

The 'happily promiscuous' woman would probably vehemently deny that she 'submits her body', a markedly sexist concept, and would certainly deny she did so 'without discrimination'. An advocate with judgement, even though without balance, would wisely avoid using such terms in cross-examination.

It is important to remember that whether he is entitled to call evidence to establish the matters he has put in cross-examination or not, the advocate, in order to serve the interests of his client to the best of his ability, is entitled to range at will over the life history of any or all the witnesses he has to cross-examine. Upon most matters witnesses are obliged to answer all the questions that are put to them. If they do not, they can be committed to prison for contempt of court. This fact alone should induce the advocate to be discreet in his use of this method of attack. Because it would be tactically unwise, however satisfactory it might be to the client to see witnesses racked on their own past, the advocate is inclined to be sparing in the use of the power he has. Because too, advocates are generally drawn from those who have some sensibility as well as some sense, they are loath unnecessarily and perhaps irreparably to damage those whom they have to attack. When he defended Mancini for murder Lord Birkett had to suggest to two young women, one of whom was seventeen years old, that they were prostitutes. To one of them he prefaced his question about her character by saying,

I hope I shall be understood. I want to deal with you as kindly and gently as I can.

To the other he said,

I am sorry to have to do this. I am very sorry indeed. But you haven't been a waitress in any sense of the term for years, have you?

When Marshall Hall defended Robert Wood at the Old Bailey (the Camden Town murder), he refused to embarrass a young prostitute who gave evidence against Wood by asking her about her life. Instead he obtained the evidence he needed by questioning the police officer about her.

In 1917 the governing disciplinary body of the Bar adopted a number of rules which apart from subsequent slight amendments continue to control the conduct of a barrister faced with the task of making suggestions of fraud or dishonesty or attacking the credit of witnesses he has to cross-examine. They do no more than state the broad principles which should guide him, for the substance and the form of the questions which may be put by the advocate must be a matter for his own choice.

The rules begin by enjoining him 'to guard against being made the channel for questions which are only intended to insult or annoy either the witness or any other person'. In the Peasenhall case (tried fourteen years before the rules were evolved) Wild had to attack the credit of a man named Rouse whose evidence was that he had seen Rose Harsent and Gardiner continuing their association after the scandal although both had sworn they would not do so. Gardiner denied everything that Rouse said. There could be no half measures in Wild's cross-examination, and his eleventh question to Rouse made that plain:

This story of yours is a lie from beginning to end, and a concocted story.

Later, when he came to attack Rouse's credit Wild sought to minimize any damage his questions might do to the person who was not, and by the rules of evidence could not be, in court to answer his suggestions.

WILD: Let me ask you something else. You were the victim of a scandal at Wrentham [where the witness had previously lived] were you not?
ROUSE: No.
WILD: I do not want to mention names. Read this. (*A piece of paper was handed to the witness with a name written on it.*)
ROUSE: It's Gooch there.

The witness having mentioned the name there could be no point in Wild continuing to try and conceal it, so the cross-examination continued:

WILD: Was not your name connected with Mrs Gooch for immorality?
ROUSE: No.
WILD: Was not there a scandal?
ROUSE: It was said they thought I went backwards and forwards to Gooch's.

When Wild went on to ask him about his relationship with another woman he was careful to see that the name was not mentioned at all.

WILD: Look at this name: don't read it out. (*A piece of paper was handed to the witness with a name written on it.*)

ROUSE: I do not know it.

WILD: It commences with a B. Have you heard the name?

ROUSE: Oh yes, plenty of times.

WILD: I suggest to you, you misbehaved with this lady.

ROUSE: You, nor any other person can bring it forward [*sic*], if they did you would bring them forward to prove it. I never heard any scandal with regard to this person.

As already explained, Wild was not entitled to bring anyone forward to prove it. The matters went to the credit of the witness and not to the issue before the court which was the murder of Rose Harsent.

The rules go on to require that an advocate should not undertake a cross-examination like this unless he has ' "reasonable grounds" for thinking that the imputation conveyed by the question is well-founded or true'. If his instructing solicitor tells him that in his opinion the imputation is well-founded or that he believes it to be true then he has the necessary 'reasonable grounds'. If someone other than his instructing solicitor gives him the information then he should not make the imputations unless that person can give 'satisfactory reasons' for his statement to him. This really boils down to this: the advocate is required to cross-examine his client to satisfy himself about the reasons for his client's belief, but is relieved from the burden of treating his solicitor in the same way.

The position is different however if the cross-examination of the witness is one which goes to an issue in the case. Provided the advocate has no reason to believe that the imputations he is instructed to make are solely to impugn the witness's character, he is at liberty to suggest fraud, or misconduct, or even the commission of a criminal offence. He may do this, and will be forced to do so, even if he has no evidence other than his client's instructions to support the allegations and even if he has no intention of calling his client to support the allegations by evidence on oath. At first sight this may seem improper. But no man, in a civil or a criminal case, is obliged to go into the witness-box to answer a claim or a charge made against him. If the rule were otherwise, then he would be forced into the box simply because his advocate had exposed to the court the bad character or evil motives of the witnesses called against him.

In civil cases the character of witnesses on both sides can be explored. In criminal cases the defendant carries an immunity which has already been explained (there are a few unimportant exceptions under the Theft and Vagrancy Acts), and which he loses if he dares to impeach the honour of the witnesses called against him. This is so even in those cases where he has to take that course: where his defence is, 'I did not do it. Mr X, the prosecution witness, did'. The harshness of this rule, which can work intolerable injustice, is mitigated by allowing the Judge of trial a discretion to refuse to allow such questions.

The advocate has no such discretion. His duty is 'to put his client's case'. This means he must challenge the evidence called by the other side where he sees that it is in conflict with the instructions he has received. Wild was 'putting his case' to the witness Rouse in the extract already set out. Following the general challenge he made and the cross-examination about Mrs Gooch and the unnamed woman 'B', Wild asked Rouse about his relationship with a third woman which had led to an interview with a man named Curtis.

WILD: I put it to you that you refused to have it [the scandal about that relationship] out with Mr Curtis.
ROUSE: Anyone who says so is a false man.

Elsewhere in his cross-examination of Rouse, Wild used a different form of words. The three questions preceding the general challenge all began:

I suggest to you, you did . . .
I suggest you have added in your evidence . . .
I suggest to you also that . . .

There is no magic in these words, although some advocates seem to think that what is convenient is in fact compulsory. Both these empty formulae ('I put' and 'I suggest') came into use late in the nineteenth century, and are now widely used to challenge the truth of a witness's evidence and to put to the witness what the advocate's client or witnesses will later swear occurred. There is no need to use either of these alternatives provided he makes the challenge clear to the witness and the court. Scarlett never used either. When he had to cross-examine one of Wakley's witnesses, a man named Lambert who had written the article containing the libel, Scarlett got him to admit that before going into the witness-box he had demonstrated on another body what he believed had happened when Cooper had performed the operation to a group which included some of the witnesses already called by Wakley. He then asked these two questions:

SCARLETT: Was it not with a view to their evidence in the cause to assist them in their scientific knowledge?
LAMBERT: It was with a view of refreshing my own memory.
SCARLETT: Was it not with a view of giving them more knowledge?
LAMBERT: No, I did not go down for that purpose.

The alternatives of 'I put' and 'I suggest' are also open to objection in that the use of the personal pronoun brings the advocate into the case, and makes it appear that he is giving evidence. This he must avoid as scrupulously as he must avoid voicing his own opinion. For the same reason he must never say in cross-examination to a witness, 'My client will say . . .', or 'My instructions are that . . .'. The first is mere hopeful speculation, and the second is giving evidence.

Once these minor difficulties are overcome the advocate will find that the form of words he chooses to make his challenge with is not very important. What is important is the manner of it. It is not obligatory to make a bold frontal attack similar to Wild's on Rouse (page 122) simply because he has to challenge the whole or part of the witness's testimony. Mendacity is not yet a national disease. The vast majority of witnesses are doing their best. To assault an honest but mistaken witness with words like Wild's would certainly be offensive to the witness and, by alienating the sympathies of the jury, probably disastrous to the client. Challenges can be made without inveighing against the witness's bona fides. This is Slade cross-examining Mr Opie, the shorthand writer of the *Newark Advertiser*:

SLADE: Now, you are, I hope, quite clear that I am not making the slightest imputation of any impropriety upon you; do you understand that?

OPIE: Perfectly, thank you.

SLADE: I want to make that quite clear. What I want to ask you is this: although you would not necessarily hear everything that transpired, I suppose I may take it that you would not take down in shorthand something which did not transpire? Do you appreciate the difference?

OPIE: No, I'm afraid I do not.

JUDGE: Although you may not have written down everything you heard, you would not have written down something you did not hear.

OPIE: No, I certainly should not have done.

The extract also allows two points to be made which have already been referred to in earlier chapters: the advocate must make himself clear and unless he has some particular purpose to serve he must avoid using unusual words. The use of the verb 'transpire' here is wholly inappropriate. There was no purpose to be served. Its use could only divert the attention of the audience by causing them to delay while absorbing and interpreting it. The word 'said' or any other equivalent should have been used. It is plain and simple and crystal clear. There is only this difference: whereas in his other tasks the advocate should seek to be clear, in cross-examination he has a duty to be so. Simple language and clear and direct speech should be used not only because it eases the task of the jury but also because it is fairer to the witness. Muir understood this well. Crippen claimed that he had last seen his wife alive at about 2 a.m. on 1 February 1910; that he had not murdered her by hyoscine poison and buried her body in the cellar of their house, and that she must have walked out of the house and gone to America before he awoke in the morning. Muir's first questions to him in cross-examination were:

MUIR: On the early morning of the 1st February you were left alone in your house with your wife?

CRIPPEN: Yes.

MUIR: She was alive?

CRIPPEN: Yes.

MUIR: And well?

CRIPPEN: Yes.

MUIR: Do you know any person who has seen her alive since?

CRIPPEN: I do not.

These are easy questions for the witness to understand. The implication behind them is also easy for the jury to understand. Two more, and the jury had displayed before them the strength of the case for the prosecution.

MUIR: Do you know of any person in the world who has had a letter from her since?

CRIPPEN: I do not.

MUIR: Do you know of any person who can prove any fact showing that she ever left your house alive?

CRIPPEN: Absolutely not.

The passage serves to illustrate another of the duties lying upon the cross-examiner. If the advocate wishes in his final speech to make comments upon the evidence then he must lay a foundation for it in the cross-examination so that the witnesses have the opportunity of disputing or explaining the facts on which the comment will be made. From these questions Muir went on to ask Crippen what inquiry he had made of local tradespeople when he found his wife had gone. Eventually he obtained this answer:

CRIPPEN: I have made no inquiries.

The Lord Chief Justice intervened.

That answer covers everything; you can make any comment on it you like Mr Muir.

That does not mean that the cross-examiner is required to cross-examine upon every detail of the evidence that is given with minute particularity before he can comment on it to the jury. Prolonged cross-examination places unnecessary and often unfair strain on the witness and is a waste of public and private time and money. The example shown by Muir in his last questions to Crippen should commend itself to all advocates. Crippen had obtained five grains of the poison hyoscine on prescription a fortnight before he said his wife had disappeared in order, he said, to make up and dispense 'homoeopathic preparations'. He claimed to have dispensed three grains in pill form to his patients and to have left the other third in a cabinet in his office. He admitted that his solicitor could find no trace of that third. Muir asked:

Have you got anywhere any homoeopathic preparations into which you put this hyoscine?

CRIPPEN: They were all sent out as they were made.

MUIR: You have none left?

CRIPPEN: I have none left.

MUIR: Have you got here any patients to whom you sent such preparations?

CRIPPEN: Mr Newton [his solicitor] has been looking the matter up. I do not know.

No patients were called as witnesses. In his final speech Muir commented:

Three grains he said he dispensed in medicines . . . but not a patient has been called who ever got a pillule of it.

It will be seen that there is no comment included in Muir's questions. He does not ask: 'If you dispensed hyoscine to your patients, can you tell the jury why none are here to be called as witnesses?' He left all such comment until he came to make his speech. Today the question in that form, or one very like it, would probably be asked, since it is now the fashion to include comment either direct or indirect in cross-examination. This is largely due to the influence exerted upon all modern advocates by Hastings's style of cross-examination. In the Laski case Hastings put this question to one of Laski's witnesses.

HASTINGS: Did you hear anything of this sort: 'Great changes were so urgent in this country that if they were not made by consent they would be made by violence?' Did you hear him [Laski] say that?

WITNESS: No, not in those words.

HASTINGS: Dear, oh dear, Mr Laski seems to be so unfortunate. He must not have been very good at hearing himself; he said that is what he did say . . .

Whether he employed comment or not (he always did, and a great deal of it too) Hastings was invariably short in his cross-examinations. With Laski he was unavoidably lengthy, but he asked no more than forty questions of any one of Laski's other witnesses. It should be the aim of every cross-examiner to be as short as possible. Charles Gill said, 'if you don't strike oil in the first five minutes, then stop boring'. Lengthy cross-examination can cause positive damage to a client's case by 'rendering the witness's story more circumstantial, and impressing the jury with a stronger opinion of its truth'. It is in fact extremely dangerous because of what one Attorney-General called 'the sad uncertainties of the criminal law' (i.e. trial by jury). A jury, quick to spot an advocate's failure to undermine a witness or his evidence, and whose sympathies are more with the hunted witness than the hunting advocate, thereafter may attach a disproportionate importance to the evidence that witness has given, and a significance to the advocate's defeat which is quite unwarranted.

It was his realization of this that led Sir Henry Curtis Bennett to maintain that no question should be asked unless the cross-examiner knew what the answer was going to be. This does not mean that the advocate should shun his duty to put his client's case. Nor does it mean that he should only put questions which must receive favourable answers. An advocate who has to cross-examine a witness who has already sworn that white is white knows that he is unlikely, simply because he is under cross-examination, to agree that white is black. What it does mean is that the cross-examiner must avoid asking the witness why he says white is white (the answer to which he cannot know in advance) unless he proposes to use the answers he gets to his client's advantage. He must never give a witness an opportunity to elaborate on the evidence he has already given so as to bolster and support what he has previously said.

It is with these aims, duties, and dangers in mind that the advocate rises to his feet to begin his cross-examination. It is the moment for him to remember the advantages he possesses over the witness. He, and not the witness, chooses the parts of his evidence on which to ask the questions. He may not choose to cross-examine about his evidence at all. He may choose to attack in an entirely different quarter. He, and not the witness, chooses the words with which to do it. He, and not the witness, knows the rules which bind them both. He, and not the witness, knows the foibles of the Judge who is to referee the contest. He, and not the witness, is familiar with and at home in the court in which they both stand, and he is dressed in a medieval armour sufficient to intimidate most well-brought-up children and quite a few adults. He, and not the witness, knows where to start and when to stop. Above all, no witness knows how much the advocate knows.

Despite all these advantages he can still make a fool of himself, to the great joy of all those who have to suffer at his hands. It was an Irish advocate who was unwise enough to ask an Irish Prelate:

Am I wrong in thinking that you are the most influential man, and decidedly the most influential Prelate or Potentate in the Province of Connaught?

and obtained the reply,

Well, you know, they say these things, but it is in the sense that they would say that you are the very light of the Bar of Ireland: these are children's compliments.

Chapter 7

The Weapons of
Cross-Examination

If an advocate were to be cross-examined on his own cross-examinations he would probably be able to supply some of the details from many of his cases, but it is unlikely he could give the methods he used to reach those points of detail and improbable that he could classify them. So much, he would say, depends on instinct and atmosphere. It is inevitable that continual practice in the courts causes him gradually and unconsciously to assimilate the techniques of cross-examination without necessarily giving him the inclination or the leisure to inquire into them.

Yet it may be possible to categorize all the methods of cross-examination. That no one has so far attempted to do this indicates that it would be a fruitless occupation. Mr J. H. Munckman, in probably the best, certainly the shortest, book written on advocacy, divides the methods of cross-examination under four heads which he calls techniques: the technique of confrontation, of insinuation, of undermining, and of probing. The question and comment of Patrick Hastings on page 128 contain elements of the first three of these techniques. One aspect of the fourth has already been dealt with in the last chapter and another is dealt with in the next. Since the advocate rarely uses these techniques in their plain form this does not help the aspiring advocate who wants to know how to go about a cross-examination or the interested observer anxious to understand how the advocate achieves the destruction of a witness.

It is best to acknowledge at the outset that there is no magic formula by which the curiosity of either student or observer can be satisfied, and that the title of this chapter is no more than a short and convenient label with which to describe the exploitation of the advantages of the advocate, some of which are listed at the end of Chapter 6. Really the advocate has only one weapon: words. How he uses them varies enormously, for two distinctions need to be noted. If the advocate is appearing for the Crown in civil or criminal proceedings he cross-examines in order to get as near to the truth as he can and not to secure a verdict. If he is defending in a criminal case or appearing for a private individual or concern in the civil courts he is under no duty to continue with questions which might establish facts unfavourable to his client and favourable to his opponent. Subject to the rules and duties already explained he has an absolute discretion as to how far he goes. Secondly, there is a marked difference in the use of cross-examination in front of different tribunals. Although there may be drama latent in a building dispute over the drains of a bungalow in Palmers Green, and there is at least one case in recent years of an expert being brought to tears by perfectly fair and proper questioning at a planning inquiry, it would be courting disaster for the advocate to conduct all his cross-examinations as if he were attacking a dishonest police officer in front of a jury. The weapons available to him are the same whatever the tribunal. But before expert assessors of fact – a single Judge as opposed to twelve laymen – he needs fewer histrionics, much more subtlety and much more speed.

With these caveats in mind, the best approach is to explore cross-examination with the eye and the ear of the advocate involved. In the examples which follow it means asking oneself repeatedly: 'What form of words should he have used to obtain the reply most favourable to his client; what questions must he ask; what questions should he avoid asking?'

The advocate ought to know the answers to all these questions before he rises to his feet. The time spent by the witness during his examination-in-chief should be spent by the advocate waiting to cross-examine in absorbing the evidence and gauging the witness. He will not be able to do this if he has not mastered the framework of his cross-examination before going into court. Ideally he should have prepared much of his cross-examination in advance, including the form and substance of some of the questions. He should certainly know the first questions that he intends to put. If the witness is one whose evidence is to be challenged they should be designed to take advantage of the first weapon the advocate holds, surprise. Rufus Isaacs's first question to the poisoner Seddon was this:

Miss Barrow [the murdered woman] lived with you from the 26th of July 1910 till the morning of the 11th of September 1911?

There was only one answer: Yes. Isaacs paused. The advocate's second weapon is timing. He dictates the speed of the cross-examination by the length of his questions and the tempo at which he puts them. In this instance Isaacs wanted the jury to have enough time to calculate the period between the dates. Then he asked:

Did you like her?

This was a question which could have provoked Seddon into betraying his whole character. Asked later in the cross-examination, when he had got accustomed to the form of Isaacs's questions, it would probably have been ineffective. As it was it jolted Seddon very badly.

SEDDON: Did I like her?
ISAACS: That is the question.
SEDDON: She was not a woman that you could be in love with, but I deeply sympathized with her.

His first answer was plainly buying time. It has been pointed out in Chapter 5 that the examiner of a witness who constantly repeats the answer exposes himself as being slow and dull-witted. The witness who does so is liable to be thought devious, that he needs to weigh his words carefully in order to create the right impression. His second answer, despite the extra thinking time, even after eighty years' change in public attitudes about the use of the word 'love' was simply distasteful.

It is not always possible to prepare cross-examination in advance. In the criminal courts prosecuting counsel does not often have advance knowledge of defence witnesses. In the civil courts, although both counsel know the issues involved, they may know little of the detailed facts relied on by the other side and nothing of the witnesses to be called in support of them until they actually go into the witness-box. Lord Birkett found himself in this position when he prosecuted Rouse for murder. The prosecution alleged that Rouse had murdered his victim and then destroyed his body by setting fire to the motor-car in which he had put the dead man. It was suggested that a brass nut on the petrol pipe which was found to be loose after the fire proved that the fire was deliberate. The defence called a surprise expert. Describing himself as an engineer and fire assessor he claimed that the fire was accidental and that the nut could have come loose in the fire. Birkett's first question occurred to him while he listened to the witness being examined in chief:

What is the coefficient of the expansion of brass?

It is so easy to be wise after the event that it should be pointed out that the witness might have known the answer, and that Birkett could not have known whether he did or not. If he did, the question would have allowed him to strengthen his credentials and the value of his evidence. He replied:

I'm afraid I cannot answer that question off-hand.

This was a reasonable enough answer. Even experts cannot be expected to carry figures running to six places of decimals in their heads. But if he really was an expert he should have been able to indicate how to determine the matter, perhaps to give some more positive assistance to the court. As it was the answer merely implied that he knew what Birkett was talking about.

It lay in Birkett's hands to change his line of questioning. It must always be within the capability of the advocate to shift with the wind. But if Birkett did he would not afterwards be able to challenge the witness's standing as an expert. It was one of Birkett's attributes that he never started on a line of cross-examination unless he was prepared to pursue it to its logical conclusion. He asked:

BIRKETT: If you do not know, say so. What do I mean by the term?
WITNESS: You want to know what is the expansion of the metal under heat.

This was an unhappy reply, and it must have been clear to Birkett that he was cross-examining an increasingly unhappy expert. The passage continued:

BIRKETT: I asked you what is the coefficient of the expansion of brass. Do you know what it means?

WITNESS: Put that way, probably I do not.

BIRKETT: You are an engineer?

WITNESS: I dare say I am.

BIRKETT: Well, you are not a doctor, or a crime investigator, or an amateur detective are you?

WITNESS: No.

BIRKETT: Are you an engineer?

WITNESS: Yes.

BIRKETT: What is the coefficient of the expansion of brass? Do you know?

WITNESS: No, not put that way.

The advocate should never be surprised at the replies he receives, though outwardly, for the benefit of his audience, he may permit himself to express astonishment. It is astonishing that this witness, an intelligent man, could allow himself the 'I dare say I am' in answer to the straight question 'Are you an engineer?' Yet replies similar to this are regularly made by every class and description of person. They need to be seized on by the cross-examiner, for he will not have the same chance again of catching the witness at a disadvantage. If his ear is partly deaf because his eye is occupied by the papers before him he may miss the significance of such replies and the opportunity to use them to his advantage.

These first questions may be used to lay the foundation for the whole cross-examination, or simply to put the issues to be decided before the court in simple terms. Sometimes they can do both. Hastings employed them in this double capacity when he began his cross-examination of Laski. Or they may, having at first seemed to have no particular relevance to the case, have tied the witness down to facts which are used to administer a *coup de grâce* at some later stage. Scarlett began his cross-examination of a young man named Clapham, one of Wakley's eyewitnesses to the operation performed by Cooper, in this way:

SCARLETT: What age are you?

CLAPHAM: Twenty-one.

SCARLETT: When did you become twenty-one?

CLAPHAM: I do not know.

JUDGE: You do not know when you turned twenty-one?
CLAPHAM: I am not turned twenty-one.
SCARLETT: You said you were. When were you twenty?
CLAPHAM: Last January.
SCARLETT: That is a very good reason for not knowing when you were twenty-one.

The episode, damaging enough in itself, appeared to be closed, for Scarlett immediately went on to challenge Clapham's description of the operation. At the end of the cross-examination he asked these questions:

SCARLETT: You say [in chief] you are a licentiate of the Company of Apothecaries [which was only open to those over twenty-one].
CLAPHAM: Yes.
SCARLETT: And you are not twenty-one?
CLAPHAM: Yes.
SCARLETT: When did you obtain your licence?
CLAPHAM: In the spring.
SCARLETT: Did you represent your age truly?
CLAPHAM: No . . .
SCARLETT: Well, Mr Clapham, I will not trouble you any further. I have as good an opinion of your judgement as I have of your veracity.

The comment rounds off the cross-examination perfectly. It leaves the jury with the devastation of the witness instead of his evidence. This is possible only if the advocate rigorously controls the temptation to go on, to ask just one more question, the question that will clinch the matter. Sometimes it does. More often it ruins all that has been built up earlier. There are no rules that can be followed to prevent this. Instinct is the advocate's only guide, and self-control his only means of ensuring that he pays proper attention to it. A young man was once charged with having unlawful sexual intercourse with a girl under sixteen. The corroborative evidence supporting the girl's story came from a farmer who said he had seen the pair lying together in a field. He was asked:

COUNSEL: When you were a young man did you never take a girl for a walk in the evening?
FARMER: Aye, that I did.
COUNSEL: Did you never sit and cuddle her on the grass in a field?
FARMER: Aye, that I did.

COUNSEL: And did you never lean over and kiss her while she was lying back?

FARMER: Aye, that I did.

COUNSEL: Anybody in the next field, seeing that, might easily have thought you were having sexual intercourse with her?

FARMER: Aye, and they'd have been right too.

It need not have been asked. It ought not to have been asked, but the temptation was too great. It destroyed all the previous effect, and it wasted another of the advocate's weapons: the last question. During the rapid flow of question and answer in cross-examination the jury do not have much time to crystallize their impressions of the witness. The pause at the end of a cross-examination may be the first opportunity for them to do so. The last question should therefore be one which will focus their attention on something to the disadvantage of the cross-examined and not to the disadvantage of the cross-examiner.

The most important weapon of all is a disguised one. Sometimes it is so well disguised that it is possible to listen to or read a cross-examination without realizing that the advocate possessed it at all. In the Wallace murder case, for instance, the prosecution alleged that Wallace had provided himself with an alibi for the time of the murder by telephoning to his chess club and leaving a message for himself. Sir Roland Oliver cross-examined the secretary of the club who took the call:

OLIVER: You had altogether quite a conversation with the voice [that left the message]?

SECRETARY: Yes.

OLIVER: At the police court you said it was a confident and strong voice?

SECRETARY: That means it was not a hesitating voice in answer to questions.

OLIVER: So far as you could judge, was it a natural voice?

SECRETARY: That's hard to judge.

It will readily be appreciated that it is one thing to cross-examine knowing what the witnesses are going to say, and quite another to cross-examine blind. In this extract the question, 'Was it a natural voice?' is a blind question, and a dangerous one, since Oliver could not know what the answer was going to be whilst it was vital to Wallace's interest that it was a natural voice. If the question had not been asked Oliver would have been entitled to address the jury on the basis that it had not been suggested that it was not a natural voice. But he wanted a more positive basis for his speech. He knew two things before he put the question: that in giving evidence-in-chief the witness had not said he thought it was Wallace speaking on the telephone, and he had described it as a confident voice, suggesting that it was not a disguised one. These were Oliver's weapons. If he got the wrong answer he could go some way towards destroying its effect by the use of these facts. Nevertheless he was careful to leave a way out for the witness, which in fact the witness took, by including the words, 'so far as you could judge' in his question.

On the surface there are no frills or subtleties about these questions. They appear to go straight to the point. The last reply was not an answer to the question asked. Oliver did not repeat it. He rephrased it:

OLIVER: Did it occur to you at the time that it was not a natural voice?
SECRETARY: No, I'd no reason for thinking that it wasn't.

Then he rammed home his advantage:

OLIVER: Do you know Mr Wallace's voice well?
SECRETARY: I do.
OLIVER: Did it occur to you at the time that it was anything like his voice?
SECRETARY: Certainly not.
OLIVER: Does it occur to you now that it was anything like his voice?
SECRETARY: It would be a very great stretch of the imagination for me to say anything like that.

In the Wallace case the weapons, the facts on which Oliver could fall back to confront the witness if he received an unpleasant reply, were already implicit in the evidence. In the trial of Lizzie Borden, Robinson who defended her had to obtain them for himself. It was alleged she had killed her stepmother because she did not like her, and that whatever the air of amiability between the members of the family given to the outside world the atmosphere in the house was frigid with hostility. When Bridget the Irish servant girl was called, Robinson had an opportunity to try to dispel this image. It was an opportunity he was forced to take because the other witnesses he could have cross-examined on this aspect of the case were certain to be hostile to him.

Robinson's manner to Bridget was quiet and confidential. (The art of cross-examination does not lie in cross-examining crossly.) At the start of his questioning he has one fact only to which he can retire: Bridget has remained in the house, whatever the conditions, for three years.

ROBINSON: You were called Maggie?
BRIDGET: Yes, sir.
ROBINSON: By Miss Emma [the elder sister] and Miss Lizzie?
BRIDGET: Yes, sir.
ROBINSON: But that was not unpleasant to you?

The 'you' in this question is important. Until this moment her attention has been focused on the Bordens; after all, that is what the case is about. No one has bothered to ask about her.

BRIDGET: No, sir, it was not.
ROBINSON: Not at all offensive?
BRIDGET: No, sir.
ROBINSON: Did not cause any ill-feeling or trouble?
BRIDGET: No, sir.

We have already seen how carefully Hastings chose the words 'troublesome' and 'tiresome' to describe Laski. Robinson is here careful to put 'trouble' in apposition to 'ill-feeling'. He follows this with another question which fixes Bridget's mind on herself.

ROBINSON: Did Mr and Mrs Borden call you by some other name?
BRIDGET: Yes sir, they called me by my own right name.
ROBINSON: Did you have any trouble there in the family?

This is the first crucial question. The attention is still on Bridget, to whom the word 'trouble', one suspects, had the servant's significance of something leading to the loss of her employment. Robinson gets the answer he wants, then switches the emphasis to a new word.

BRIDGET: No, sir.
ROBINSON: A pleasant place to live?
BRIDGET: Yes, sir, I liked the place.
ROBINSON: And for aught you know they liked you?
BRIDGET: As far as I know, yes.

The seizing upon Bridget's reply is a brilliant piece of opportunism. Now Robinson has four things to fall back on: she had stayed there for three years, she had no trouble there, she liked the place, and she thought the family liked her. Even so, he still proceeds with great care, using again the word 'family' with all the implications that word bears, and the word 'pleasant'.

ROBINSON: It was a pleasant family to be in?
BRIDGET: I don't know how the family was; I got along all right.

It is no answer to the question, but Robinson sheers away from it as quickly as possible.

ROBINSON: You never saw anything out of the way?
BRIDGET: No, sir.
ROBINSON: You never saw any conflict in the family?
BRIDGET: No, sir.
ROBINSON: Never saw the least — never saw any quarrelling or anything of that kind?
BRIDGET: No, sir, I did not.

A pedant might observe that one does not see conflict or quarrelling, one hears them. The reader will observe therefore how the questions are the more likely to provoke the answers that Robinson wants. (If the prosecution want to correct the error they can do it in re-examination.) Meanwhile Robinson turned to something else. He had got what he wanted.

It may be thought a misnomer to call the possession of facts on which the advocate can fall back a weapon, disguised or otherwise. To give them, or the use of them, any other title is to ignore the psychological pressure they exert on the witnesses. The chess club secretary knew he had never claimed the voice on the telephone was Wallace's. Consciously, or subconsciously, he knew that Oliver knew he had never claimed it was Wallace's voice he heard. What the advocate is doing is to utilize that pressure to get at the nearest equivalent to the truth a court can ever receive.

The other position, cross-examination of a witness whose answers are known in advance, can be dealt with much more shortly. The advocate has no need to tread with caution. In the

Mancini case Birkett wanted to focus the jury's attention on the dangerous nature of the steps down which he was going to suggest the dead woman had fallen to her death. (The case for the prosecution was that the defendant had bludgeoned her to death.) He asked the Inspector of police who produced a plan of the defendant's flat these short and direct questions:

Were they [the steps down to the flat] very worn?
Were they steep?
Were they narrow?
Did they call for care?
Had the area a hard stone floor?

The questions are all leading ones. Contrary to popular belief, such questions may be asked in cross-examination. It is only when examining his own witnesses that the advocate must not lead the witness. In the cross-examination he may lead as much as he likes. It is, however, unwise to lead where he is cross-examining a witness who is patently favourable to him, not because there is any rule to prevent him doing so, but because such questions expose the witness's partiality and thereby diminish the weight of his evidence.

These examples from the Wallace, Borden, and Mancini cases all show the advocate cross-examining witnesses called by the side which begins; namely, as they are all criminal cases, the prosecution. In each instance the cross-examination established facts which are new, some of which the jury have never heard before, some to which their attention has not previously been called. This can be done more rarely by the cross-examiner who has to question a defendant or his witnesses. By this stage in the trial most, if not all, the relevant facts will already be before the court. This calls for a change in the form of the questions. The weapons available to the advocate are precisely the same, it is only the way in which the questions are put that changes.

In one case Sir John Simon had to contest the validity of a will on the grounds that the testator was not of sound mind, memory, or understanding at the time he signed it. Simon possessed statements from persons describing the testator's habits at that time. In due course he would be able to call them as witnesses. Before that moment came he had to cross-examine the solicitor who drew up the will. He confronted him (borrowing Mr Munckman's technique) with the evidence to come by using questions in this form:

SIMON: If you had a client who would come downstairs in the daytime and walk about the house in his nightshirt would you call him well-balanced?

SOLICITOR: No.

SIMON: If your client had a habit of festooning the end of his bed with wearing apparel tied in fantastic knots for no reason at all, would you regard that as proof of testamentary capacity?

SOLICITOR: No.

SIMON: If your client, when he came down to breakfast, overthrew the furniture and tore down the curtains for no reason at all, would that be proof of testamentary capacity?

In the Peasenhall case when Gardiner went into the witness-box Dickens confronted him with the evidence which had already been called. The form of the questions is completely different. (The first two tie Gardiner to the time.)

DICKENS: What time was it [that he got up] on Sunday the 1st of June? [The morning of the murder.]

GARDINER: Eight o'clock.

DICKENS: Will you swear to the jury that on that morning your fire was not lit until half past eight?

GARDINER: Yes, I would.

DICKENS: You lit it, as I understand, simply for boiling the kettle?

GARDINER: That's it.

DICKENS: For that purpose you would want a very small fire?

GARDINER: It would be a small fire.

No bloodstained clothing had been found in Gardiner's possession. The doctors agreed that whoever murdered Rose Harsent must have been spattered with blood. The prosecution suggested Gardiner had burned the clothing he had worn in the big fire his next-door neighbour Stammers had seen alight at seven-thirty.

DICKENS: Is it true that the fire was alight and blazing at seven-thirty?

GARDINER: No, it is a lie.

DICKENS: Is it true that smoke was coming out of the chimney at seven o'clock in the morning?

GARDINER: No, it is not true.

DICKENS: There was no reason for your having a fire as early as that was there?

GARDINER: No.

DICKENS: Do you know Stammers, your neighbour?

GARDINER: Yes.

DICKENS: Did you hear his evidence?

GARDINER: Yes.

DICKENS: That your fire was alight at seven-thirty?

GARDINER: Yes.

DICKENS: Is all that invention?

GARDINER: Yes.

DICKENS: You never had any quarrel with Stammers?

GARDINER: No.

DICKENS: Can you suggest why, when you are on trial for murder, Stammers should have invented this story against you?

GARDINER: No.

DICKENS: How long have you known Stammers?

GARDINER: Three or four years.

Here are three of Mr Munckman's techniques in use: confrontation, insinuation, and probing, in order to undermine Gardiner's evidence. Dickens confronts Gardiner with the evidence given by Stammers; probes his relationship with him; and then insinuates that since there is no reason why Stammers should lie, that Stammers was telling the truth.

In whatever combination the techniques are used the advocate should bring a healthy dose of common sense to bear on the evidence he hears given. There is something in the atmosphere of the courts which lends a sober air of respectability to the most bizarre of explanations. Properly applied, the jury can at once see how far divorced from reality is the tale they are asked to accept. In another case in which Slade was engaged, a doctor was sued for enticing the wife of a grocer's assistant away from him. It was proved that she spent all her time in his company: driving in his car, or riding or shooting with him, or at the house where she lived with her husband. Eventually she left her husband and went to live close to the doctor where he continued to visit her as if nothing had happened. When she gave evidence for the doctor she said she had left, not because she had been enticed away, but because she could not stand her husband any more. She was asked:

COUNSEL: What are your feelings towards the doctor?
WIFE: I like him very much, as a friend.
COUNSEL: No passionate love?
WIFE: None.
COUNSEL: What used you to talk about?
WIFE (*Pause*): The weather mostly.

If the atmosphere is right, or if he is capable of creating the right atmosphere himself, then sarcasm, irony, or plain mockery are the quickest way to expose tales of illusion. The best of this class of weapon is ridicule. This is not for the advocate who holds that the distance between counsel's bench and the witness-box is an immeasurable chasm marking his social and intellectual superiority. It is surprising how often it can be employed. Curran's use of it was masterly. Carson and Hastings, who excelled in all the weapons of derogation, were adepts, yet Henry Brougham, Sir Edward Clarke, and Marshall Hall relied on it very infrequently. The best example comes from the last trial for witchcraft to take place at the Old Bailey in 1944. Defence witnesses spoke of a little girl called Shirley who was materialized by the defendant medium, and who then recited to those present at the seance. Prosecuting counsel asked one of them:

COUNSEL: What did Shirley recite?
WITNESS: This little piggy went to market.
COUNSEL: How far did the piggy go?
WITNESS: All the way.
COUNSEL: Not just the first line?
WITNESS: No.
COUNSEL: Roast beef and all that?
WITNESS: Yes.
COUNSEL: And the little piggy that had none?
WITNESS: Yes.

Of course, trials for witchcraft are rare (now prosecuted under the Fraudulent Mediums Act 1957). But the weapon is available even in the longest commercial fraud trials. One involved an evening meeting at which a decision had to be taken in respect of a share issue of a company which might have a dramatic impact on the price of the shares of the company. The decisions eventually taken were said to be fraudulent. One of those attending was the finance director of the company, who held a substantial number of shares and valuable options to purchase more. He claimed not to have been involved in any of the decisions. He said he had not heard them being taken. He was, he said, 'perched' on a window-sill looking out of the window. The word 'perch' was seized on by one of the defending advocates in cross-examination.

COUNSEL: On your version of events, you spent your evening, to use your expression, 'by my perch' looking out of the window, if your version is to be accepted by the jury. 'By my perch looking out of the window'?

WITNESS: That's correct.

. . . . .

COUNSEL: If you are in the meeting you get to know the results. If you are by your perch looking out of the window you do not get to know the result, but you want to know it; is that not right?

WITNESS: I fully believe that if the result was known, I would have been told.

COUNSEL: No, it is whether you asked.

. . . . .

I have to suggest to you that you are just not telling the truth. It is inconceivable that you, a finance director, heavily involved in this issue would have spent that evening by your perch looking out of the window and not taking an interest in all that was going on around you; is that not right, and you have tried to distance yourself for one reason or another?

WITNESS: I totally refute your allegation.

. . . . .

I think you are making too much of the perch.

. . . . .

COUNSEL: Were you alone by the window? Was anyone else on the perch?

. . . . .

WITNESS: Mr Gray and myself spent a certain amount of time talking about matters.

COUNSEL: What matters were you talking about?

WITNESS: The view, I would think at the time . . . We were not being told anything. We were not being kept abreast. The huddles were between what I would call more the principals.

COUNSEL: And the Chairman? [of the company]

WITNESS: Yes.

COUNSEL: Right. So that is established. The Chairman was not looking out of the window?

WITNESS: I don't recall that being the case.
COUNSEL: He is not the kind that looks out of windows and sits on the perch is he?
WITNESS: I don't think I can comment on that . . .

This has a fine swashbuckling ring about it. In this instance the cross-examination came perilously close to overdoing it. The advocate was inviting an intervention by the Judge to tell him to get on with the case, worse still, a more emotional swing by the jury in the witness's favour. Control must be added to the attributes which the ideal advocate should possess.

Some advocates would classify ridicule as the first of the three Rs of cross-examination. (This is not because any of them are fundamentals; they simply start with the letter R.) Repetition is the second. It has three quite distinct uses. There is the repeated use an advocate makes of one question to the witness who does not, or who will not, answer it fully and truthfully the first time it is put – as Henry Brougham used one question three times to Sir George Chetwynd. There is the repetition by a witness, generally a young child, who discloses when asked the question, 'Will you please repeat your evidence?' that he has learned it by heart. And finally there is the repetition in the replies of a witness who, cross-examined on an aspect of his story which he has not prepared, continually uses one form of words as a retreat.

The charge of adultery levelled by King George against Queen Caroline was mainly based on the evidence of her Italian servant Majoochi. His evidence was detailed and without inconsistency on all those matters which supported the charge against the Queen. Henry Brougham cross-examined him on the details which did not support the charge. An honest man would remember both with equal facility.

BROUGHAM: Didn't Sir William Gell's servant sit at that table [in the Queen's house] too?
MAJOOCHI: *Non mi ricordo*. [I don't remember.]
BROUGHAM: Didn't Mr Craven's servant sit at that table too?
MAJOOCHI: *Non mi ricordo.*
BROUGHAM: Where did Sir William Gell's servant sleep?
MAJOOCHI: *Non mi ricordo.*
BROUGHAM: Where did Mr Craven's servant sleep?
MAJOOCHI: *Non mi ricordo.*

BROUGHAM: Where did Bergami's [the alleged adulterer] child sleep?
MAJOOCHI: *Non mi ricordo.*

Yet he always remembered where the Queen and Bergami slept. Cross-examination on irrelevant matters frequently discloses untruthfulness on the relevant ones.

The third R is riveting. It has two quite separate aspects. In one form it consists in tying the witness down to a positive statement from which he cannot afterwards escape. In the other the advocate selects one small item from the whole of his evidence on which to concentrate his energies, examining it with minute, and more often than not embarrassing, detail. Hawkins used this weapon again and again during the Tichborne case. One of the issues was whether the real Roger Tichborne bore tattoo marks on his arm like those of the claimant. A man named Boyle claimed to have seen such marks on three occasions when Tichborne pulled up his sleeve to rub his arm. Hawkins put these questions:

HAWKINS: Do you know why he rubbed his arm?
BOYLE: I suppose it itched. I don't know.
HAWKINS: But what did you think when you saw him rubbing his arm?
BOYLE: I thought he had got a flea.
HAWKINS: A flea! Did you see it?
BOYLE: No, of course not.
HAWKINS: Whereabouts was it? Just show me. (*The witness pointed to his upper arm.*) What time was this?
BOYLE: Ten past eleven.
HAWKINS: On the second occasion did you think it was a flea again?
BOYLE: I suppose so . . .
HAWKINS: What time was it? About the same time?
BOYLE: Yes.
HAWKINS: Ten past eleven?
BOYLE: Yes.
HAWKINS: Then all I can say is, he must have been a very punctual old flea.

In all the examples enumerated in this chapter it will be seen that the advocate has nothing to assist him besides his own intelligence and his capacity with words. It sometimes happens, however, that the witness has already committed himself to some previous statement, verbal or written, which is inconsistent with what he now says. The advocate is entitled to arm himself with that statement and cross-examine the witness upon it. (A further portion from the cross-examination of the maid Bridget by Robinson which is set out in the next chapter deals with this position.) If he denies making the statement, then it can be proved, provided the contents are relevant to the issue before the court and do not go simply to the witness's credit.

Finally, it should be remembered that it is not only the opposing advocate who has the right to cross-examine. The Judge, counsel for co-defendants in a criminal case, counsel for the co-respondent (a male adulterer) or the woman named (a female adulterer) in the Divorce Division, and counsel for third parties brought into High Court actions also have the same right. It constitutes an array of expert assessors of mendacity which should cause the dishonest witness to pause for a long time before he tries his mettle against them. It is one of the abiding fascinations of practice in the courts that it does not seem to deter him in the least.

Expert witnesses fall into a category of their own. The cross-examination of an expert can be a terrifying and harassing experience for the advocate. Ideally the advocate should be the equal of the expert in the subject about which the evidence is given. The ideal can rarely be realized. The best he can do is to make it appear to the tribunal and, if possible, to the expert witness that he is equally well qualified or instructed. This requires a high standard of duplicity and a sizeable chunk of cheek. 'A little knowledge is a dangerous thing' is just as true for the lawyer as for the layman, and every lawyer rising to his feet to cross swords with any expert must remember how easy it is to come a cropper.

Inspiration may come to his rescue. Birkett's first question to the defence engineer when prosecuting in the Rouse murder case, cited on page 134, certainly falls into this category. But the success of the question there depended on the ineptitude of the witness.

Inspiration needs to be followed by ineptitude on the expert's part, and cannot be relied on to surface at crucial moments. Occasionally, ineptitude unprompted by the advocate, a mishearing of a question or a momentary inattention can damage the credibility of an expert witness. One of the experts in the *Herald* inquiry was asked by the Commissioner:

COMMISSIONER: How long after passing the outer Mole would you have expected the *Herald* to begin taking water over the spade?

WITNESS: I thought when I read the evidence that pretty soon after having passed the outer Mole the speed was 16 knots and she started to take in water.

COMMISSIONER: About half a minute?

WITNESS: No, not that much – 30 seconds or so. (*Laughter.*)

The advocate cannot expect such assistance in every case. He can however expect assistance from a high proportion of experts in every field in two separate ways. Many experts demonstrate an almost pathological aversion to answering the questions they are asked, and by doing so they alienate their audience. It is almost as if they refuse to listen to the question they are actually asked and instead answer the question they think they should have been asked. Many are garrulous. They talk themselves into the grave and their audience into stupefaction. Some suffer from both faults. A smaller number combine one or both with a lofty superiority which seems designed to get up the nose of the most sympathetic and unbiased listener. The wise advocate will trade on such deficiencies. He will challenge what he must in accordance with the rules and thereafter he will allow the witness to expose his own weakness rather than expose the advocate's lack of knowledge or understanding of the subject. Once he sees the witness has lost ground with the audience, he will sit down.

The professional expert witness, one who is not merely a leading figure in his field but one with experience in giving evidence to committees, tribunals and courts, rarely suffers from such obvious human frailties. He enters the witness-box without the hidden inner need to justify his opinion, usually the basic cause of the three faults identified earlier. He shows himself to be the master of his subject, to be sensible, moderate and flexible. How does the advocate tackle such a formidable opponent as this? He starts with the facts. In all cases in both civil and criminal courts statements made by experts must be revealed to the opposing parties before the expert is called. 'Trial by ambush', as it was called, the sudden unexpected appearance of an expert or alibi witness, is no longer permitted. If satisfactory notice is not given before the witness is called, the trial Judge can refuse to allow the evidence to be heard.

Expert evidence is evidence of opinion based on a stated set of facts. The stated set of facts must be included in the statement. But the facts made available to the expert might not be the same as those proved during the trial and might not have the same value. So, as in all preparations for cross-examination, the advocate ignores the opinion, he ignores the expertise, he examines the facts to see what may be missing. In the *Herald* inquiry, as in so many cases, he examined the facts to great advantage. The statement of one of the experts contained these passages:

According to the Chief Officer [from another ship in the vicinity] who was in a lifeboat there was a swell of between 1 metre to 1.5 metres. The direction of the swell is of importance but is not known, nor is the swell wave length . . .

From the statements it seems justified to conclude that: water got ingress to G deck through the open bow doors. There was a swell between 1 and 1.5 metres . . .

Points above seem to justify the conclusion that swell was an important contributing factor to water ingress to G deck . . .

The witness was challenged as to the reliability of the evidence of swell coming from the Chief Officer:

COUNSEL: What other evidence have you considered as regards the swell?
WITNESS: Mainly this one [indicating the statement of the Chief Officer]. I consider it very trustworthy that an experienced sea officer being in a lifeboat beside a big ship which is not moving with the swell like a small boat does. He must be elevated.
[This was not an answer to the question.]
COUNSEL: What other evidence have you considered as regards the swell?
WITNESS: I have heard orally that the Dredger Master reported some swell.
COUNSEL: What did you hear the Dredger Master had reported?
WITNESS: There had been some swell.
COUNSEL: What did that mean to you, 'some swell'?
WITNESS: I then investigated a few other cases. With those calculations the response of a ship could easily be determined by a significant wave height over a period. We have two programmes for this. When carrying out these types of calculations you run the model in regular

and different lengths and then superimpose the results at random. I asked one of my assistants to carry out such a run and you can see the results in the table which indicates that you have got much motion between the bow of the ship and the wave surface.

COUNSEL: The question I asked you was, what did you understand to mean by some swell reported, you understood, by the dredger?

WITNESS: There was a swell and the magnitude I got from the Chief Officer's statement.

COUNSEL: Did you consider the evidence from the *European Trader*?

WITNESS: No.

COUNSEL: Did you consider the evidence from the *Arko Avon*?

WITNESS: No.

COUNSEL: Did you consider the evidence from the Port Authority?

WITNESS: No.

COUNSEL: Did you consider getting evidence as to the height of the sea and swell from the buoy which is outside the breakwater to record the sea and swell?

WITNESS: I saw them first the other day.

COUNSEL: Had you not sought to discover that before?

WITNESS: It was not so important.

COUNSEL: It was not important?

WITNESS: No. In my view it was not necessary to know there was a swell because I have no experience of a totally calm sea. You always have movements which are important when you are discussing the effective freeboard between the bow and the sea surface and that is sufficient for me to realize you cannot judge only after the calm water, but the possibility of having relative motion between the ship and the swell.

COUNSEL: You cannot assume that the sea is rough or you cannot assume that it is smooth. You want to know what the sea is doing. Would you not consider the measurements taken from the buoy outside the outer breakwater as the best evidence as to the height of the sea and swell?

WITNESS: I cannot answer that. I do not know exactly how they measure – swell and sea, wind-generated fresh sea state, so to speak.

COUNSEL: Have you come across buoys that measure sea and swell?

WITNESS: No.

By the time another fifteen questions were asked, the court was reminded that the Chief Officer on whom the expert relied had not launched his lifeboat until an hour and a half after the capsize, during which time sea conditions had deteriorated, that he was then substantially further out at sea, where impliedly sea conditions were worse, and that his measurement had been made there in the dark. The other available evidence showed that even at midnight the wave height (the witness agreeing that swell is simply 'a low frequency wave') was 0.72 of a metre. Pressed further, the expert said:

Indeed I am of the opinion that the swell must have been a contributory factor but not to the extent which I thought at the beginning.

Later he was asked:

COUNSEL: [So] this is part of your conclusion, that the swell must have played a contributing factor?
WITNESS: Yes.
COUNSEL: Of course, another contributing factor might be that the draught was greater than calculated [i.e. that the ship was lower in the water]?
WITNESS: Yes.
COUNSEL: It could have been greater than calculated by the other experts?
WITNESS: Yes. I based this on the available information I had then.
COUNSEL: Yes, I follow.

These last three words are very important. The sub-text of the last answer of the witness is (a) an unqualified acknowledgement that there were other theories besides his own about swell which could equally well account for what he believed happened, and (b) an apology for relying on a single piece of evidence (from the Chief Officer of another ship) instead of all the evidence now available to the Court of Inquiry.

The answer was a patently honest admission and deserved to be received, as it was, with courtesy and apparent understanding. In bare, cold print such words may seem patronizing. They could be delivered with a patronizing inflexion. It is difficult for many advocates not to be patronizing to some degree in court to at least one person a day. It is impossible for any advocate after about ten years in practice not to be patronizing to a significant proportion of experts whom he believes should more appropriately be guests of honour at the Mad Hatter's Tea Party. There is, however, a much more significant proportion of experts who cannot be so dismissed. These generally give evidence in areas where the public have some knowledge of the subject before they come into court, fingerprints, physical and genetic, blood group-ing and dentistry are good examples. Their evidence is confined to facts, not theories, save for the single final opinion, devastating in its stark simplicity, delivered in a flat unemotional tone.

Better than any other single class of witness, the expert can demonstrate that, faced with an honest and accurate witness, the powers of the advocate are slight to non-existent. He may be a verbal conjuror, but he is not a genie. He cannot make bricks without straw. Such witnesses have nothing to fear from the advocate.

Chapter 8

Style in Cross-Examination

Probably more nonsense has been written about style in cross-examination than about any other single aspect of forensic advocacy. The fault lies mainly with the writers of legal biography who attribute the successes achieved in cross-examination by the subjects of their work to their virtues and not to their questions. This sort of eulogistic description is typical:

His whole style of address to the occupants of the witness-box was soothing, kind, and reassuring. When he came down heavily to crush a witness it was with a resolute decision, but with no asperity, nothing curt, nothing tart.

The reader is invited to believe that since the possessor of all these virtues (the American Rufus Choate) was a successful advocate these are virtues which will inevitably lead to success, and the style is one to be followed. If he then turns to read a biography of Hastings he may be led to believe that if he adopts a style which is brusque and tyrannical he too can be successful. It is undoubtedly true that Choate was as kind as Hastings was rude. It is also true that both were immensely successful. But it is wrong to draw the conclusion that the adoption of either style will automatically lead to success.

The truth is that style does not matter in cross-examination at all. What matters is effect. In fact the possession of a particular style can be a distinct handicap. The soothing approach will not do at all if it is a Bottomley who has to be cross-examined. Similarly a harsh approach towards a young child in cross-examination will do more harm than good. It is for this reason that few advocates possess a distinct style of their own. Style is not adaptable, and adaptability is everything for the advocate called upon to cross-examine people in every walk of life.

Some advocates, however, do develop a recognizable style of their own. Rufus Isaacs was subtly and coldly analytical. Muir was painstaking, no point was too unimportant for him. Hastings had the gift of crystallizing in a few questions the whole essence of the case he had to present, and the courage to do so. Simon was always detached: Marshall Hall passionately involved. All these advocates achieved great forensic successes as a result of questions to hostile witnesses. But they did not achieve them because of their style but because the direction of their questions was right and the development of their cross-examination was appropriate. When he cross-examined Laski, Hastings wanted to show the jury the gulf existing between the robust common sense of twelve ordinary men and the convoluted dialectical prognoses of a political economist. At one stage he read a long extract from one of Laski's books, *Reflections on the Revolution of Our Time*:

HASTINGS: '. . . The issue is whether the premises of their rulers are near enough the premises of the masses to make possible a revolution by consent . . . It is indeed, seen fundamentally, the issue about which this war is being fought, for the real purpose of Hitler is to turn the world into a vast latifundium.' That was not intended, I suppose, for the lower class, for the more humble class? That was more for the Professor. What is a latifundium?

LASKI: A latifundium was a great estate held by a Roman owner at the period of the Republican Empire.

HASTINGS: That would want an explanation if it went to the very substratum of society . . . (*Continues reading.*)

This is a typical example of Hastings's style: the highlighting of one word out of a great mass of words, the comment standing outside the framework of the question and the sarcastic arrogance with which he rounds the passage off. But it is not the style alone which makes the point. Initially, it is the decision to use this one word at all. Others would probably have used the passage for the same purpose. They too would have used comment in much the same sort of way. It is not very difficult to imagine Carson, who invariably put his comment within the framework of his questions, putting the question in this sort of way:

Are you suggesting to the jury that the lower class of person, the more humble class, would know what you meant by a latifundium? Would you be kind enough to tell *me* what it means?

The subtlety of Rufus Isaacs might have led him to ask:

Doubtless *Professor*, you are very familiar with latifundiums. Would you enlighten *us* as to what they are?

While the mischievous informality of Fearnley Whittingstall might have put it even shorter as:

And what the devil, Professor, is a latifundium?

These differences, whether they are differences in style or not, are unimportant. They are all ways of achieving the same end. They all have precisely the same effect on a jury. It is because the end that is pursued is right and because the right effect is made on the jury that the question is right and not because the style has added anything to that end or to that effect.

The direction taken by the advocate in cross-examination then is of paramount importance. Once he is able to decide on that direction, which as already pointed out he may not be able to do until he has actually risen to his feet, he must not allow anything to intrude which is inconsistent with it. During his cross-examination of Mrs Robinson, Simon's good nature frequently overcame him. At one stage he produced her passport application:

SIMON: . . . there is a photograph on it which, if I may be allowed to say so to this lady, was a very bad and unflattering one.

The allegation he was putting to her was that she had sold her body to an Indian prince as she had to other men before and since, thus enabling her 'husband' to blackmail the prince to the tune of £150,000. There was no necessity to be rude to her, but he was certainly not obliged to call her a 'lady', and still less to make comments dignifying her physical charms.

Once the advocate has decided on the direction that his cross-examination is going to take, the development along that path must seek to take advantage of everything that presents itself to him. The quickness with which Hastings seized upon infelicitous replies of witnesses is a prime example of this. Throughout the Sievier case, for instance, he matched every jest of Sievier's with biting comment:

HASTINGS: Did you marry your first wife in 1882?
SIEVIER: Unfortunately for me, I did.

HASTINGS: Unfortunately for her, too. Did she divorce you in 1886, four years later?
SIEVIER: She did.

This is an ability given to very few people, but all have the same opportunities to develop the cross-examination as Hastings in the passage which followed this extract:

HASTINGS: For desertion?
SIEVIER: Yes.
HASTINGS: And adultery?
SIEVIER: Yes.
HASTINGS: And cruelty?
SIEVIER: I know nothing about cruelty.
HASTINGS: I have her petition here . . .

This is doing the case 'in style', and this is the only style in cross-examination that matters. There is no particular style in its generally accepted sense about these questions, but putting them as three separate matters, piling them one upon the other, gains for this passage its particular effect. This is obtaining every legitimate advantage by every legitimate means at the advocate's disposal.

Some situations lend themselves more readily than others to a display of this kind of style. In cross-examining a witness on a statement he has made previously which contradicts what he is now saying the advocate is given an opportunity to wound the witness, or if he handles the situation correctly, to destroy him utterly. In the previous chapter, part of Robinson's cross-examination of Bridget, the maid in the Borden household, was examined. Later on Robinson came to ask her about the side door opening on to the yard at the back of the house. One of the further peculiarities of the house was that the doors were always kept locked even when there were people in the house. If this practice was followed on the day of the murders then there would have been no opportunity for an unknown person to enter the house and commit them. Attention has been drawn to Robinson's gentleness in handling the girl. In this passage he demands exact answers to his questions.

ROBINSON: Do you think you told us today just as you told us before?
BRIDGET: I've told all I know.

157

ROBINSON: I don't ask you that. What I want to know is whether you've told it today just as you did before?

BRIDGET: Well, I think I did.

So far the jury can have no idea what Robinson is coming to. That there is something coming is obvious. If this form was designed for no other purpose than to rivet their attention it is successful. But it does more than this for it is also a test of the witness. If Bridget is going to lie about this part of the matter, she may well remember that there is some difference between the evidence she now gives and the evidence which she gave at the inquest. Her reply shows Robinson that she is being patently honest. Yet Robinson still does not go directly to the conflict but only to the subject matter of the conflict.

ROBINSON: What did you do to the side door when you came into the yard?

BRIDGET: I hooked it.

ROBINSON: Did you say so before at the inquest?

BRIDGET: I think so.

ROBINSON: Do you know so?

BRIDGET: I am not sure.

ROBINSON: Let me see if you said this [reading]: 'Question: When you came in from the yard did you hook the side door? Answer: I don't know whether I did or not.' Did you say that?

BRIDGET: Well, I must have hooked it because . . .

ROBINSON: That isn't it. Was that the way you testified?

BRIDGET: I testified the truth, Sir.

ROBINSON: I don't imply that you did not. I merely want to know if you recall saying that, that you couldn't tell whether you hooked the door or not.

BRIDGET: It's likely that I did hook it because it's always kept hooked.

In such a cross-examination as this there are always two stages: did the witness make the previous statement now being attributed to her, and secondly, was that statement true? There can be a third stage, unless the advocate believes that will provide the witness with an opportunity of slipping out of the difficulty in which she finds herself, namely, why are the two accounts different? Robinson's aim was to show uncertainty. He jettisoned any plan he may have had to go through the formal stages. The word 'likely' led him to ask:

ROBINSON: Do you positively recollect one way or the other?
BRIDGET: I generally hook the side door.
ROBINSON: That isn't what I asked. Did you hook it or did you not?
BRIDGET: I must have hooked it, for I always . . .
ROBINSON: That isn't it. Did you hook the door or did you not?
BRIDGET: I don't know. I don't know whether I did or not.

Having got what he wanted he at once went on to something else.

In the examples quoted so far it is relatively easy to see the direction taken by the cross-examiner and the development the advocate employed. This is always so where the cross-examinations are short or where the topics for cross-examination can be divided up into distinct parts so that each bears its own individual label. It is not so in a long cross-examination which has to range over many, and often unrelated, topics. In such a case the advocate can claim style only if he carries the jury along in his narrative so that they can follow the significance of the course he is pursuing. It is vital that he makes his points plain to them, that each can be seen to relate to a matter which he has already touched on, or to some matter which is yet to come.

In 1909 Carson defended the *Evening Standard* in an action for libel brought by Messrs Cadbury. Between 1901 and 1908 Cadburys obtained a large part of their supply of cocoa and consequently their profits from the Portuguese islands of San Thomé and Principe off the coast of Angola. The cocoa was grown by slave labour shipped to the islands from the mainland. The Cadburys had first learned of this fact in 1901. In 1903 the British Minister in Lisbon had advised them to allow their protests to be made to the Portuguese Government by him. By 1907 nothing had changed so they made further representations to the Foreign Office. Meanwhile they continued to get their supplies of cocoa from the islands. It was only in 1908, when they saw it was hopeless to expect any improvement, that they discontinued buying.

Rufus Isaacs, in opening the case for Cadburys, described the libel as labelling his clients 'a bunch of canting hypocrites', for the article in the *Standard* claimed that their known Quaker benevolence and philanthropy was ill-contrasted with their secret financial support of a trading system under which slavery flourished. Carson's task was far from easy. The defence he had to put forward was that the libel was true, that the respectable and respected white-haired figure in the witness-box was in truth a 'canting hypocrite'. He had other difficulties to contend with. The case was tried at Birmingham Assizes, Cadbury's home ground, at the height of a General Election. Cadbury, the *Daily News*, in which his family had the controlling interest, Rufus Isaacs, indeed, Birmingham itself, were all Liberal. The *Evening Standard* and Carson were Conservative, and strangers on hostile territory. When Isaacs finished his opening there was cheering in court. Few cross-examinations can have opened in more unfavourable surroundings. The first dozen questions were harmless enough. They established the financial size and scope of the Cadbury Empire. Then followed what Simon, Isaacs's junior, later described as the most scarifying ten minutes' cross-examination he had ever listened to. One general question preceded it:

CARSON: May I take it that the San Thomé cocoa used by you in your factory for the past eight years has been, to your own knowledge, slave-grown cocoa?

CADBURY: Yes ... I am quite satisfied that 'slave-grown' describes the conditions.

At first sight this question has no particular significance. In fact Carson was to make it his central theme. This was a man who despite his protestations of horror at the conditions in San Thomé had continued to make his living for eight years from those very conditions.

CARSON: The men who were producing the cocoa you were buying procured it by atrocious methods of slavery?

CADBURY: Yes.

CARSON: Men, and not only men, but women and children were taken forcibly away from their homes against their will?

CADBURY: Yes.

CARSON: Were they marched on the road like cattle?

CADBURY: I cannot answer that question. They were marched in forced marches down to the coast ...

CARSON: How far had they to march?

CADBURY: Various distances: some came from more than a thousand miles, some from quite near the coast.

CARSON: Never to return again?

CADBURY: Never to return again.

In every trial thousands of words are poured into the jury's ears. The amount they can carry into the jury room with them when they retire can only be a minute fraction of the whole. It is part of 'style' in advocacy to fasten upon words which the jury will retain. It is 'style' in its finest form to choose a word like 'procure' with its particular connotation. Even more so, those last four words 'never to return again' bring home to the jury the contrast between their own security and slavery. Perhaps Carson paused to let the full impact of the words sink in. Then he went on:

CARSON: From the information you procured did they go down [to the coast] in shackles?

CADBURY: It is the usual custom, I believe, to shackle them at night on the march.

CARSON: Those who could not keep up with the march were murdered?

CADBURY: I have seen statements to that effect.

CARSON: You do not doubt it?

CADBURY: I do not doubt that it has been so in some cases.

CARSON: The men, women and children are freely bought and sold?

CADBURY: I do not believe, as far as I know, that there has been anything that corresponds to the open slave-markets of fifty years ago. It is done more by subtle trickery and arrangements of that kind.

CARSON: You do not suggest it is better because it is done by subtle trickery?

There was to be no escape for Cadbury. The pompous half answers, 'I have seen statements to that effect', and the last answer were pounced on and waved under the jury's noses as evasions. Then, from this display of bestiality, cruelty, and murder, Carson returned to his foundation stone:

CARSON: Knowing it [the slavery] was atrocious you took for eight years the main portion of your supply of cocoa for the profit of your business from the islands conducted under this system? . . .

CADBURY: Yes, for a period of some years.

CARSON: You do not look on that as anything immoral?

CADBURY: Not under the circumstances.

As a cross-examination develops the advocate who performs his task with style is constantly introducing fresh themes upon which to build fact and suggestion. At first they may appear to have nothing to do with the matters which have already been dealt with and it is only much later in the cross-examination they can be seen to link up with what has gone before. This was so of the next part of Carson's cross-examination:

CARSON: Were you anxious to keep back from the public during those years the knowledge of the conditions of that slavery?
CADBURY: No.
CARSON: Never?
CADBURY: Not from the public, no.
CARSON: Do you think, sir, that if the public had known the conditions under which your supply was produced, if they had been *advertised* to the public, it would have been detrimental to your firm?
CADBURY: Yes, I think it might have been.

The development of the idea implanted by the last question and the significance of the carefully chosen word 'advertised' was not made immediately. Carson examined first how much cocoa had been imported from San Thomé ('fully half our supply') and the value of it ('over £1,300,000'), and the profit made from it ('the profit has been good'). With those before the jury he returned to his foundation stone:

CARSON: Then it was not against the principles of Cadbury & Co. to make a considerable profit out of slave-grown cocoa?
CADBURY: In certain circumstances, as stated before.
CARSON: For eight years after you became acquainted with the facts?

This was to be repeated again and again. As each new set of facts was established the jury were reminded: 'This is a man who made his profits from the labour of slaves.'

Carson went on to the second theme arising from the use of the word 'advertisement'. Cadbury had agreed the conditions were atrocious, that the public, had they known of them, would have protested, and that he had not advertised the position. What had he advertised?

CARSON: One of your advertisements shows how you treat your own employees. In fact, your 'Bourneville paradise', as it is described, is largely exploited as a reason why people should buy your cocoa.

CADBURY: We have often put photographs of Bourneville in our advertisements.

CARSON: It is more than that. One advertisement calls it, 'the girl workers' paradise'. (*Laughter.*)

CADBURY: I objected to the use of the word paradise. If it was there it has slipped in inadvertently.

CARSON: It refers to their, 'simple and happy life', (*Laughter*) and, 'comfort for workers in beautiful Bourneville'. (*Laughter.*) Let me read from another describing conditions for Bourneville employees in Trinidad.

'The welfare of the workers has every consideration, and their prosperous condition is well-known.' There is no reference to the San Thomé paradise there. Instead of shackles the women in the picture are shown wearing bracelets on both arms. (*Laughter.*)

CADBURY: Some of those in San Thomé do.

CARSON: You don't think it would have added anything to that advertisement to have given particulars of conditions on San Thomé?

This apparently simple and in fact immensely skilful question pointed what Carson wished the jury to see: Cadbury advertised that part of his work which was commendable and not that part of his work which he knew could be criticized. This constant portrayal of contrast is one of the aspects of style in cross-examination at which Carson excelled. He immediately followed it with another:

CARSON: What supply of cocoa do you get from Trinidad?

CADBURY: Only two or three days' supply a year.

Another contrast and another point made. Cadbury advertised a small source of supply where conditions for the workers were good, and did not advertise a large source of supply where conditions were bad. Unless the jury had it well fixed in their minds that Cadbury could hardly be expected to advertise the living conditions of workers employed by others they might well find hypocrisy replacing honour.

By this stage in any cross-examination of length it becomes almost impossible to keep distinct the issues which have been raised. Subsequent questions no longer have clear reference to only one aspect of the case, but touch equally upon several. For instance, the next part of Carson's cross-examination made a close study of the mortality figure of the slaves employed in the eight-year period and in the increase of Cadbury's purchases of cocoa from the islands. Then he suddenly asked:

CARSON: Did it not strike you that by increasing the output from the islands the numbers of workers in conditions of slavery would thereby be greatly increased?

CADBURY: I don't think that the islands would have produced any more or any less if we had stopped buying.

CARSON: But your money was going to pay for all this. Did that not give you a feeling of personal responsibility in this matter?

CADBURY: Yes, as I have told you, it added to my responsibilities seriously.

All that it is possible to say is that mortality figures, 'money', and 'responsibility' are designed to fit within the general framework of the cross-examination and are designed to increase the jury's feelings of contempt for Cadbury.

Carson held copies of the minutes of the Board meetings of the Cadbury Company. He referred to one held in 1901 when the directors discussed the valuation of an estate in San Thomé:

CARSON: The circular [of the sale] values 200 labourers at £3,555. Did you think that was a pleasant thing?

CADBURY: No.

CARSON: It describes their food as chiefly bananas, their clothing as costing little, and their treatment when ill, as of little importance . . . Did you discuss whether you should go on buying the stuff?

CADBURY: We certainly discussed the proper thing to do.

CARSON: Did you ever discuss wiping your hands of the tainted thing?

This was at once followed by establishing that it was not until 1903 that Cadbury had first gone to Portugal to try and do something about the conditions, and that in 1904 he had written a letter in which he said, 'I suppose we must wait until 1908 [when an international convention on slavery was to be held] to see any change.' Cadbury explained:

Unfortunately, many of these international questions do entail very serious delay – much more than one would wish.

CARSON: This was not an international matter. It was the question whether you ought, knowing the conditions of slavery, to go on buying cocoa.

This was the very question Carson wanted the jury to decide put before them in one sentence. He then took it a stage further. Had Cadbury continued buying from misguided motives or because he was able to keep the truth from the public? Was he a fool or a rogue? Carson put to him his family connection with the *Daily News*, and a minute in one of the company meetings recording that the *Daily News* had promised help in bringing an end to the slave conditions in the islands. He forced an admission that there was no reference in the *Daily News* to those conditions until 1907. Then he pointed the contrast again:

CARSON: Were you aware that the *Daily News* were carrying on a vigorous agitation against contracted Chinese labour in South Africa?

CADBURY: Yes.

CARSON: They did not wait six or eight years before beginning their campaign. Doesn't it strike you as inconsistent that the Cadbury firm should be spending hundreds of thousands of pounds buying raw material from a slave-worked country while the *Daily News*, controlled by your family, were carrying on an agitation against indentured labour in the Transvaal?

CADBURY: No, I don't think so. One member of the family was doing his best to put down one evil and another member of the family was doing his best to put down another.

CARSON: Had the *Daily News* dealt with slave cocoa in the same way as it was carrying on its other campaign, it would have ceased at once.

CADBURY: Yes, I have no doubt that it would . . .

CARSON: There was no difficulty about making the facts known?

CADBURY: There would be no difficulty.

CARSON: You could have made the facts known and the public would have condemned them?

CADBURY: Yes.

CARSON: But then you would have had to give up buying San Thomé cocoa?

CADBURY: We could not have given up. We had started a definite policy recommended by the Minister in Portugal and we had no intention of departing from it.

CARSON: If you had made known the facts, public opinion would have condemned the conditions of labour and you couldn't have gone on buying?

CADBURY: I think so . . .

CARSON: Do you think that if the public had known the conditions under which your supply was produced that would have been detrimental to your firm?

CADBURY: Yes, I think it might have been.

On this general question, repeated after each fresh theme was introduced, Carson got no further than he could have expected. But he had further ammunition in store, which he went on to examine in detail, suggesting at the end of each stage that Cadbury had deliberately withheld the truth from the public. The whole cross-examination lasted for five hours.

Finally he came to his last questions. What should they have covered: the profit, the prevarication, the attempts to suppress publicity, or perhaps something new saved right to the end, a sudden, and unexpected death blow? In fact the first condensed Carson's whole case into a single question. The second, from the form of the first, casually tossed at the witness, remains one of the most horrifying questions ever asked in an English court.

CARSON: Now I have come to the end, and I ask you only this one question. From 1901 down to 1908 when you ceased trading, was there anything effective you did at all?

CADBURY: I think so myself. I admit that my efforts resulted in a good deal less than I should have liked, but I do not admit that I did nothing at all.

CARSON: Have you formed any estimate of the number of the slaves who lost their lives in preparing your cocoa from 1901 to 1908?

CADBURY: No, no, no.

If the cross-examination had failed to achieve its purpose this last question would probably have doubled the damages. As it was the jury found that Cadbury had been libelled but assessed the damages at a farthing.

Generally it is difficult to choose the last question to put to a witness in advance. Yet for all its apparent spontaneity Carson's to Cadbury may have been so chosen. Such occasions are rare. More often than not the advocate must seize on some point arising during the cross-examination. As already pointed out he ought never to conclude when he is at a disadvantage. Hastings invariably ensured his advantage by making his last question a comment and not a question. In the Laski case it is likely that the end of his cross-examination was made obvious by the beginning. These are Hastings's first two questions to Laski.

HASTINGS: Mr Laski, do you believe that the use of violence to achieve your political ends is practically inevitable?
LASKI: No, in a country where there is a long constitutional tradition of mature and literate people, I think that consent . . .
HASTINGS: Is the answer, 'No'?
LASKI: The answer is no.

For Laski suffered from that most debilitating of witness diseases, the incapacity to answer questions. Again and again he made long statements where he could, and should, since it would have been much wiser, have said yes or no. So after a day and a half of cross-examination, Hastings interrupted him in the middle of an answer:

LASKI: . . . was that the situation of the people, if we go back to pre-war conditions, would be intolerable . . .
HASTINGS: I am afraid you must go on by yourself Mr Laski. I cannot go on.

It will be appreciated that cross-examinations like Carson's of Cadbury and Hastings's of Laski require an immense amount of preparation. Muir never began any cross-examination without a voluminous sheaf of notes, cross-indexed and marked with pencils of every colour in the rainbow. Hastings rarely had a single note in front of him. Everything was carried in his head. Such differences in individual temperament do not matter so long as the advocate adopts a method which enables him to lay his tongue accurately and immediately on any detail he wants when he wants it, and without causing his mind to miss the significance of the answers he receives. This is important for a number of reasons. (One has been stated in the previous chapter.) Nothing looks worse to a client than an advocate who cannot remember his name. Nothing looks worse to a jury than an advocate who cannot remember the details of the case they are trying. Nothing gives greater confidence to a witness and improves his standing in the eyes of a court than an opportunity to correct the inaccuracies of a cross-examiner.

In all criminal trials taking place before a jury the preparation for cross-examination should begin in the Magistrates' Court. All criminal cases begin there. About 98 per cent end there, too. The major crimes go through the Magistrates' Court where, with some notable exceptions (enough to fill a separate book) both prosecution and defence have the right to ask that some or all of the prosecution witnesses are called into the witness-box to give their evidence both in chief and in cross-examination. In the majority of cases this is not necessary. It is generally not necessary if the case is one where it is known that the accused is going to plead guilty. It is generally not necessary where the statements taken by the police under the guidance of the Crown Prosecution Service show clear evidence of proof of the offence charged and where all the questions that should be asked have been covered in the statements served on the defence. In these instances the Magistrates will be asked to commit the accused for trial 'on the nod'; they do not have to even read the statements, both sides, prosecution and defence, confirming in court that they are content with this short procedure, which usually takes no more than five minutes.

But in a significant number of cases any defending advocate worth his salt knows that what appears on paper is not always the same as what is said in the witness-box. All prosecuting advocates should know this too. Both therefore have the opportunity to call the witnesses to test the true worth as opposed to the paper worth of the case. It can be that a full examination of the evidence, with or without cross-examination of the witnesses, exposes some fundamental flaw in the prosecution case and leads to the Magistrates dismissing the case altogether. This then means that no trial in front of a jury takes place at all. The saving of time, trouble and expense is immense. Even if the Magistrates do commit for trial, that is, having heard the evidence they come to the conclusion the case is fit to be tried by a jury, the savings can be equally significant, for the case will have been fully prepared and the real issues made crystal clear.

Cross-examination in the Magistrates' Court in these circumstances is very different from that which may follow in the eventual court of trial. The defending advocate is not at this stage required to put his case, so he can avoid confrontation completely. What he is really seeking to do is to establish exactly what the witnesses are saying in order to tie them to precise statements from which they cannot subsequently resile. The cross-examinations of Cadbury and Laski highlighted in this chapter are wholly destructive in nature. Those in the Magistrates' Court are almost 100 per cent constructive. They seek to build a foundation from which an attack with style, in the sense used here, can be made on the prosecution case at trial.

This is what was done over a period of twenty days in front of the Chief Stipendiary Magistrate (a qualified lawyer sitting on his own as distinct from a bench of lay Justices) in the *Herald* case. Notice was given that nine or ten of the Masters of the Spirit class vessels should be called. The prosecution contention was that the Master of the *Herald* was operating an unsafe system, that on 6 March 1987 when the disaster occurred there was an obvious and serious risk that the vessel would go to sea with the bow doors open, and that that was either known to him and he ignored it and went on to take it, or he simply did not consider the possibility of it when he as a prudent man should have done so. The prosecution further said that the same recklessness or gross negligence was shown by shore management, and so they too and the company itself, of whom they were the representatives in law, were equally guilty. That was the prosecution case, that was their assertion. What did the Masters say, those who had operated the system since 1980 when the Spirit class vessels had first come into service? One of the defending advocates took a statement made by one of the Masters as his starting point. He read part to the Master in the box:

COUNSEL: (*reading*) ... 'At completion of loading, harbour stations called' ... paraphrasing ... 'by loading officer'. Correct?

MASTER: Yes, sir.

COUNSEL: Is the Loading Officer normally the Chief Officer?

MASTER: Yes, sir.

COUNSEL: The calling of harbour stations should provoke the attendance [to close both sets of bow doors] of the Assistant Bosun at the control panel on G deck?

MASTER: Yes, sir.

COUNSEL: The Chief Officer to be there, watching?

MASTER: Yes, sir.

COUNSEL: And the words you use, 'when all secure and bow doors either shut or shutting, to bridge'.

MASTER: Yes.

COUNSEL: That is the Chief Officer to the Bridge?

MASTER: Yes, sir.

COUNSEL: The Chief Officer, when all secure and bow doors either shut or shutting, is to go to the bridge, correct?

MASTER: Yes, sir.

COUNSEL: The phrase 'either shut' is quite plain. It means the doors are then closed.

MASTER: Yes, sir.

COUNSEL: By the word 'shutting', and it may be very obvious, did you mean that the doors are physically moving towards the closed position? Is that what you meant by 'shutting'?

MASTER: Yes, sir.

COUNSEL: So the system that you understood was the Chief Officer was to observe either that the doors were closed or were closing or shutting before departing from G deck for the bridge?

MASTER: Yes, sir.

COUNSEL: That system, if faithfully observed, you viewed then as a safe one?

MASTER: Yes, sir.

There are no histrionics here, no trace of the courtroom/stage drama that excites public attention to the advocate at work. This is plain, straightforward and immensely workmanlike. It in fact masks its importance, for the answers will be valuable at trial in relation not only to this one Master but to all other Masters too, for questions can now be put to them in this fashion, 'Do you agree with Master X when he says . . .'.

This advocate could have stopped at this point; he had obtained all he needed. But he did not. He wanted to explore further, which in the absence of a jury it was safe to do. To begin with he got what appeared to be a wrong answer:

COUNSEL: That system, if faithfully observed, you would view now as a safe one, would you not; if faithfully observed?

MASTER: No, sir.

COUNSEL: You think because of the casualty it's no longer a safe system, even if faithfully observed?

MASTER: If faithfully observed . . .

COUNSEL: You see the point, Captain?

MASTER: I do take the point. I would not refer to that system now.

COUNSEL: Because you'd be worried about whether it was observed?

MASTER: Exactly.

COUNSEL: Because the tragedy has taught us that it failed to be observed in two respects, correct?

MASTER: In two respects, sir?

COUNSEL: Yes. Well, first of all, the Assistant Bosun did not close the doors, correct?

MASTER: Yes, sir.

COUNSEL: We know that, that's uncontroversial. And, secondly, the Chief Officer never saw the doors shut or shutting.

MASTER: Yes, sir.

COUNSEL: But I repeat, if the system as you describe it is followed, is faithfully observed, it is a safe system?

MASTER: Yes, sir.

COUNSEL: And until this casualty occurred, your experience and understanding was that this system was indeed followed.

MASTER: Yes, sir.

Having obtained all he could from the witness on this central part of the case he turned to another area, once again preparing for the future trial. The wreck inquiry had stated that shore management had been aware before the disaster of occasions when ferries fitted with clam doors had sailed from harbour with these doors open. Masters were yet to be called who would speak of these incidents. The advocate turned to this.

COUNSEL: You have said, Captain Martin, that you had no personal experience of any ship setting sail to the open sea with the bow doors open before the casualty?

MASTER: No, sir.

COUNSEL: If as a Master you had learnt of such a thing, you would expect it to be reported to shore management? You would expect it to be reported by the Ship Master to management, would you not, if it had ever happened?

MASTER: Yes, sir.

COUNSEL: My learned friend asked you about the report-writing this morning. Do you remember that? Do you remember being asked about the writing of reports this morning?

MASTER: Yes, sir.

COUNSEL: And if a Master had experience of a breakdown in the system we've been talking about, so that the ship – a ship under his command – was in jeopardy of sailing on the open sea with the doors open, you would expect such an incident to be reported?

MASTER: Oh, yes, sir.

COUNSEL: In writing preferably, but certainly reported—

MASTER: Reported, yes, sir.

COUNSEL: to shore management.

MASTER: Yes, sir.

With these answers as to what the other Masters who knew of the incidents should have done, and with the knowledge that none of the incidents had been reported, the defence advocate was now fully armed for cross-examination of these future witnesses.

The kind of detailed and painstaking preparation needed to achieve a cross-examination like this is sometimes called 'fact management' or 'case management'. It is a convenient modern label. Like most labels it fails to tell the whole truth about itself. A better title would be 'structured drudgery'. It is simply identifying from a mass of material that which is important and that which is dross and can safely be discarded, and then putting what is retained into the most suitable order to achieve the objective which the case demands. The effect of this can be seen in the style attained when the Masters came to give evidence before the jury.

Below is the central part of the cross-examination by the same advocate of a different master, the first of the many who were to be called. This was day fourteen of the trial. The advocate first asked in detail about his sea-going experience. Then he went straight to the system.

COUNSEL: Now, with all that experience, I want you to give us the benefit of your professional assessment of what the system truly was, how you understood it over those years, to see if I have got it right. First of all, the first duty fell upon the Assistant Bosun to physically close the bow doors, correct?

MASTER: That's correct, yes.

COUNSEL: The second human check was the Loading Officer, normally and usually the Chief Officer?

MASTER: That's correct.

COUNSEL: His duty as you carried it out in practice and understood it as a Master was to ensure that the Assistant Bosun was at the panel to close the doors, correct?

MASTER: Correct.

COUNSEL: And in the process of closing them, before he left G deck to come to the bridge?

MASTER: Yes, correct.

COUNSEL: It was a double human check, as I have described it, is that correct?

MASTER: Yes.

COUNSEL: Which in your experience, which is extensive, worked well and efficiently over the years?

MASTER: Correct.

COUNSEL: If you as a master of a vessel taking hundreds of people to sea had thought that system unsafe, you would not have hesitated to say so, is that correct?

MASTER: Correct.

COUNSEL: It follows that you, and I shall put it to all your fellow masters, you thought before this most tragic casualty that that system as laid down if carried out properly by the individuals concerned was a safe system, that's correct, isn't it?

MASTER: Yes, that's correct.

The words 'and I shall put it to your fellow masters' impose a burden on the advocate. A promise, or threat, like this must never be made unless it is kept. If it is kept then the advocate must strive to vary the way in which he keeps his promise. Mere repetition makes all material stale to the ear and diminishes it in the mind. The following day he rang the changes by undermining at the same time another proposition of the prosecution: that an electrical circuit could have been introduced with warning lights on the bridge indicating when the two pairs of clam doors were open and when shut. He asked:

COUNSEL: If a master considers in his judgement that it is unsafe to go to sea because the ship lacks vital safety equipment, it is his duty to say so, is it not?

MASTER: Yes.

COUNSEL: Even after your knowledge of these incidents, if you had thought this ship was unsafe to sail on the existing system of closing doors, it would have been your duty to say so as it would be indeed of any fellow Master, that is so, is it not?

The day after that he rang the changes again, this time giving the jury a bird's-eye view of the uniform strength of the defence: it was believed by everyone that the system was safe and that there was no risk at all.

COUNSEL: When you heard that this most unfortunate accident occurred because the *Herald* sailed to the open sea with both bow doors opened, did that come as a complete shock to you?

MASTER: Total and complete surprise, I could not believe that it had happened.

COUNSEL: Was that because in your mind, first of all, it was something you had never foreseen would happen, is that right?

MASTER: That's correct, sir, yes.

COUNSEL: Second, because you thought up to the moment of the accident that the system was indeed a safe one?

MASTER: Undoubtedly, sir.

COUNSEL: On this disaster ship, the *Herald*, you are the longest sailing master on that ship together with the Captain of the Bridge that night, you cover the whole span of its seven years of sailing?

MASTER: That is correct, sir.

COUNSEL: I just want to take stock of that. We know there are at any one time either four or five serving masters on any Spirit class vessel?

MASTER: At that time, five or six.

COUNSEL: Five or six. And that applied across the three ships, the *Pride*, the *Spirit* and the *Herald*?

MASTER: That is correct, sir.

COUNSEL: So, at any one time, there were something like fifteen to eighteen serving masters on the three sister ships?

MASTER: There would have been six masters on two of the ships and five masters on the other one on Zeebrugge during the winter and during the summer when all ships were on the Calais service, there would have been six on each, eighteen, sir.

COUNSEL: Of course with the passage of the seven years, there is a change in personnel?

MASTER: There is, sir.

COUNSEL: People retire and people are promoted. We are talking perhaps something like, would this be a fair figure, something in the order of twenty-five or so masters covering the three sister ships in the seven years from when they were commissioned?

MASTER: Well in excess of that figure, I would suggest.

COUNSEL: Have you ever heard of any single master or senior master of the Spirit class vessel in the seven years that you were Master express the view that the system of closing the bow doors was unsafe?

MASTER: No, sir.

COUNSEL: Had you ever heard any chief officer who served either under you or in a sister ship express such a view?

MASTER: No, sir.

COUNSEL: Had any of the many chief officers who served under you ever said to you, I cannot do my duty at the bow doors with safety?

MASTER: No, sir.

COUNSEL: In your assessment of the matter, could the Chief Officer fulfil his duty with safety?

By day twenty-two of the trial he had compressed the cross-examination into two questions:

COUNSEL: Before this tragic accident, prior to March 1987, did you ever think for one moment there was an obvious risk of this ship sailing to sea with her bow doors open?

MASTER: No, sir.

COUNSEL: And the like question, before this tragic accident in March 1987 did you ever think there was a serious risk of the ship sailing to sea with the bow doors open?

MASTER: I never thought there was any risk whatsoever, sir.

Five days later on day twenty-seven of the trial the Judge directed the jury to acquit. The facts established by these cross-examinations played an important part in that decision. (See Chapter 9.)

It is obvious that all the extracts in this chapter are from cross-examinations which were successful. Many are not. There are cases where even the most ingenious advocate simply has no room to be constructive, however hard he plays at being so. There are even more cases where he will fail miserably at his attempts to be destructive. There are as many of these as there are truthful and accurate witnesses who listen to the questions they are asked and do their best to answer them. The advocate meets examples of both every day. If he can, he will ask them no questions at all. If he must, then the best he can hope for is that he will be allowed to resume his seat without having done permanent damage to his client's cause. It is in such circumstances that the last test for style can be applied. Has the advocate done all he should for his client in testing the value of the evidence that has been given? Few situations are as intimidating as the prospect of controverting a witness when one's private belief is that the witness is speaking the truth. But if then the advocate makes a distasteful display of his right to cross-examine he will forfeit all claims to style.

Chapter 9

Remainders

Like Caesar's Gaul, all trials are divided into three parts: the case for the prosecution or plaintiff, the case for the defence, and the judgment. But there is no more certainty about these boundaries than there was about the boundaries of Gaul. If the plaintiff or prosecution fails to establish its case against a defendant then the second part can be omitted altogether, and judgment is delivered without hearing the case for the defence at all. This is what happened in the criminal trial for manslaughter in the *Herald* case. After cross-examination of some of the Masters of the Spirit class vessels, some of which has been referred to in earlier chapters, the Judge expressed doubts about the validity of the prosecution case based on 'an accident waiting to happen'. Although only part way through the prosecution evidence, he heard full argument from all the advocates in the case as to the correct tests he ought to apply in deciding whether, on the evidence so far called and assuming all the further evidence was called, a case of manslaughter could be established against the Master of the *Herald* and the management ashore. If it could not, then those individuals and the company would have to be acquitted. He decided the prosecution had failed to prove the case against those defendants. But he could not acquit them. A jury had been sworn to try the defendants. It was only the jury who could pronounce the words 'not guilty', even if it was as a result of the Judge directing them to do so and thereby giving them no option but to do what they were told.

Such a direction is a mini-exercise in advocacy of its own. Many juries and individual jurors resent suddenly being told they have no more meaningful part to play in a case. The Judge without warning adopts a role-reversal. Having been told the law is for the Judge and the facts for them, without so much as a by-

176

your-leave the Judge announces that the facts are for him first and he is going to deprive the jury of what by then they believe to be their right to decide the issues in the case on those very same facts. If he wishes to avoid, as he should, alienating the jury, a Judge in directing them in such circumstances needs to use the same care and tact as displayed by the Coroner in opening the inquest cited in Chapter 4. In the *Herald* case the Judge began like this:

Members of the jury, out of respect to you and the very close attention with which you have been following this case, I will repeat to you the substance of the rulings which have led to the present situation.

I am about to direct you that, as a matter of law, there is no evidence upon which you could properly convict the Master or any of the shore-based personnel.

Let me please – because of the interest and assiduity with which you have followed the evidence in this case – just recap for your benefit what it was that I said to Counsel for the prosecution yesterday and some of what I said to him as long ago as 10 October [nine days previously].

He went on to explain in detail how and why he had made his ruling, what it was that had caused him to reach that conclusion. He referred to the evidence of the Masters, to whom

... the risk that has been talked about in this Court simply did not occur. Specifically, in evidence in this Court, to none of the Masters – even those who had been privy to previous open-door incidents – did the possibility of an open-door sailing present itself as something which was remotely possible in real life.

In all, he took fifteen or twenty minutes. Such matters cannot be rushed if a Judge is to retain the confidence of the jury in court and the public outside.

In many cases, whether coming, like the *Herald*, to an abrupt end or not, two separate battles are waged at once. In the old type of divorce action, where a wife petitioning for divorce had to establish a 'fault' in her husband, if the petition was for adultery the husband might cross-petition for cruelty. The wife was then plaintiff and defendant, except that in the Divorce Division, as it used to be called, plaintiffs were called petitioners and defendants, respondents. In many road-accident cases there are more than two parties. An injured passenger may sue the driver of the car in which he was travelling and the driver of the other car, leading to a tripartite fracas. In such a case, the advocate for the passenger can adopt the happy attitude 'I did nothing wrong, one or other of you is to blame, the court can sort it out between the two of you', unless, of course, the passenger forgot to fasten his seat-belt, in which case he will be blamed for contributory negligence and will be forced to join the fray.

Whatever the complications caused in multi-handed cases (as they are inappropriately called) throughout the case for the plaintiff the defendant or defendants are making frequent incursions by way of cross-examination into the territory of the plaintiff. These may be repulsed by the witnesses. If they are not, then the plaintiff's advocate can come to his assistance by asking questions in re-examination, in order to explain or expand upon what he has said. If the witness has been badly mauled by the cross-examination then the re-examination can attempt to put Humpty-Dumpty together again.

Such questions must not be leading, and must only cover issues raised by the cross-examination. If there is no cross-examination then there cannot be any re-examination. Re-examination cannot be used to elicit evidence which should have been dealt with in chief. If the examining advocate has forgotten to ask about something or has failed to get the answer he wants then it is better for the opposing advocate to ask no questions in cross-examination at all, for if he does he allows his opponent a second bite at the cherry. This happened in the Sievier and Wootton libel case. Wootton's final allegation against Sievier in his broadsheet was that he was a blackmailer. To prove this Hastings called a man named Mills who was expected to say that he obtained from Jack Joel, the South African racehorse owner, £5,000 in cash which he handed to Sievier. This was in return for Sievier's promise not to publish a photograph of Joel in his paper between two photographs of South African murderers. Mills was a friend of Sievier's. Although he gave evidence of the passing of the money between Joel and himself and then between himself and Sievier, he insisted on describing the transaction as a loan and, despite considerable pressure from Hastings to tell the full story, omitted all reference to the photographs. When Hastings sat down the Judge asked Sievier:

JUDGE: Now Mr Sievier, do you want to cross-examine this witness?

SIEVIER: My Lord. I see no need to cross-examine. As I have said, I refused to have any transaction with Joel and would only borrow the money from Mills.

JUDGE: It is a matter for you Mr Sievier.

SIEVIER: I can see no need.

But he changed his mind, and put a series of quite unnecessary questions to Mills. It enabled Hastings to make another attempt to get at the truth.

HASTINGS: Before the loan, did Mr Sievier show you any documents in his office?

MILLS: I really can't say.

HASTINGS: Did he or did he not . . .

SIEVIER: My Lord, this is cross-examination.

JUDGE: Well, I won't say anything about it at present.

Sievier was quite right. Mills was an obviously hostile witness, but Hastings could only cross-examine his own witness if he first made an application to treat him as hostile. If the application had been granted the Judge would have been obliged to direct the jury that his evidence was not worthy of credence. Instead Hastings moderated his tone:

HASTINGS: Before the loan was made to Mr Sievier, did Mr Sievier show you any documents in his office which might relate to Mr Joel?

MILLS: I am not sure.

JUDGE: Mr Mills, at the present moment you are in court giving evidence on your solemn oath, and all we want you to do is to tell us, as best you can, what happened.

Judges' incursions into the field of battle frequently upset the most carefully laid plans. They can become the most powerful of allies or the most feared of foes, depending on whose side they intervene. Outwardly divorced from partisanship and wielding great authority, a dignified interjection like this can provide a stimulus to truth unlike any held by the advocate. Mills's memory suddenly returned. He had been shown, he said, two photographs of South African murderers.

HASTINGS: Did Sievier tell you what he was going to do with those pictures if the £5,000 was not paid?

MILLS: He said they would be in the next issue of the *Winning Post*.
HASTINGS: In what way connected with Mr Joel?
MILLS: I forget.
HASTINGS: You forget! Did he say he would use them if the £5,000 was not paid?
MILLS: He may have done.
HASTINGS: Tell us what he was going to do if the £5,000 was not paid.
MILLS: He said they would be in the next week's issue, and ... that a picture of Mr Joel would be published between the two pictures.

At last the truth had come out. If Sievier had not asked any questions in cross-examination it could not have done so.

Re-examination rarely produces such dramatic results. Many advocates believe that it is better to affect a lordly disdain and dismiss the witness after the cross-examination with an airy, 'I have no need to re-examine', thus conveying a contempt for the attempt to diminish the evidence which has been given. Sir John Simon once said to a witness who had withstood a whole day's cross-examination:

You are a witness that does not need re-examination, thank you.

Others rightly believe that it can give the impression of concern, that the advocate believes his witness to have been so badly mauled by cross-examination that he needs to be bandaged. There remain a large number of occasions when witnesses must be re-examined, in order to explain what has been said in cross-examination. One witness admitted in cross-examination that he had been convicted of felony. He was asked in re-examination:

COUNSEL: When were you convicted?
WITNESS: Twenty-nine years ago.
JUDGE: You were only a boy?
WITNESS: Yes, My Lord.

The report adds that, 'a just and manly indignation burst from all parts of the court'. If there is need to elucidate any matter, to set it in context then there is a need to re-examine. There was plainly such a need in the Cadbury case, and Rufus Isaacs asked:

ISAACS: Has your ceasing to buy San Thomé cocoa in 1908 had any effect on the output or consumption of cocoa from there?
CADBURY: No, nor on the conditions of native labour.

ISAACS: In order to do anything effective about those conditions what view have you always taken?

CADBURY: That it was necessary to have the combination of the other chocolate manufacturers: that alone we could do nothing to ameliorate the conditions.

ISAACS: Did you take any steps to that end?

CADBURY: We attempted to get the American manufacturers to join us in our action but without success.

ISAACS: Has the action you have taken by continuing to purchase or ceasing to purchase cocoa from the islands had any effect on your profits?

CADBURY: None at all.

This is an ideal re-examination. The questions are not leading. They do not go outside the matters raised in cross-examination. They allow the witness scope to deny the suggestions made in cross-examination, and to re-establish the basis of his case and his own honesty. Similarly, the expert savaged in the *Herald* case about swell (see p.151) was asked in re-examination:

COUNSEL: You have explained the equation [the witness's explanation of how the disaster developed] and your work based on it. Does the swell affect in any way the consequence or the working out of the equation?

WITNESS: No.

COUNSEL: Does the current affect in any way the working out of the equation?

WITNESS: No.

COUNSEL: So are the conclusions on page 166 [of the witness's report] onwards depending in any way upon either swell or current?

WITNESS: No.

This is just as it should be: crisp and to the point. There is not a single superfluous word and it says to the expert tribunal exactly what is needed while the witness is still in the witness-box: 'No matter if you think the witness has been damaged, he has been damaged on a peripheral matter. It leaves the important substance of his report untouched.'

In most trials the re-examination of the defendant or the last of his witnesses is the last stage before the final speeches begin. The law, however, does make some allowance for human imperfection and in some cases further evidence can be called by the plaintiff or prosecution in rebuttal. But this may only be done where they have been taken by surprise; where something has arisen in the evidence given by the defence which 'no human ingenuity could foresee'. In one case a man was charged with forging a cheque. Although they possessed the evidence of a handwriting expert the prosecution did not call it but relied on the other evidence they had available. After the defendant had gone into the witness-box and denied it was his handwriting on the cheque the Judge suggested the prosecution should call the handwriting evidence and said to the jury: 'I think it is better we should have this case properly investigated.'

He was obviously right from the public point of view, but he was hopelessly wrong legally and the Court of Criminal Appeal immediately quashed the conviction which resulted. The evidence, they said, was not fresh, for it had been in the hands of the prosecution all the time, and it was not directed to a matter which had arisen for the first time when the defendant was in the witness-box, for by his plea of not guilty at the outset of the case he had put the prosecution upon proof that he had written the document. It did no more than remedy an obvious defect in the case for the prosecution.

This means no more than that evidence cannot be withheld and then tendered after all the evidence for the defence has been given, and the defence has been disclosed. Gilbert ran into this trouble in 1880 in one of the host of actions he brought against the Comedy Opera Company. He swore an affidavit over the run of *H M S Pinafore* which was filed with the Chancery Court. When the defence answered with twenty affidavits Gilbert filed fifty-one more in reply. They all could, and should, have been filed at the same time as his own, and the defence tried to get them struck out of the action. In fact no harm was done for the action was eventually settled.

Less fortunate was a Mr Barker in 1896, who suddenly found that all his furniture had been sold by a man named Shalless through a firm of auctioneers. Counsel for Mr Barker was confident he could prove his case against both Shalless and the auctioneers for 'converting' the furniture (selling it against his will and keeping the proceeds) by cross-examining Shalless. Mr Shalless was of the same opinion, and although present in court during the hearing, he declined to give evidence on his own behalf. Determined not to be foiled by this ruse counsel then applied to the Judge for leave to call Shalless himself. The Judge pointed out that if he had wanted to call Shalless he should have done so as part of his own case. He went on:

... in granting the Plaintiff's application ... I should be making a precedent which would, if established, lead to an improper amount of laxity in the conduct of the plaintiff's case.

This is a convoluted way of saying that the advocate must make up his mind before the case begins how he is going to conduct it: that he cannot wait until he sees which way the wind is blowing and then call extra evidence. The basis of the rule is more fundamental. A defendant, whether in criminal or civil courts, is entitled to know the whole of the evidence proving the case against him before he is obliged to answer it. That is the principle. Practice demands its enforcement if only because trials last quite long enough already. If purely confirmatory evidence in rebuttal were allowed, it would be difficult to prevent evidence in surrebuttal (evidence called by a defendant in rebuttal of rebuttal evidence) being called with equal frequency, and it would be difficult to see the end of any trial.

However, the courts will not allow defendants to gain verdicts by fraud or to spring surprises on plaintiffs, if they can prevent it. In 1876 a Mr Hollis very nearly succeeded in doing so. He was a manufacturer of tar and sulphate of ammonia with premises in south-east London. Mr Bigsby, who lived and worked nearby under the arches of the then London and Greenwich Railway, was a manufacturer of varnish, in particular of Brunswick and Japan Black. Bigsby claimed that Hollis's factory emitted sulphuretted hydrogen which injured the health of himself, his family, and the plants in his garden, and he sought an injunction to prevent Hollis from continuing to poison the local atmosphere. No suggestion was made to Bigsby in cross-examination that he too emitted sulphuretted hydrogen from his work, but right at the end of the evidence called for the defendant an expert gave evidence that the manufacture of Brunswick Black and Japan Black from mineral asphaltum also produced sulphuretted hydrogen. He even performed an experiment in court to prove his point which nearly asphyxiated the Judge. Mr Bigsby, knowing that he used vegetable asphaltum which gave off no vapour at all and not mineral asphaltum, promptly applied to call that evidence in rebuttal. The Judge refused the application and refused to grant an injunction, saying that not only was Mr Bigsby responsible for his own misfortune but that he had sought to conceal the truth from the court.

Happily Mr Bigsby could afford to go to the Court of Appeal who reversed the decision, though only after three days' argument. One of the Judges said:

At no period of a cause is it too late to show that confusion and error have arisen from two persons, or two things passing by the same name, and more especially to show that through such confusion the Court had been deceived by a misleading experiment performed in its presence.

The Court made no direct reference to the fact that the advocate for the defendant had contributed to that 'deceit' by failing to cross-examine Mr Bigsby properly. Had he suggested to Mr Bigsby that he also produced sulphuretted hydrogen Mr Bigsby would have been able to deal with it as part of his own case, and the need for calling evidence in rebuttal would never have arisen.

In fact, were it not for the occasional error by the lawyer and the more frequent commission of perjury by the parties and their witnesses, the need for and the rules for rebuttal evidence would never arise. Some of them are of appalling complexity. They are incomprehensible to the layman and unjustifiable by the lawyer. In one Irish murder case (the fact that it was an Irish case has no significance) it was suggested in cross-examination to a witness who identified the defendant as the murderer that he had told four men the police had arrested the wrong man, and that he had told a police officer he did not know who the murderer was. In due course two of the four men and the police officer gave evidence for the defence. The prosecution then called the other two of the four to rebut the evidence given by the first two, but were not allowed to call a Sergeant and an Inspector of police to whom the police officer said he had reported the conversation with the witness, who could have said that he did no such thing.

The fact is that the courts have always looked with unfortunate and unnecessary dislike on any evidence which might delay the speedy conclusion of a trial once it was under way. Nothing irritates a Judge more than to be unable to finish in haste today a trial he could finish at leisure tomorrow. Happily, since the end of the war, there has been a marked improvement in the patience of the Judges. The proper conclusion of a trial involving a single citizen is at last recognized to be of more importance than the full employment of the Judiciary. Things have changed a great deal since the 'Black Book' case when Mr Justice Darling refused to wait more than ten minutes for the Chief of Admiralty Intelligence to come to the Old Bailey from his office in Whitehall to give evidence which Darling had himself described the previous day as 'vital'.

Less happily, this improvement in the patience of the Judges has led to 'an improper amount of laxity in the conduct of a case' by counsel, which the Judge in the *Barker* v. *Shalless* case feared so much. Witnesses are continually being recalled so that they can deal with some point which should have been put to them before, but which was not put because counsel had not been properly instructed by his solicitor or because he had not read his brief. It is only with the leave of the Judge that witnesses can be recalled. The same Lord Darling silenced attempts by Simon and Halsbury in the Mr 'A' case to re-cross-examine and re-re-examine with a testy: 'Really, this case must be cleared up once and for all.'

The Judge himself has always had power to recall a witness, or, with the agreement of both sides, to call a witness they are unwilling to call themselves. This does not happen very often. The advocate is not very pleased when it does. Subject to the wishes of his client, it is his function to decide who shall or who shall not be called. It is to be expected that he will look with disfavour on any usurpation of his powers. But no one is more aware than the advocate that a nod is as good as a wink, and that to ride roughshod over nods and winks from Judges or juries that they want to hear a particular witness is not the way to win cases.

Juries have no rights on questions of evidence at all, except as the final arbiters of fact. It is one of the contradictions of English legal procedure that those who are required to decide questions of fact have no power to require fact to be laid before them. They can, of course, ask questions. But they cannot require witnesses to be called to answer them, or even insist that witnesses who are called do answer them. (Grand juries had power to do both. They were abolished in 1933.) This may be a shock for the layman who believes in the infallibility of the jury system without understanding what a jury undertakes to do. Their oath is to return a verdict, 'according to the evidence'. Their oath is not to return a verdict, 'according to the evidence which we think should be called'. So, if the question they ask requests information which by the laws of evidence is inadmissible (for instance, in a criminal trial, 'has the defendant done this before?'), then it cannot be answered. Put more shortly, they cannot ask questions which could not be asked by the Judge or either of the advocates. As a rule questions come from the jury after they have retired to consider their verdict, when they cannot be answered. This may seem harsh. But the line must be drawn somewhere. There must be a point when no further evidence can possibly be called by whatever name it may be known. That point is reached when the Judge finishes his summing-up.

Until then great attention will be paid to any question asked by the jury on the nod and wink principle referred to. Counsel will do anything they can to answer, or to explain why they cannot answer, the question that is put. Some can be very embarrassing. The one cited in the last paragraph would probably lead to the discharge of the jury if the defendant did have any previous convictions since by refusing to answer the question the jury would be bound to infer that he had, thus taking from the defendant his right to anonymity of character. The best question from a jury was put to an advocate in the middle of his final speech. He was defending two men from East London charged at a country Crown Court, with possessing housebreaking implements by night. They had been seen at three o'clock in the morning in a motor-car, which was later found to be stuffed with the implements. When the police appeared on the scene they decamped across the marshes. When finally caught they said they were interested in ornithology and looking for partridges' eggs. To substantiate this defence, one said that he had canaries at home which sat on the eggs and hatched them. Neither counsel nor the Judge questioned the improbability of this explanation. Defending counsel was waxing eloquent on the perils of law-

abiding ornithologists being arrested by over-zealous police officers
when a juryman said to him:

JURYMAN: Excuse me; mind if I ask a question?
COUNSEL [who minded very much but could not say so]: No, please do.
JURYMAN: D'you mind telling me how canaries sit on partridges' eggs?

The Final Speech

'Stand up, speak up and shut up' is the standard advice to the novice. It might be added: 'and keep your fingers crossed that you don't keel over half way through'. There is no ideal way to begin any speech, so much depends on the nature of the tribunal, the nature of the case and even the atmosphere which the speaker finds imposed on him. A common technique, for there is no art in this, is to promise to be short. So at the end of a long City fraud, in fact day 164 of the trial, one advocate began:

Before I start, I am going to tell you roughly how long I am going to be, because I am very conscious that the last time you were subjected to a speech from me it took four days, and you are probably a bit apprehensive when you see me getting to my feet again, especially when you see this great wodge of notes . . . I am hoping to finish tomorrow afternoon. That is not an absolute promise but I will do my best.

Perhaps there the circumstances justified it, but ordinarily to make such a forecast is a mistake, since the number of advocates who can keep to a time limit can be counted on the fingers of one hand.

Another advocate in the same case started with a joke about the court room, a converted office like a small scale aircraft hangar so large and with such bad acoustics that everyone had to use microphones to be heard. The witness-box was so far from the jury that they had to have television screens in front of them to relay pictures from a camera focused on the witness's face.

Members of the jury I hope you can hear me . . . I am told the main reason you have not been able to hear me is because I have not switched it [the microphone] on. Perhaps in a moment or two you will wish I had left it that way. I am going to be addressing you, members of the jury, over the next little period in relation to corporate liability. Immediately

I can sense that has all the tantalizing appeal of a party political broadcast. You have the disadvantage, however, that I am on all four channels at once and you cannot switch me off. You will bear with me, I am sure, however, for this single opportunity that I have on behalf of the company to address you.

The last sentence is the important one. Although buried in the designedly trivial and ingratiating preliminary, it focuses the jury's mind on the importance of what is to come solely because this was the 'single opportunity' for the speech.

The first defence speech in the same case following immediately after the prosecution's final speech attempted to do something much more fundamental: to alter the atmosphere created by that speech.

May it please your Lordship, members of the jury, shall we now come down to earth? Shall we get back to the real world and instil a little simplicity, commonsense, reality and some balanced regard to the evidence in the presentation of this case because that is what we think you would now like to have to help you reach your proper conclusion in this case.

In front of tribunals, atmosphere plays a very subservient role, though it may surface in the most surprising ways and at the most unexpected moments. Jokes, even successful jokes, are virtually taboo, especially as an introduction. The approach is business-like, and increasingly often preceded by a written summary. Some courts now require such a document to be provided days in advance of the actual delivery of the speech. It may flatten the language which is used, rhetoric cannot survive in print, but it does concentrate the mind quite wonderfully. Some of those advocates appearing in the first part of the *Herald* inquiry used their document to structure their speeches. One, the best, began like this:

Sir, as you will have seen from my outline submission which I handed up last night, there are four topics upon which I would wish to address the court, and I will go straight to the first one, which is to certain of the facts relating to the final voyage. Sir, the first fact upon which I want to address the court is the loading condition of the vessel. The cargo consisted of some eighty-four cars and forty-two lorries and various other items of freight. You can see the precise details, Sir, from the evidence of . . .

Chapter and verse for each statement of fact were faultlessly given, interleaved with appraisals of the contentions of the other advocates in the inquiry. At the end of each section a conclusion was drawn. The end of this one was as follows:

We accept on the available figures that the vessel was loaded below her C2 marks and apart from that we have no particular case on trim and draughts . . . I invite a finding that the vessel was not loaded below her C1 mark.

Each section was dealt with in the same way. There is a golden rule to be found here: 'Begin as you mean to go on.' There is a corollary to the rule: 'Do not antagonize your audience at the outset.' To do so is to invite less attention, possibly less respect, being paid to everything you say later.

One of the other advocates addressing the Commissioner and his four assessors at the end of Part I of the inquiry, which had dealt with the capsize of the *Herald* and the safety aspects of the operation of the ship, had described the approach of the Commissioner as 'robust'. Outside observers might have used different and stronger language. One of the witnesses, a Master of a sister ship, had written to the Court saying, 'due to the rather intimidating atmosphere in which questions were asked, some of my answers were not a true reflection of the facts . . .' At one stage, because of the hostile nature of the questions to some of the witnesses, Counsel had had to remind the Court that unless notices were served on the witnesses warning them that they might be subjected to criticism in the eventual Report, and such notices had not been served, the Court could not name them critically in the report. At another point, the Court indicated that technical material available to one of the assessors should not be shown to a witness before he could be cross-examined on them. It had required the intervention of Counsel to ensure the rules of natural justice were complied with. The atmosphere during the twenty days occupied by Part I was highly charged. The room used for the hearing was packed day after day with over 200 spectators, survivors and victims' relatives. The advocate for the company protested that the approach of his client had been responsible and that every assistance had been given to the tribunal. He went on:

Despite that approach, those instructing me and their servants have sometimes felt involved in not just a robust inquiry, but one which has sometimes been conducted somewhat aggressively, perhaps not entirely fairly.

Later he used words which seemed to indicate that the words 'not entirely fairly' were limited to questions put to one witness only, 'he was treated unfairly'. He was challenged by the Commissioner. There was an unpleasant confrontation. The word 'unfair' was not persisted in. The word 'aggressively' remained, although a later speaker sought to blunt its use by suggesting that a tribunal of this nature cannot do its work properly if it is conducted like a parish council meeting.

There are two morals here. Never make a claim which you cannot justify, and never start out by saying something contentious which is unnecessary to the prime purpose of your speech. It was obvious to anyone attending the inquiry that it had been conducted aggressively, but by the time speeches were due this was water under the bridge. If it was to be referred to at all it should have been by way of a by-line not a headline.

If there is no ideal way to begin, there are ideals to be pursued for the remainder of all speeches. Hastings pretended that there were not. Soon after he began to address the jury in his final speech in the Laski case he said:

I may say after long experience that I have never yet known a case in which anything I have said has had any effect on a jury one way or the other, and therefore I have come to the conclusion that the shorter the time I take in saying it the better for everyone.

As a means of gaining a substantial tactical advantage over Slade who had yet to speak this was a sound if hypocritical and well-tried formula. As an accurate statement of fact, however, it was nonsense. Unfortunately many modern advocates seem to have taken Hastings seriously, and behaving as if this were the advocate's eleventh commandment, stumble through the odious task of addressing the Judge or jury, boring themselves almost as much as their audience.

Many excuses for this (apart from Hastings) lie ready to their hands. It is said that the technicalities of the law or of the particular courts in which they practise are unfavourable to oratory and eloquence; that twentieth-century Judges and juries are not won by the grandiloquent and artificial language and phraseology of the nineteenth century, or that it is fact and not fancy that wins cases. Like all excuses these do not excuse; nor do they exonerate the advocates whose dull words, ungrammatical sentences, and commonplace thoughts delivered in flat and monotonous tones pass for speeches in many courts. More important still, they ignore the truth; for the demands of the greatest teachers of oratory for order, clarity, and coherence are as necessary in plain speech as they are in the highest flights of rhetoric. And they ignore the necessity; for no advocate ever yet started a case without the certain knowledge that he would not end it without making a speech.

Unhappily truth and necessity are forgotten. The example set by Demosthenes who cured his stammer by constantly speaking with small pebbles in his mouth, and his weakness of voice by reciting aloud on the seashore until he could be heard above the waves, gives rise to amusement rather than a desire to emulate his determined fight to overcome his handicaps. In the same way the lessons to be learned from a study of the speeches of the past are spurned on the general grounds that they have no relevance to today's racy and casual mode. The fallacy underlying this argument can be judged from these four extracts. From what centuries do they come?

Before I go any further I will ask you to consider how far we have already got in the case you are trying. It is admitted, indeed it cannot be denied, that an Englishman has a right, which no power on earth can take away from him, to form an opinion.

What is conspiracy? It is the agreeing together of a number of individuals either to do some illegal act or to do some lawful act by unlawful means, which is, perhaps, much the same thing.

Gentlemen of the Jury: the charge against the prisoner is murder, and the punishment for murder is death; and that simple statement is sufficient to suggest to us the awful solemnity of the occasion which brings you and me face to face.

When one thinks of trust funds one thinks of widows and orphans and the wistful savings of a vanished hand.

The first three extracts come from speeches made during the nineteenth century. The first is part of Brougham's speech in a libel case in 1811; the second, part of Sir James Scarlett's argument in the High Court seeking a new trial in 1820; and the third is the opening of Dean Inglis's speech to the jury in the trial of Madeline Smith for murder in 1858. Only the last extract comes from the twentieth century. It is from a speech of Fearnley Whittingstall's in a fraud case tried at the Old Bailey in 1956. (I know of no more beautiful sentence spoken in an English Court.) Each one of the first three extracts carries lessons for the modern speaker. Brougham's points all the dangers of badly prepared parenthetical speech, as vividly as the last extract in this chapter demonstrates the force it can impart if the material is carefully selected. Brougham's is diffuse and places the emphasis on the wrong part of the sentence. Scarlett's definition of conspiracy is a model of condensation, and is in almost daily use in the criminal courts; while as a means of grasping the attention of an audience at the outset of a speech the Dean's opening has yet to be improved upon.

It is much too easy to be scathing about the manners and methods of the older advocates. Hastings introduced the words set out on p. 191 by saying:

You may remember in the old days it was the habit of advocates sometimes to make long and eloquent speeches on all sorts of subjects, including comments on the Goddess of Justice who sits with scales above the court.

This kind of derogatory dismissal is far too common. It is largely founded on the belief that emotion is an unreliable guide to a true decision on fact, and that there is therefore something suspect in evoking or displaying emotion. This both distorts reality, for most human action is prompted by feeling and not by facts, and supposes that there is an infallibility about fact which produces verdicts with the accuracy of a Pythagorean equation. There is not. But the belief encourages speeches of an appalling flatness. One longs for a Curran or a Patrick O'Connell with their gusto and flamboyance. They were, of course, impossibly verbose; but their speeches live. There is a swaggering profligacy of words which is immediately and immensely attractive. One simple statement of the facts is never enough. Allusion is piled on analogy, metaphor, and simile, and the whole edifice lighted with a burning brand of syllogism. This is part of Curran's speech in 1804 on behalf of a young and poor clergyman whose twenty-four-year-old wife was enticed away from him by the rich and elderly Marquess of Headfort. The Marquess actually made off with the wife while her husband was safely preaching in his pulpit.

This Cornish plunderer [the Marquess came from Cornwall] intent on spoil, callous to every touch of humanity, shrouded in darkness, holds out false lights to the tempest-tossed vessel [the wife], and lures her, and her pilot [the husband], to that shore on which she must be lost for ever; the rock unseen, the ruffian invisible, and nothing apparent but the treacherous signal of security and repose; so this prop of the throne, this pillar of the State, this stay of religion, this ornament of the Peerage, this common protector of the people's privileges and of the Crown's prerogative, descends from these high grounds of character to muffle himself in the gloom of his base and dark designs, to play before the eyes of the deluded wife and the deceived husband, the fairest lights of love to the one and the friendly and hospitable regards to the other, until she is at length dashed on that hard bosom where her honour and her happiness are wrecked and lost forever ...

It ought to be recorded that the wife left her husband voluntarily, and, according to the chambermaid who gave evidence, spent the first night of her elopement sharing the Marquess's bed at a nearby inn with every sign of enjoyment.

The advocates of the eighteenth century, which saw the beginning of forensic advocacy as we know it today, were not embarrassed by emotion. But this was before the morality of Victorian England had turned it into mawkish sentimentality. Erskine from Scotland, Thurlow from Suffolk, Curran and O'Connell from Ireland all understood the truth in Lord Chesterfield's letter to his son written in 1746:

Wherever you would persuade or prevail, address yourself to the passions; it is by them that mankind is to be taken. I bid you strike at the passions ... If you can once engage people's pride, love, pity, ambition (or whichever is their prevailing passion) on your side, you need not fear what their reason can do against you.

This was a period in English history when Lord Chesterfield could advise his son to speak well not because of what people would think of him if he did not, but because it was foolish to neglect an accomplishment which would serve him well in later life. Manners were an end in themselves and not merely a means to achieve propriety by conformity. It is not surprising that a deliberate cultivation of language should have taken place at the same time. This is part of Sheridan's opening on the impeachment of Warren Hastings:

The coolness and reflection with which this act was managed ... proves the prisoner to be that monster in nature, a deliberate and reasoning tyrant; other tyrants of whom we read ... were urged on to their crimes by the impetuosity of passion. High rank disqualified them from advice, and perhaps, equally prevented reflection. But in the prisoner we have a man born in a state of mediocrity; bred to a mercantile life; used to system, and accustomed to regularity; who was accountable to his masters and therefore was compelled to think and deliberate on every part of his conduct. It is this cool deliberation I say, which renders his crimes the more horrible and his character the more atrocious.

The studied perfection of this language falls unseasonably on modern ears. It is some measure of the unreasonableness of the age that the greater the care with which a speech appears to be fashioned the greater the distrust it arouses in the audience. The era of the common man invites common speech. Of course, words are the cheapest commodity on the market. Spoken words are also the most ephemeral. It is not surprising that less and less attention is paid to the construction of speeches or to the choice of the individual words from which they are built.

This should not be so. A speech on which time has been spent in preparation need not smell of long hours and guttering candles, and need not be unnecessarily prolix. If the occasion required it, Curran could be as short as anyone, yet he spent days fashioning his speeches. In one he completed the devastation of a witness, who had informed against his client, in a single sentence:

I conjure you, suffer him not to take an oath; the hand of a murderer should not pollute the purity of the Gospel; if he swear, let it be upon the knife, the proper symbol of his profession.

Of course, the advocate must heed the practicalities of the situation. Even O'Connell realized that, and reminded himself of them by writing on a piece of paper: 'A good speech is a good thing, but never forget the verdict is the thing.' The most devoted admirer of Curran and O'Connell would realize that the style of neither would fit the cold realities of a Town and Country Planning Inquiry, or an application to the Divisional Court of the High Court for an order for mandamus against a Bench of Justices who had misinterpreted part of the Ministry of Transport's Construction and Use Regulations governing the emission of smoke by articulated lorries. In such courts, clarity of thought and directness of speech are the paramount virtues. There must also be complete mastery of the facts so that at the outset the advocate can set out the points on which he wishes subsequently to enlarge. In the following case an advocate was addressing the Commissioner of Wrecks inquiring into the loss of a ship at sea. At the end of the inquiry the Commissioner was obliged to answer over a hundred questions as to why the ship twice caught fire and how she was eventually lost. After reading the agreed statement of facts prepared for the guidance of the Commissioner, he said:

My submissions are that the main things to be considered really arise out of Question 23: first, what caused the fire on the 6th November; secondly, what caused the fire on the 8th–9th November which was the fatal fire; and thirdly, could the second fire have been put out. We know the first fire was. We have to consider how it started, how far it advanced, and how it could have been dealt with.

This simplification of the issues enabled him to pass on to the technicalities of the case, knowing the court would be able to follow him. The technicalities were formidable. The modern advocate is in fact a jack-of-all-trades. Building disputes will oblige him to learn brick sizes and the diameters of drain pipes, industrial accident torques and metal fatigues, while a running down practice, which deals with insurance claims arising out of motor-car accidents, will give him a medical knowledge shared only by a hospital consultant. After the extract set out above, the advocate told the court they would have to consider:

The position of the port settling tank; the filling of the port settling tank including the evidence about the electric oil transfer pump, a float indicator and the electrical cut out . . . the exhaust manifold on the after part of the port engine . . . the removal of the exhaust valve on the number three unit starboard engine and the fitting on it of a deflector plate . . . fire extinguishers . . . emergency fire pump, as to why it would not sound although the motor worked . . . spray nozzles on the hoses . . . vents, skylights, and doors . . .

This sort of technical jargon in this sort of dose is quite a common experience. Passion and emotion, and the use of fine language do not enter into recitations of this type. Speeches on these topics require prodigious feats of memory, not eloquence. Quintilian, writing in the year A.D. 70, understood this well, and included memory in the five attributes he said were required by the forensic advocate. Curran was especially gifted in this. In 1783 he delivered a speech as long as a third of this book. He had in front of him a note of only thirty words. The word 'drowned' gave rise to this passage:

. . . when the liberty of the Press was trodden underfoot; when venal sheriffs returned packed juries to carry into effect those fatal conspiracies of the few against the many; when devoted benches of public justice were filled with some of those foundlings of fortune, who, overwhelmed in the torrent of corruption at an early period, lay at the bottom like drowned bodies, while soundness or sanity remained in them; but at length, becoming buoyant by putrefaction, they rose as they rotted, and floated to the surface of the polluted stream, where they drifted along, the objects of terror and contagion and abomination.

The great advantage of mastery of material, whether of fact or thought or plain rhetoric, is that it leaves the advocate's eye free to gauge the effect of his words. The point has been made elsewhere already. This should be added: that it also leaves a part of the mind free to arrange the order of the next sentence. If while speaking he is a prisoner of his writing, the paper on which he relies becomes a barrier between himself and his audience.

But whatever the practicalities of the situation, anything which allows the advocate to 'lend variety to sameness and charm to the commonplace' should not be neglected. It was the half-remembered lines of Tennyson which permitted Fearnley Whittingstall to complete the sentence on page 192 with the words 'of a vanished hand'. It may be that the memory of these words put the whole passage into his mind. One of the recurring difficulties facing the advocate springs from repetition. He quickly becomes known as a commercial man, or as a divorce specialist, or more crudely as 'being in crime'. When he begins in these specialized fields he usually feels it unsafe to go outside the certain limits he has heard during his pupillage. Once he has gained enough confidence to do so, it becomes immensely difficult. One cannot be original about bills of lading, or constructive desertion, or offensive weapons indefinitely. Indeed, it is a positive disadvantage to use fresh language in front of some Judges. They have grown so used to the hackneyed phraseology of the courts that it has acquired the advantages of a verbal morse code. In appeals on questions of law a freshness of language is particularly required. Nearly every kind of problem has come before the courts in one form or another. For some there are precedents from cases previously decided stretching back for centuries. On corroboration, which is always sought when an accomplice gives evidence and in sexual cases, there is a classic definition formulated in 1916:

What is required is some independent testimony ... that is evidence, direct or circumstantial, which implicates the accused, and which confirms in some material particular not only the evidence given by the accomplice [or complainant in sexual cases] that the crime has been committed, but also the evidence that the prisoner committed it.

Since then the number of appeals touching on this question runs into hundreds. Not one has said anything fresh on the subject. Is the advocate simply to learn this by rote and trot it out whenever it is required? Why not look back to Sir William Jones's opening speech in 1679 when he was prosecuting the murderers of Sir Edmund Berry Godfrey, the magistrate killed in the Popish plot?

You will easily believe that most of these particulars [of the murder] must arise from one who was a party to the fact [i.e. an accomplice], yet, My Lord, I will undertake before I have done, so to fortify almost every particular he delivers with concurrent proof of other testimony, and the things will so depend one upon another and have such a connection that little doubt will remain in any man's mind.

Although it is jury advocacy which catches public attention it is by argument on matters of law that many lawyers earn their bread and butter. In these cases mere skill with words, eloquence, and powers of oratory are no substitutes for knowledge and understanding of the law. Marshall Hall was a supremely good jury advocate, but he was no lawyer. The same was true of Hastings. The converse was true of Slade. But law cannot be wholly divorced from fact. The advocate must be ready at any moment when he is dealing with fact to answer questions of law. In the middle of his cross-examination of Laski, Lord Goddard interrupted to ask Hastings:

The jury may come to the conclusion that the plaintiff did use the words [printed in the paper] in which case, it seems to me, *caedit questio* [that's the end of the case]. It is equally possible that the jury may come to the conclusion that the plaintiff did not use the words ... What then is the position? If he did not use those words is it open to you to justify something else? That is a plea of justification of some other libel ...

A little later he said:

Is it open on a plea of justification to say: 'Well, we cannot justify that you committed a crime on the day we say you did, but we justify to this extent, that we show that on the previous day you committed a crime'?
HASTINGS: Yes.
JUDGE: I should like to have authority for that.
HASTINGS: I think there is an old authority which says ...

He could not produce it. Slade produced two authorities on the point within a minute of the question. This ability to lay hands immediately on relevant cases and statutes is a very important one. One Judge is reported to have said his elevation to the Bench was not due to his abilities as a lawyer, but because he knew where to find his law, and could therefore be expected to render invaluable assistance to the other Judges. In speeches to the Appeal Courts this ability, combined with the orderly presentation of those authorities, is of supreme importance. The requirements for securing and retaining interest in a lay audience can be entirely discarded. When Sir James Stephen opened the appeal in the Folkestone Ritual case in the House of Lords in 1877 he quoted from over thirty different authorities on the first day. He spoke in all for four full days, his authorities ranging upwards from the Injunctions of Queen Elizabeth I and the Rubric of

1662. In such a setting the tone of his voice, the rhythm and the length of his sentences were of little significance.

Nevertheless it would be foolish to neglect Quintilian's advice: 'the advocate who seeks to persuade should first seek to please'. This bribery of the senses takes many forms. One lies in promising to be short. Sometimes it can be very effective. More often it is not, because lawyers are always underestimating their own loquacity. In the Laski case Hastings began his speech:

HASTINGS: May it please Your Lordship: Members of the Jury, I can start what I have to say to you with perhaps the only bit of good news you have heard in this case so far. That is that I am only going to address you for a very few minutes. I want to explain why, because I do not want you to think, and I hope you will not think, that the value of anything that is said to you is to be measured by the number of words.

The Laski case does not fit into the usual mould of cases in which similar promises are made. Time had been standing on Laski's heels from the beginning. On a number of occasions Lord Goddard had intervened to speed the case on its way. Secondly, if Hastings promised to be short, he was going to be short. And thirdly, he knew Slade was to speak after him. This was the first exploitation of the tactical advantage he had created to which reference was made at the beginning of this chapter. Exactly three quarters of the way through his speech he said:

I told you I was only going to be a few minutes. I have been fifteen, and I am afraid that is too long. I wish you good luck that Mr Slade will not be four times as long. Whether you will get that good luck or not, I do not know. I doubt it.

It was a cheap gibe. And as a forecast it was not particularly accurate, for Slade spoke for two hours, not for one. It gave Hastings the whip hand over Slade by leaving in their minds an antipathy towards him which would grow with every passing minute.

This was as nothing, however, compared with Hastings's ascendancy over Slade in style. The one advocate was the complete antithesis of the other. They were engaged in a case where style mattered a great deal, and which the stylist won hands down. This is how Hastings finished his speech:

I am going to ask you to say that these words were spoken and in addition that the whole of this report is a fair and accurate report of what was said on that murky evening when incivilities were so happily exchanged between these two gentlemen ... I ask you to say that this action ought never to have been brought and probably no one regrets it more than the plaintiff himself.

Slade ended with these words:

Now, Members of the Jury, I ask you to take all those matters into consideration together with the plea of justification which has been persisted in right up to this moment, and if you come to the conclusion that the plaintiff is entitled to succeed – and it is only in that event that you have to consider the question of damages at all – I say, subject to My Lord's direction, that you are entitled to take into consideration the whole of the matters I have mentioned in aggravation of damages, so that when a man comes to vindicate his character he shall not be subjected to treatment of this kind, and I ask you to do so. That is why I ask you, if you are in Mr Laski's favour, to award him exemplary damages, as I say, not for the purpose of the money itself, but so as to mark your reprobation of that treatment of a plaintiff who comes to the courts for the purpose, as I say, of vindicating his character. That is all I desire to say.

This was a sad and spiritless performance. It is diffuse and impossibly repetitive. It leaves an impression of tiredness amounting almost to depression and an unfortunate lack of confidence in the outcome of the case. Hastings on the other hand swept through the issues in fine, gladiatorial style. Every word presumes upon the verdict being his within minutes of the jury's retirement. It does more, for the words, 'incivilities so happily exchanged', compress the whole case within the Hastings-brand teacup. Few advocates mark out the boundaries they wish to draw in the cases they do as clearly, or as shortly, as did Hastings. But then few have his presumptuous courage. The way in which it is done is of secondary importance to the fact that it is done. Whatever the audience, the advocate must know the limits he wishes to set on the case, and then do all in his power to persuade his audience to accept them.

This is the prime requirement in every speech. The advocate addressing the Commissioner of Wrecks was doing it. Sievier in his opening was attempting to do it. It does not matter whether the case revolves round one single fact, or whether it involves many. It does not matter if the theme is a momentous one, or the advocate believes he is appearing for a worthless scoundrel. In 1940 Sir Winston Churchill spoke in the House of Commons about the military situation following the invasion of France. The greater part of the speech is recitative. The sentences are in the main short, and the construction of them simple. Then, at the end of the speech, he turned to the future. It is impossible to describe his object as the drawing of a boundary or the setting of a limit, yet in a sense it was, for he sought to unite his audience in order to achieve a particular end. He began this part of the speech:

Even though large tracts of Europe and many old and famous states have fallen or may fall into the grip of the Gestapo and all the odious apparatus of Nazi rule, we shall not flag or fail. We shall go on to the end, we shall fight in France, we shall fight on the seas and the oceans . . .

The power of the speech mounted with each pair of nouns until it reached a crescendo –

. . . we shall fight in the fields and in the streets, we shall fight in the hills; we shall never surrender . . .

It was magnificent. And it was not the end. Having brought his audience to a point where he could not be expected to continue, he did continue –

. . . we shall never surrender, and even if, which I do not for a moment believe, this island or a large part of it were subjugated or starving, then our Empire beyond the seas, armed and guarded by the British fleet, would carry on the struggle, until in God's good time, the new world, with all its power and might, steps forth to the rescue and the liberation of the old.

With its command and authority and simplicity, this is advocacy in its finest form. This should be the aim of the advocate each time he rises to his feet to say,

May it please Your Lordship, Members of the Jury . . .

Chapter 11

Style in Speeches

In speeches, unlike cross-examination, style matters a great deal. In final speeches clarity of thought and expression are required above everything else. In an opening speech an advocate may permit himself a looseness of language, at least a lack of precision in the language he uses, since at that time not all the issues may be capable of proof and the case will depend on the effect of the evidence yet to be given. It may be unwise at that stage to tie oneself down too tightly. No excuses are available for an advocate who fails in his final speech to speak with clear, simple and direct language. This requires a capacity to summarize sometimes the most complex of ideas so that the audience can be in no doubt as to what they are being asked to consider and decide. He must show a capacity to do this both in relation to the facts in the case and in relation to the law which has to be applied. By the time the Coroner reached the end of the evidence in the *Herald* case it was clear that he had to instruct the jury how to approach a verdict of 'unlawful killing' manslaughter. This is the central part of his direction to them:

(i) Are you satisfied so that you are sure that what he did or omitted to do was something which it was his duty to do? Something which, in the eyes of the ordinary prudent Officer or Petty Officer (as appropriate) would have created an obvious and serious risk of causing injury to passengers and crew? If you are not satisfied that this was the case, for example, if you felt that to the individual concerned, in the light of his knowledge at the time, the risk was not both obvious and serious, then you do not need to consider the second question. The ingredients for unlawful killing would not have been made out in respect of that individual. If, on the other hand, you are satisfied so that you are sure that the risk, in the eyes of a prudent Officer or Petty Officer, was both obvious and serious, then you must consider the second question. And the second question is this.

(ii) Given that there was an obvious and serious risk, are you satisfied so that you are sure that that individual did not consider the possibility of the risk, in other words, was indifferent to the risk, or that he recognized the risk and nevertheless decided to go ahead and take it?

I must emphasize that a failure to recognize that there was such a risk at all would not by itself amount to negligence of the required degree.

If you are satisfied so that you are sure, that the answer to question two is yes, in other words, that he was indifferent to the risk or recognized it and decided to take it, if you are sure about that, and you are also sure that you, that an individual, that that individual owed a duty and that his acts or omissions were a substantial cause of the death, then the ingredients for unlawful killing have been made out.

In the subsequent criminal trial at the Old Bailey it had become clear from the cross-examination of the Ship Masters and Officers that the real question was now limited to whether the risk was an obvious one. Without exception all the witnesses had said that at the time it was not obvious to them. Before the prosecution evidence was finished the trial Judge called on prosecuting Counsel to explain to him how then he put his case. The advocate must always be ready to deal with such interventions. They invariably come at inconvenient and unexpected moments, often having nothing to do with the part of the case then being examined. In this instance the question went to the heart of the matter.

JUDGE: We have heard a body of evidence which I assume for present purposes to have been relevant, probative and therefore admissible, to the effect that experienced seaborne personnel never thought for a moment that with the system in force there was any risk of that event happening . . . Where does that leave the case in terms of obvious risk?

The discussion which this question provoked lasted almost three days, but the prosecution were able to put their contention into no more than five sentences right at the beginning of their argument:

In our submission, the risk was still obvious even when masters and others who have given evidence about it say they didn't think there was a risk. What they mean in our submission is they didn't see the risk. Our submission is their failure to see the risk does not alter the obviousness of the risk. Again, in parenthesis, Mr Hartwell dealing with the question of positive reporting said words to the effect, I didn't think of it at the time. That doesn't mean, in our submission, it wasn't a visible risk at the time which could have been avoided.

As we have seen from Chapter 9, this advocate was unsuccessful in persuading the Judge that there was evidence which ought to be considered by the jury. The case he was presenting was fatally flawed. But there was no lack of 'style' in the robustness and persistence with which he presented it.

But the advocate does not live by style alone. The extracts from the *Herald* trial show that well enough. Facts are the bricks with which he builds and style at best the mortar to bind them together. Without some facts to help them even the most imposing advocates are impotent to affect the result of a case. With the facts that he has the advocate must use all the skill and style he can muster to persuade the Judge and jury to view them in the light most favourable to his client. His skill should lead him to adopt the style most suitable to the case rather than the one most suitable to himself. His style should lead him, as in cross-examination, to extract from the facts every advantage they can be made to admit.

To a very large extent the advocate cannot help carrying with him the stamp of his own individual traits. Inevitably they in part dictate the manner of his court behaviour. It is for this reason that Muir became a prosecutor in the criminal courts, while Marshall Hall invariably appeared for the defence. But whatever his personal characteristics, his style while prosecuting will be markedly different from his style when defending. The duties of counsel on opposing sides in criminal cases have already been examined in Chapter 3. They impose on counsel appearing for the Crown a restraint which led the normally rumbustious Serjeant Davy to end his speech for the prosecution in the trial of Elizabeth Canning in this way:

Those, gentlemen, are the remarks occurring to me upon the various circumstances in this very long trial. Many of them may have been unnecessary, or improper, whilst some, which I have omitted, should have been enforced; but whatever errors are imputable to me in the course of this prosecution, I solemnly protest that the misstating or misapplying any fact has been entirely foreign to my intention throughout the cause; in the merits of which I have at no time been engaged otherwise than, as I conceived, the duty of my profession directed me; and this duty I have discharged to the best of my abilities.

In prosecuting, counsel is acting on behalf of the community as a whole, who have as great an interest in securing the acquittal of the innocent as they have the conviction of the guilty. He is not therefore to strain after conviction like a bloodhound after a fresh scent, but to present the facts fairly and dispassionately. He is not required to abandon his abilities as an advocate. His passion may be a little muted; it does not disappear. Davy was free to comment on the improbabilities in the story told by Canning to account for her disappearance and her month's confinement in the depths of winter in the Enfield attic of Mother Wells's bawdy house, after she and the gipsy Squires had failed to persuade her to adopt a life of prostitution. And he did so with all the lusty vigour of the century.

Is it creditable on coming thither that the gipsy, an artful procuress, hackneyed in the ways of women, should only slightly ask her to go their way, and because she said no, should give over all further attempts? Was this acting like the President or Lady Abbess of such a house as Mother Wells? Was this any proper trial of the prisoner's virtue? I hope, for the honour of the female sex, that there hardly ever was a young woman not above eighteen years of age [this was 1753] who did not say no, once at least, especially if solicited by an ugly, decrepit hag. And yet this faint, this half-consenting, no-refusal, is the only reason given for her long and barbarous confinement. Her confinement! To what purpose was it? What, starve a young woman out of her virtue? Rich food and strong liquor may do much, but bread and water, cold and hunger are not apt to inflame the passions.

This is the only distinction between the roles of the advocate in the courts which needs to be noted. Another, that between speeches in the courts and in other forums, is less well recognized. It arises from the structure of the trials within which the speeches have to fit, and from the uncertainties implicit in every trial. In the rapid shift of events in jury trials few speeches can be set pieces of verbal pyrotechnics. Furthermore, they are mainly concerned with facts and not ideas. This leads to a narrowing of the scope available to the advocate, and to this strange paradox, that at any given moment, the fullest use of the material in the hands of the advocate is not necessarily its best use. If, for instance, in opening his case the advocate explores one point in it to the full, he may find from the unexpected failure of the witness upon whom that point depends the whole case collapsing about his ears. It is impossible therefore to judge an advocate's speech from what appears on the surface, for what he says and the way he says it, and what he does not say, may be dictated by the stage the case has reached and the certainty with which he can speak.

In most cases there are four speeches: the opening for the plaintiff or prosecution, the opening for the defence, and the two final speeches. But there is nothing immutable about the laws the lawyers make for themselves. If the defence are calling no evidence in addition to the defendant's, then they lose the right to open. In both the Laski and the Peasenhall cases four speeches were made. The following extracts all come from the Peasenhall case. They show the danger referred to in the previous paragraph, and the concentration on minute and petty detail which an advocate must employ if he is to perform his task properly. All the extracts deal with only one of the points in the case. The first is from Dickens's opening. An attempt had been made to burn the body of the murdered girl Rose Harsent with paraffin so as to hide her pregnancy. Where had the paraffin come from?

DICKENS: On the floor too, was found a broken bottle, and by the fireplace, where it must have rolled, was found the neck of a bottle with the cork jammed tightly in. So tightly was it that you could not get it out, but on that part of the bottle was found a label giving instructions as to the doses to be given to Mrs Gardiner's children. The doctor will tell you that that was a bottle which he gave to Mrs Gardiner for her children some little time before, and what we suggest took place was this – that the murderer, whoever he was, with that cold-blooded brutal premeditation, had gone there with the object of meeting the girl and getting rid if he could of all trace of her shame by burning the body. For that purpose, we suggest, he took with him the bottle filled with paraffin oil, but in putting the cork in with a view to putting it in in such a way that it was not likely to come out, he put it in so tightly that when the murderer took the bottle from his pocket he could not move the cork. He thereupon tried to get the oil out of the lamp [this is 1902, there was neither gas nor electricity in the house] as was suggested by the way the lamp was taken to pieces, but not being able to get the top off he broke the bottle in order to obtain the paraffin ... In breaking the bottle the accused forgot he was leaving behind the label, and which we suggest is damning proof against him. It is for you gentlemen to say whether the man who murdered the woman brought the bottle with him.

Much of this is a bare recital of fact couched in plain, even pedestrian, language. But much of it is superfluous supposition. Why say that the neck of the bottle 'must have rolled' to the fireplace? There was no need to. It did not advance the case against Gardiner at all. And from the words 'what we suggest took place' to the end of the extract is all theory, and very dangerous theory. Other facts, adduced either in cross-examination of his own witnesses, or established by the witnesses called for the defence, could give rise to other, and equally attractive theories. The fresh facts might utterly destroy the basis of Dickens's theory. In the particular circumstances of the Peasenhall case it was madness for Dickens to theorize about the bottle in his opening. This was a re-trial. (The first jury had failed to agree.) Dickens knew the evidence which Wild was going to call. He knew Wild had an explanation for the bottle with the Gardiner label. It would have been far safer to have allowed the inferences arising from the facts, that Gardiner took the bottle filled with paraffin and having broken it forgot the pieces, to speak for themselves.

When Wild began his opening speech the jury knew nothing of this. All they had before them was Dickens's theory and the established facts from which it had been woven. Wild first commented on those facts in the safe certainty that the case for the prosecution was closed.

WILD: ... the bottle which is the cause of this case. But for it Gardiner would never have been accused in this case. But the police in Peasenhall had the bottle, and they said to themselves: Gardiner did this murder, and he has left his card. Out of consideration for us, in order not to tax our brains too heavily, Gardiner has considerately brought a labelled bottle with his name on it – and, of course, he did the murder. If this was not a murder case it would make us laugh. Is it the sort of mistake that an accomplished murderer makes? Happily, we can explain this to you without a doubt.

A dose of good, thumping sarcasm, spiced with a short, sharp rhetorical question or two, has always been one of the most effective weapons in the advocate's armoury. Rushing on from 'accomplished murderer', a suggestion which had never been made against Gardiner (one might be inclined to think that accomplished murderers are those uncaught and not those who make the mistakes by which they are caught), to the simple facts by which Wild was to explode Dickens's theory makes this passage doubly effective. He went straight on to open the evidence he was about to call: Mrs Gardiner to say that she gave a bottle with camphorated oil in it to Rose Harsent to cure a cold, and Mrs Walker, the local midwife, to say that Rose Harsent told her she had used camphorated oil given her by Mrs Gardiner to cure a cold.

Then Wild advanced his own theory, for the bottle found by the girl had contained paraffin and not camphorated oil.

WILD: The bottle was taken by Rose Harsent, and then what did she do with it? I do not know. I can only guess and so can you. It is not an uncommon thing for servants, and particularly if they are a little slovenly, to use a little paraffin to make up the kitchen fire and replenish the lamp. I suggest that, having used the [camphorated] oil, she filled the bottle with paraffin. Of course, if the paraffin had been in the bottle some time there would be no smell of the camphorated oil remaining.

This only goes part of the way. It does not explain how or why the bottle came to be broken. Should Wild lay his own explanation for that before the jury at this stage or should he wait for his final speech? If he does so now this theory may be exploded in cross-examination. But if it is not, and Wild knew the strength of Dickens's cross-examination in advance for he had heard it on the previous trial, then it would gain weight with the jury by remaining uncontroverted by evidence unlike Dickens's own theory. Wild took one tiny fact, that a shelf in the kitchen behind the door leading up to the girl's room had been broken in the struggle between her and her assailant, to launch his suggestion.

WILD: In all probability the bottle was on that shelf which was broken because you remember that shelf was standing above the side of the door [sic] and the bottle fell down, and the pieces were found on the left of the girl's head. It would be exactly where they would be found if they fell off the shelf. The very fact of this paraffin falling in the scuffle that ensued made the man suddenly think: 'I will try to burn the body.' So he at once went to get the paraffin out of the lamp, and in his hurry neglected to hide the bottle.

It will be seen that the main body of this theory rested on five suppositions: that Rose Harsent herself had a bottle with a Gardiner label on it, that she had used up all the camphorated oil it had contained, that she was a slovenly servant and had refilled the bottle with paraffin, and that she kept the bottle on the shelf in the kitchen. (There are other suppositions implicit in the theory which are dealt with later.) None of these limbs was yet established fact, and Wild had not cross-examined Mrs Crisp, Rose Harsent's employer, who had been a prosecution witness, to try and establish them as facts. Perhaps he believed, as he was entitled to do if he so wished, that it was too dangerous to the interests of his client to ask about them, and safer to rely on theory. In the Wallace case Oliver had refused to adopt this course. He had cross-examined the secretary of the chess club (pp. 137-8) so that he had positive facts on which to address the jury. Wild recognized that he had not and that his argument was therefore based on speculation. He finished this passage of his speech by saying:

That is only a theory, but I submit that my theory is as entitled to consideration as the theory of my learned friend, and I have the privilege, if I can put before you a theory which is possible, it is entitled to consideration, but my learned friend's theories are such that they must be right, and there must be no mistake, because, as I have said, this is a question of life and death.

Nothing dignifies an argument so much as placing the opposing view in immediate and unfavourable contrast to it. Cicero's example is the most apposite. A simple statement like, 'my witnesses are honourable men', is powerful enough, but if the speaker can go on to say, 'but those called on the other side have unsavoury reputations', he doubles the worth of the honourable at the expense of the unsavoury.

Dickens did not challenge the evidence given by Mrs Gardiner and Mrs Walker in cross-examination so that Wild's first, and most important, supposition became established fact. Perhaps it was with the feeling that his theory had been enhanced in the eyes of the jury by Dickens's failure to question a part of it that Wild's final speech on this issue was hardly more than a catalogue of fact.

WILD: Not only did Mrs Gardiner give a reasonable account how the bottle got into the possession of Rose Harsent, but Mrs Walker told you that Rose Harsent was suffering from a severe cold shortly before Easter, and she said that Mrs Gardiner gave her camphorated oil in a bottle ... Mrs Gardiner said: 'I gave her a bottle, I do not know which.' Mrs Walker said: 'She had a bottle, and she rubbed oil on her chest.' That disposes of the most serious point in the whole case. When you are asked to believe that Gardiner was such a fool as to take a bottle with six ounces of paraffin in and bearing his name upon it, you will probably say that the bottle story goes.

Some advocates believe that this was a dangerously cavalier way of dealing with this issue. Others advance the view that there is no more effective method of denigrating the arguments of one's opponents than by appearing to pay them no attention. Wild could count on the fact that the jury had heard one of Dickens's theories undermined by the evidence of Mrs Gardiner and Mrs Walker, and would therefore be less likely to pay any attention to any other suggestions he might offer as alternatives. One thing was certain. Dickens could not afford, any more than any advocate in similar circumstances can afford, to ignore scoring points made by an opponent. So he started with a concession.

DICKENS: With regard to that [the medicine bottle] it may be that they are perfectly right in what they say that some months before a bottle had been given with camphorated oil to Rose Harsent. The bottle found there undoubtedly came from Gardiner's house.

This is not very well expressed, for it can be taken to concede that *the* bottle was the one given by Mrs Gardiner to Rose Harsent and not that *a* bottle had been given. However, there were other facts with which Wild had not dealt at all from which Dickens could make himself clear. One was that the burning had been largely confined to the girl's body and the nightclothes she wore. There was only a little burning of the surrounding floor. Dickens went on:

The suggestion of my learned friend is that the girl had placed the bottle in an out-of-the-way place and the door banging to [this is not what Wild said] the bottle was knocked down, and the paraffin spilt over the floor. How the murderer picked up the paraffin to set the body alight I do not know. It is for you to say whether the suggestion is a reasonable one. The suggestion on the other side is that the murderer, whoever he was . . .

It is incredible that Dickens should have continued with the words, 'the murderer, whoever he was', when his whole case was that Gardiner was the murderer. An advocate who is seeking to persuade a tribunal to adopt one set of facts in preference to another cannot afford to use words which imply that he thinks the other set of facts a reasonable one.

The extract is important for another reason. It contains one of the crucial points in the case which was never made clear to the jury. The agreed facts at this stage, so far as facts can be agreed in a criminal case, included these: that the murderer had tried to get the paraffin out of the lamp and had failed; that the only other known place from which he could have got paraffin was the medicine bottle, and that the murderer had set light to the body with paraffin. If Wild's theory was right and the medicine bottle had smashed on the floor spilling the paraffin, one vital question remained to be answered: where had the paraffin come from to set light to the body?

The murderer might have had another bottle of paraffin in his pocket and used that. It sounds very unlikely but it is possible. But what makes Wild's theory quite impossible is that there was no burning of the floor under the shelf. Since there was no burning of the floor under the shelf, and since if the bottle had broken there so close to the body there would have been burning, the bottle must have been broken when it was held above or on the body so that the paraffin all ran down over it. Dickens never made this point to the jury. The reference to it in the sentence, 'How the murderer picked up the paraffin to set the body alight I do not know', is put in a number of sentences all of equal weight and of outward equal importance. Neither the sequence of words, nor the thoughts preceding it point its significance. They do not even make the point clear, for there is no reference to the places which were burnt and those which were not.

However, there are other points for Dickens to make. If the jury can be persuaded to accept the plain facts instead of being hypnotized by Wild's speculations, those facts show that the body was burnt with paraffin from the bottle bearing a label prescribing doses of camphorated oil for the Gardiner children. If the murderer did not take the bottle to the house himself, how did he know that the bottle contained paraffin with which to burn the body and not camphorated oil with which to cure a cold? Dickens dealt with the point like this:

Supposing that the bottle was on the dresser [it was to be supposed that the bottle was on a shelf, not a dresser]: supposing that the girl for some extraordinary reason had kept paraffin oil in that bottle. It is clear it was so tightly corked that you could not get the cork out, and therefore the alternative suggestion must be that the unknown murderer, coming in, made up his mind to burn the body, saw the medicine bottle on the dresser, so many doses to be taken a day, jumped to the conclusion at once, by a sort of intuitive instinct, that it must be a paraffin bottle, and broke it to get the paraffin out.

A Suffolk jury of 1903 can be forgiven if it failed to grasp the essential ingredients of an argument which did not distinguish for it the points which Dickens was seeking to make. They were asked to assimilate an argument which was without order and which did not highlight the points they were asked to approve or contrast those of which they were asked to disapprove. How much easier for them if the speech had read like this:

You are asked to suppose that the bottle was kept on the shelf. There is no evidence that it was. Mrs Crisp, the lady of the house, who might have been asked whether such a bottle was kept on the shelf was not asked if that was so. However, let us suppose for the moment that it was. You are then asked to suppose that Rose Harsent was a 'slovenly servant' and had put paraffin in the bottle. There is no evidence that she was, or that she kept paraffin in such a bottle. Again, Mrs Crisp, who might have been expected to know if her servant was slovenly and given to such habits, was not asked if it was so. However, let us suppose for the moment that it was so. The evidence is that the bottle was so tightly corked that you could not get the cork out. Do you believe that a slovenly servant, keeping that bottle to fill the lamp or make up the fire, would do that?

This may be the counsel of perfection, but it is perfection in everything that he does that the advocate must seek. It really requires that he should proceed in argument before a jury by logical stages. There are no short cuts. The jury must be shown how the advocate's arguments fit into the facts and how they controvert the counter-argument. It is only after an exposition of this kind that Dickens's final point can be driven home. In the re-written speech it might read like this:

If it was not Gardiner who brought the bottle to the house, the only possible alternative is that the unknown murderer saw the medicine bottle and broke it so that he could use the contents to burn the body. But it was a medicine bottle. The label said, 'so many doses a day'. How could Mr Wild's unknown murderer have known it contained paraffin, the very thing he wanted to burn the body? What intuitive instinct led him to know it was paraffin and not camphorated oil in that bottle?

It is obvious that a close scrutiny of fact must be an accurate one. The advocate cannot afford to misstate the evidence. If he does his opponent cannot afford to leave the misstatement uncorrected. In his opening Wild had said, '... [the pieces of the bottle] were found on the left of the girl's head. It would be exactly where they would be found if they fell off the shelf'. This was not correct; only some of the pieces were found there. The most important piece, the neck and the part bearing the label, was found by the fireplace, nowhere near the girl's head. Dickens did not correct Wild's inaccuracy. It allowed the jury to believe Wild's statement to be an accurate one, and Dickens's unnecessary comment in his opening, that it had 'rolled there', a proper inference to be drawn from the facts.

Nothing is easier than to ignore the pressures of engagement in a trial and to be wiser after the verdict has been delivered than either of the advocates actually engaged in the case, but there was another point which Dickens could and should have made at this stage in the case. Wild had asserted that his unknown murderer might have thought of burning the body when the bottle fell on the floor. Why should he? The murderer was not trying to destroy the evidence of the murder. Harsent's throat had been cut. It was the lower part of the body which had been burnt. The burning was an attempt to hide the fact that she was pregnant. Who, other than the man who was responsible for her condition, would be anxious to conceal that? Who, other than the defendant, had had his name associated with hers? Dickens did not make this point in this form at any stage in his final speech. The nearest he got to it was in an earlier part of his speech when he listed the ten conditions the unknown murderer would have to fulfil if that murderer was not Gardiner.

DICKENS: First, he must have written extremely like the accused; he wears shoes invariably with bars like the accused; he must have walked backwards and forwards on this night from the accused's house to Providence House and back; he had a knife of the same character as the accused had – a knife with which this crime must have been committed; he is brought into connection in a marvellous way with the missing bottle, as we see undoubtedly the accused was; he is a man who uses buff envelopes, as we see the accused had; he must have told her to put a light where it could be seen, as was undoubtedly the case with the accused; he must have been looking out for the signal at about nine o'clock that night as the accused was looking out; and he must have been a man in such a position that it was imperative upon him to conceal his shame.

To summarize the points of argument before dealing with them individually is the simplest and one of the most effective ways of bringing their cumulative force home to any tribunal. However, it is foolish to think that a jury could retain the last one on the list in their minds so that they would automatically slot it into place when Dickens dealt with the facts to which it related. How much more weight is added to Dickens's speech if, when he is dealing with the attempt to burn the body, he reminds the jury that it was only to Gardiner that the burning of the body was 'imperative'.

The reader may by now be unpleasantly aware of how much time, and how many juries, will be exhausted by a full and proper exploration of the facts of any case. The advocate must remember that he does not double the strength of his argument merely by doubling its length. Instead he should remember Clemenceau's compliment to the English advocate: 'I see you pay your lawyers not according to the length but according to the quality of their speeches.'

To acquire quality needs practice. The rules and their exceptions are easy enough to state. They are more difficult to put into practice, and it takes considerable time before the advocate has developed the automatic mental reflexes which allow him the freedom to cultivate style. To begin with there are so many contradictions. He must be convincing in his manner and with his material: yet concessions, hesitations, and even self-corrections can lend an air of truth to his subsequent statements. There must be variety in his language and in the tone of his voice, he must avoid monotony like the plague: yet repetition of a word or phrase can be a valuable weapon. One part of a case may demand a rapid summary of fact, and another require him to dwell at length on a single point. His remarks must have relevance to the facts before the court: yet, a healthy digression may enable him to return to the issues with renewed force. Two of these endless contradictions are worth noting. He must be capable of simple, plain, and direct speech, but he must learn how to sharpen its effect by deliberate interruption and by ornamentation.

The quotation from the speech of Fearnley Whittingstall in the previous chapter,

When one thinks of trust funds one thinks of widows and orphans and the wistful savings of a vanished hand,

was inessential to his argument, but it was an essential part of his speech. In it the impact of the nouns, 'widows', 'orphans', 'wistful savings' is increased by expressing it as 'widows *and* orphans *and* the wistful savings', simply by delaying the mind, easing and directing it from noun to noun.

The second, the need for ornamentation, is sometimes misunderstood. Ornamented speech does not have as its object mere display, which flatters the speaker, but an enhancing of the speaker's purpose, which flatters his speech. To say, for instance, that a man has been 'struck by old age', is to recite fact. To say, as Virgil did, that he has been 'struck by sad old age', is to make the words live. It gives sharp reality to the condition that is described, it maintains the interest of the audience in what is being said, and it makes its retention by them much more likely. The chief criticism of the speeches of the past is that such embellishments were overdone. It was for this reason that Charles Phillips was known in England as 'Councillor O'Garnish'. An

English opponent once triumphed over him after describing one of Phillips's speeches to a jury as 'the horticultural address of my learned friend'.

The modern advocate must practise moderation if not in all things, then at least in the use of these verbal condiments. Alliterations may run as happily from his tongue as they did for Phillips opening a libel case in 1830:

Who shall estimate the cost of a priceless reputation – that impress which gives this dross its currency, without which we stand despised, debased, depreciated . . .

but he must not play the same trick twice in one speech. Similarly, the use of hyperbole, metaphor, simile, inversions of language, parallels, and allegories should be carefully controlled. Arguments should seem to rely more on force of logic than extravagancies of language.

Part of the art of advocacy lies in its concealment. Even where he follows Aristotle's order in his speech of Exordium or Introduction, Statement (of the issues before the court), Proof (being the arguments in support of one's own case and the refutation of one's opponent's), and the Peroration, there should be no obvious display of these divisions since it serves only to interrupt the sequence of thought the advocate should have induced in his audience. It may be to avoid this particular pitfall that many advocates seem to follow no order at all. It may be also that they seek to avoid the controversy as to which part of their speech should be devoted to their most important point. Two schools of thought exist. One demands it should be put first. This assumes such a lack of skill in the advocate that his audience is liable to be asleep within five minutes of starting. The other advises it should be put last on the basis that at least the jury will carry that point with them into the jury room. This assumes that all the other points have been put so clumsily that none but the last will be remembered. Since both are arguments of defeatism, both should be ignored. If the advocate really feels he has only one point worth making then he should make it quickly and cleanly and sit down.

If he does so he will deny himself many pleasures, principally that of delivering himself of a peroration. Modern advocates tend to eschew the use of this peculiarly forensic extravaganza. Yet, until quite recently, it was possible to see counsel winding themselves up to sweep into the majestic spontaneity of their carefully prepared final onslaughts on the emotions of the jury. The peroration stood quite apart from the rest of the speech. Most Victorian advocates had it written out in longhand. As a result it is possible to take a pencil to their speeches and mark off where the peroration begins. Some, but only a few, were brief. Most, as the relative clauses piled higher and higher, were long. This is part of one from a speech of Sir Edward Clarke's delivered at the Old Bailey in 1872 when he was defending a man with the same name as himself:

CLARKE: Gentlemen, you, I know, will do your duty; but while it is part of your duty clearly and peremptorily to pronounce guilt where guilt is well established, it is the highest and best privilege that you have to scout from the judgment seat the perjured witness, and to send out the innocent man with an unchallengeable verdict of Not Guilty to hold up before his fellows. Judge in this case as you would be judged. Use diligence, discretion, and discrimination in dealing with the verdict; and I do hope confidently – I trust it is not the mere advocate's feeling that speaks in my words at this moment – that Clarke may go out from this court, not discharged because a jury could not agree; not with some bastard verdict of not proven to hang round his neck for the rest of his life, the irremovable stigma of suspicion of crime; but with the straightforward, honest Not Guilty that sends him back to his friends an honoured man; that sends him back, for the rest of his life, to enjoy the love, obedience, honour, troops of friends, and all that should accompany old age; to leave his children when he goes an heirloom richer than wealth can purchase, grander than power can create – the splendid heritage of an unsullied name.

Finally, the advocate should not only seek to persuade his audience, he should also seek to please himself. He must not get these priorities in the wrong order. The advocate who performs an intellectual war dance of triumph in celebration of his own speeches while he is delivering them is unlikely to persuade anyone to adopt any view except to convince them of his own overweening conceit. But if by a speech which is finely wrought and well delivered he can arouse the interest and secure the minds of his audience then he will secure a pleasure and satisfaction for himself which can be found in no other occupation.

Chapter 12

Verdict

In a criminal trial where it is alleged that a publication is obscene, the jury will be instructed by the Judge that they have to decide whether the publication has a tendency to affect its likely audience so as to corrupt and deprave it. The judgement of the jury must focus entirely on this question of the effect of the publication on its actual or supposed audience. It would be tempting to apply the same or at least a similar test to the advocate in court, for the effectiveness of an advocate can in a sense only be judged by the verdict which he gains from his audience at the end of a case. Those who are not admirers of our be-wigged advocates would probably succumb to the temptation and take the parallel even further. But one cannot judge the advocate by the result in a single case. One cannot judge the advocate by studying a line of cases of a particular kind or in a particular court. Still less can one judge him by studying the cases of particular advocates. Any reliable verdict on the advocate – which is the purpose of this chapter – can only be reached by examining the court system in which the advocate operates and the freedom that system gives him. The freedom goes far beyond that which is allowed to an advocate appearing in any other court system and there are few curbs contained within it. If this is not already apparent, then a simple example will demonstrate it.

A few years ago a man was arrested on the business premises of an auctioneer on the viewing day before an auction of valuable jewellery. On the man was found an imitation diamond ring. On view was an identical ring but with a real diamond. The man had not done anything towards switching the rings, but since – the prosecution said – he was obviously waiting for the opportunity to do so, he was taken to the police station and charged with attempted theft. When he appeared in court his 'clever lawyer', as the auctioneer described him, obtained the man's acquittal by arguing that acts done in the preparation of the commission of crime are not attempts to commit a crime. Therefore the charge was not the appropriate one.

For the auctioneer, and perhaps most laymen, the defending lawyer had become the villain of the piece. For them the moral of the tale was clear: yet another example of disreputable pleading on the part of a skilful advocate had brought about yet another miscarriage of justice. Some of the auctioneer's audience might have added a second villain, the prosecuting advocate who failed to prefer the correct charge of being found in a warehouse for an unlawful purpose. Some in the audience would have gone further and attacked the Judge for failing to circumvent the wiles of the defending advocate and remedying the deficiencies of the prosecuting advocate by suggesting that a new charge should be preferred against the defendant.

In the last thirty years, since the first edition of this book was published, there has been an immeasurable shift in public opinion about the service which the advocates and the courts in which they operate give to the public. No reader will have got this far without being impressed – possibly disagreeably impressed – by the dominance of the advocate in our common-law, adversarial system. As already pointed out, the Judge presides rather like a referee on the football field, blowing his whistle from time to time, but not actually kicking the ball. The system under which their roles have developed has evolved over the last 600 years. Many will now say that the system has solidified. In the example of the auctioneer, why should the Magistrate trying the case not have amended the charge so that the defendant could be convicted? The defendant was plainly engaged on a dishonest course of conduct. His intentions were so plain that it was likely he had done it before. He obviously deserved to be convicted, and the courts exist to do justice. The Judge should have intervened. The public requires protection against such men. Why should the courts adhere to an old system, letting the advocates play their intricate games, while the public suffers?

In the criminal courts, Lord Chief Justice Taylor has stated the present position as recently as May 1992:

Trials on indictment in England and Wales are adversarial. The prosecution decide who to charge and with what offences. They present the case for the Crown. Counsel for the defence presents the case for the accused. The judge is there to hold the ring impartially and to direct the jury on the law.

This summary is undoubtedly correct. It applies in both criminal and civil courts. And if our system is to continue to require the Judge to maintain a lofty, detached and ostensibly impartial stance, then the two squabbling advocates must be permitted to act in the way the first eleven chapters of this book show. Is this wise? Is there no improved approach which has surfaced over the last 600 years? In the medical field leeches were employed over a period of about a thousand years. They have now been discarded. Research had shown that better methods of treatment were available. Research should be capable of showing the direction in which we should go in the legal field.

There is some research, but it is not broadly based. What does exist is confined to corners, and not the core of our legal system. This is the Anglo-Saxon and Celtic approach: we show ourselves to be pragmatists and not philosophers. A problem emerges, a scandal erupts. A Bill is drafted and presented to Parliament. The Bill becomes law and the scandal subsides. The Government of the day congratulates itself on taking firm and effective measures, while the Opposition of the day congratulates itself on goading the Government into taking firm and effective measures. The media correctly believe they have extracted every inch of linage they can from the subject and until the next scandal they, and the public, evince no particular interest in the subject. So, for instance, in relation to childcare, an enormous stride has been taken which affects how the courts approach and deal with cases touching the welfare of children, and necessarily affecting the way in which the Judges and the advocates for contending parties share this power over the destiny of the child. No one could disapprove of this improvement. A moment's thought will show that the change needed to be taken recognizing the basic principle that children need protection. A further moment's thought will show that parallel, if not identical, legislation is essential for all those who similarly need protection: the mentally disturbed and a significant proportion of the aged. The legislation was put through Parliament without reference to these two groups. The problem, the scandal did not affect them. So they must wait until some scandal does.

The ability of the courts and advocates to resolve or alleviate the problems of the public should not depend on such chance incursions by Parliament into such fields. There should be an identified overall concept of what it is that we in the courts should do. At the moment there is none. One division of the courts acts in one way, and another in a way which is totally at odds with the first.

In some types of case the courts do possess interventionist and inquisitorial powers. The Companies Court has two functions,

> ... one to decide rights between the parties and the other to administer estates. In administering estates, whether in Chancery, bankruptcy or the winding-up of companies, the Court itself by its officer often finds itself in the position of a quasi-litigant.

More recently (1991) Mr Justice Millet described the powers given to the Court by section 236 of the Companies Act 1986 with these words:

> The process is an extraordinary and secret mode of obtaining information required for the proper conduct of the winding-up (effectively the death and interment of a company). The section – earlier versions of which stretch back to the middle of the last century – has been described as conferring an extraordinary power of an inquisitorial nature and even compared (not, I think, favourably) to the Star chamber ... The Court's powers under the section are backed by powers of arrest and seizure. The power is potentially oppressive and is exercised with caution, especially against persons who are not former officers of the company.

The powers are exercised by registered insolvency practitioners appointed and supervised by the Court. They can summon and interview witnesses, requiring them to answer questions and produce documents. As the Judge went on to say in the same case from which this citation is drawn, given the powers exercised directly or indirectly by the Court, it is not surprising that requests for information and/or documents made by the liquidators are instantly complied with by 'responsible people' for they know perfectly well what would happen to them if they did not:

they would be cited for contempt of court and would be liable to a fine and/or imprisonment.

Similarly, though in a very different manner and not with the same powers, the courts are now required to intervene in all cases involving the welfare of children. The parties seeking or disputing the custody, care or control of children still appear before the court still fighting the age-old conflicts between mothers and fathers and others claiming the body of the child by claiming already to have secured the heart of the child. But under the Children Act 1989 a positive duty is imposed on the courts to take their own course independent of the wishes of the squabbling parents and/or local authority. In every case of any complexity a 'directions hearing' must take place. One text book on the subject describes this as enabling the court, *'to take control* of the proceedings by giving directions about those steps which must be taken by the parties before the substantive hearing . . .'

The italicized phrase is crucial. The court is given power to set a timetable for the proceedings, to appoint a guardian *ad litem* (that is, someone whose sole task is to consider and represent the interests of the child) and to order the submission of evidence, including expert reports and welfare reports. The court is in fact required to set a timetable for the preparation, hearing and disposal of the case. To facilitate the operation of such orders, a uniform procedure has for the first time been introduced for the handling of such cases in the Magistrates' Courts and County Courts, and power given to transfer cases from any one court to any other in order to speed their disposal. Section 1(2) of the Act requires the court to have regard to the principle that any delay in determining a question in relation to the upbringing of a child is likely to prejudice its welfare. These are healthy and positive reforms. They introduce a necessary urgency, and provide sharp teeth to the courts to prevent delay, provided the courts themselves are capable of dealing with the volume of work which will be generated by the Act.

It will be realized that a court that exercises these new powers to the full will be cutting down the freedoms previously allowed to the advocate practising in this field. In one very significant respect the Act goes further, by restricting, except under supervision, the preparation which an advocate can undertake in such cases.

No examination of a child by an expert is permitted except with the leave of the court. An application for leave to conduct such an examination must be made to the court and must be served on all the parties to the case, so no longer may an attack based on some medical or psychiatric basis be prepared in secret. This is a shift affecting one of the fundamental principles on which court procedure has previously been conducted.

Few will quarrel with these changes, and most will applaud them. These proceedings involve children: their present health and their future destiny. The interests of the child should be paramount. The interests of the parents should be protected and respected, of course, but by hiring a pair (one on each side) of hack lawyers they should not be permitted to fight out their own bitter battles over the bodies of their innocent offspring. If at the same time it cuts the lawyer down to size, so much the better.

The public, if asked, would be likely to demand similar reforms in other fields. They might say, since the Commercial Courts have in matters of insolvency taken hold of cases by the scruff of the neck for over 100 years, and since the Family Courts can now do it, why can it not be done in the other courts dealing with civil disputes? Better still, why can it not be done in the courts dealing with criminal cases? With a fair wind and good judges we might be able to get rid of these expensive lawyers altogether. Alas, this is a Utopian dream, though some steps have been taken which appear to point towards this end, on the criminal side through the new procedures adopted following the setting up of the Serious Fraud Office and on the civil side through the Small Claims Court. In fact, neither provides more than a glimpse of the direction that law reforms should take.

It is the unpalatable and intolerable number of miscarriages of justice in respect of convictions recorded in the criminal courts that has attracted most public attention and aroused the greatest public disquiet in recent times. Even though the most notorious of these involved impropriety by the police or services associated with the police, the police have shown themselves most vociferous in their complaints. That made in October 1992 by the Chief Constable of the Thames Valley Police is typical:

People depend on our whole system of justice to support them. Many feel it is letting them down. It has evolved over centuries, but public confidence is decreasing because it is now incapable of doing the job it should be doing ... Old-fashioned procedures and practices leave our legal system backward-looking and lacking any clear direction for the future. The system, despite many good points, tends to serve the needs of its rules and rituals rather than the people - victims, witnesses, defendants and jurors - caught up in it. It needs a clear vision for the future, and this it does not have ... getting at the truth is not even a part of our present system. Instead, it is a game, an adversarial combat, a contest between lawyers doing their very best for their clients, be they prosecution or defence. They are required to obtain a conviction or an acquittal, not to discover the truth ... The whole system lacks a clear sense of direction. And it may be that we need an inquisitorial justice system in which everyone works together to establish the truth. Because if the truth is determined, then the question of innocence or guilt will follow naturally.

Sir Peter Imbert, formerly Commissioner of the Metropolitan Police, is less tentative in his recommendations, wishing to see reform of the entire British justice system from the adversarial to an inquisitorial pre-trial procedure along French lines.

Court room drama is exciting stuff, but the opposing Counsel's gladiatorial content, their verbal ability to play on jurors' minds, sometimes amounts to thespian trickery.

The impression created by the steady stream of such criticisms, more appropriate to the activities of Rumpole of the Bailey than to any living advocate practising in the Central Criminal Court, is that there is no virtue left in the basic principles of our common-law system. For reasons which lie outside the scope of this book, that impression is wholly wrong save to the extent that the judiciary should be given more power to intervene in criminal trials in order to direct and control the course that they take. The arguments in favour of this step being taken are now overwhelmingly strong and are recognized in the new procedures introduced following the creation of the Serious Fraud Office.

In cases of serious fraud the trial Judge combines the traditional role of referee with that of physiotherapist to both teams, prosecution and defence. The 1987 Act that created the Serious Fraud Office and the new procedures allows him in preparatory hearings before the trial begins to require the prosecution *and* defence to disclose their cases to each other and to him and to prepare their evidence in such form as to:

identify issues which are likely to be material to the verdict of the jury, assist the jury's comprehension of such issues, expedite the proceedings, and assist the Judge's management of the trial.

In order to achieve these plain and plainly sensible purposes, the trial Judge is given power to force both sides to agree facts and to admit documents and the truth of the contents of the documents. The Court of Appeal has already said that 'Judges must not be reluctant to exercise their power in order to secure a manageable and therefore fair trial.' They have said that the approach of the Judge should be 'robust'. This, together with separate requirements imposed by other Acts of Parliament to give advance notice of, for instance, alibis and reliance on expert evidence, means that the prosecution/police complaints about 'ambush' defences taking the prosecution unfairly by surprise and distorting the criminal trial process cannot be sustained.

But – and it is a substantial but – even the provisions of this 1987 Act do not go far enough. These new powers of the Judge exist only during the preparatory hearings. They do not continue into the trial in front of the jury. The preparatory hearings are held in private, which enables the Judge and the advocates to speak 'robustly'. Once the jury are sworn and the public admitted the old rules apply, the Judge's powers wither and his ability to intervene in the case is just as limited as it was previously. The public may ask why this should be. The public may further ask why this line should be drawn between what happens between Judge and advocate in private and what happens between Judge and advocate in public. After all, the course of any trial to which this legislation applies is affected by the pre-trial rulings made by the Judge as well as the events occurring during the trial itself.

The answer to these questions lies once again in the piecemeal approach of Parliament to virtually every aspect of reform of the courts and court procedure. This is exemplified by the response to the problem of long and complex fraud cases. A part of the Criminal Justice Act 1987 was assigned to deal with that problem without attempting to examine the whole process of a fraud trial. So the Act created the new department called the Serious Fraud Office and gave it new and extensive powers. The Act provided an accelerated procedure to bypass the preliminary hearing in the Magistrates' Court in order to eliminate delay. In the preparatory hearing procedure the Act gave the powers briefly described to the trial Judge to get his teeth into the case and if need be into the advocates. The Act then totally failed to ensure that there were courts available to try the cases and totally failed to ensure that the trial Judge had the ability to keep his teeth embedded in the case and if need be the advocates. If curbs on the power of the advocate are needed, which may be open to question, then this would be an ideal opportunity to impose them. In fact what is needed is a check on the advocates' work while the trial is in progress. This can be done if power is given to a trial Judge fully to monitor the powers exercised by the advocates and to intervene in the conduct of trials if and when he sees it is desirable in the interests of justice. That should include an untrammelled power to ask questions of witnesses called by the two sides, a power to call witnesses himself and a power to call for documents to be produced. This would give the Judge an interventionist role which in the criminal courts he does not at present play. Some commentators would call this an inquisitorial role. It is a role which Judges in the civil courts and in tribunals are increasingly playing.

The best example is provided by the Small Claims Courts. These were established in 1973 as an additional arm of the County Court. They deal with all claims, save for cases of exceptional difficulty, for sums less than £1,000. They are a laymen's, as opposed to a lawyers', court. The sittings are in private, there are no rules of evidence, evidence is not given on oath, and the court sits anywhere at any time convenient to the parties. There is not a wig in sight. There is no stuff and nonsense. They are immensely successful, except that there are not enough Judges to dispose of the cases within an acceptable time. The Judges are the former Registrars of the County but are now called District Judges and arbitrators, while the cases are called 'arbitrations' to add to or at least continue the informality and flexibility which are the hallmarks of the proceedings. The costs of administering the system and the costs to the parties, including the costs which can be ordered to be paid by an unsuccessful litigant, are minimal. About 50,000 claims are disposed of each year, which is twice the number of actions tried in the civil High Court of Justice. The system has more than shown its worth. It is now seen as an important adjunct to the more formal trial system applied in the County Court. A higher claims limit ought to be set and greater financial resources allocated to it so that it can function as efficiently as it has shown it can.

The proceedings, however, remain adversarial in exactly the same way that proceedings in our criminal and other civil courts are adversarial. Party faces party, one pitted in combat against the other, no matter that a different name is given to the proceedings. As the Court of Appeal has said, it is fundamental to such a system that each party is entitled to present his own evidence and that the opposing party is entitled to test its accuracy in cross-examination. So, a Registrar who attempted to interfere in this basic right by insisting that questions in cross-examination should only be put to the witness through him was slapped on the wrist by the Court of Appeal. In October 1992 the Lord Chancellor issued fresh rules which say that:

the arbitrator may adopt any method of procedure which he may consider to be fair and which gives each party an equal opportunity to have his case presented; having considered the circumstances of the parties and whether (or to what extent) they are represented, the arbitrator –
(a) may assist a party by putting questions to the witnesses and the other party . . . ;

This gives the greenest of green lights to a District Judge sitting wearing the artificial hat of arbitrator to become an interventionist and adopt an inquisitorial role. The perceptive reader will have noticed that the rule is carefully permissive, it uses the word 'may' rather than the word 'shall'. It may therefore be thought to be pretty wishy-washy. It certainly cannot be identified as a clarion call to the troops in the camp marked inquisitorial system. But it points unmistakably to the route that they should take, provided that those who are going to be given inquisitorial powers like these are properly trained in their use. The organization Justice, while promoting the award of such powers, has correctly noted that 'such a change in procedure must be accompanied by better and more intensive training' for those who are to exercise them. It is a sad fact that those who show themselves most skilled in asking questions when carrying the banner of a client are not the best at asking questions when clad in only the white sheet marked 'the search for justice'.

The perceptive reader will also have noticed that the arbitrator is not required to obtain any consent from a party or the advocate to a party before embarking on an exercise of his powers under these new rules. The drafting of the rules makes clear the need of the arbitrator to demonstrate that a proper balance is maintained between the parties. It contains an implied compliment to the advocate: that his appearance on one side against an unrepresented opponent puts his client in a more favourable position. So it should. He is not concerned about balance when he is about his business as an advocate. Even under the Children's Act to which reference has already been made, although his heart may bleed for the child about whom the parents are destructively fighting like alley-cats, his mind and his tongue must be engaged solely to advance the interests of his client.

So the changes in the court system which have been noted, even when circumscribing his activities, carry with them no valid criticism of the advocate in court. If confined in this way, the 'verdict' on the advocate should not be an adverse one. But any verdict on any aspect of human activity cannot sensibly be based solely on his visible, public performances. Nor can any verdict ignore changing standards and attitudes. How far has the advocate discharged his responsibility outside court to influence legislation or to mould public opinion so that the systems under which he operates reflect the needs of changing values? Better than anyone else he knows what can be done, what should be done and how it should be done. He has a uniquely experienced and authoritative voice. Outside the court he has no client to circumscribe his actions or the expression of his views. Has his voice been heard?

The answer is: only faintly, and by the public hardly at all. Judged in this way, if the verdict was to be given by the public, it would probably be an adverse one. What is visible to them is a seemingly endless squabble between the two most recognized groups of lawyers, the barristers and solicitors, about rights of audience, the right to act as advocates in a court system in which there is a decreasing amount of work, or an increasingly bitter battle between the two groups and the Lord Chancellor about how, when and to what extent each will be paid under the Legal Aid Act. What is not visible to them is the patient, endless and, most surprisingly, unpaid work undertaken for example by the Criminal Bar Association which led to the introduction of preparatory hearings, by the Family Bar Association and its sister committee from the Law Society which led to the drafting of the Children's Act, and the work by members of both groups on Rules Committees which has enabled the Lord Chancellor to introduce, for instance, the new rules for small-claim arbitrations referred to above. This work has been supported, and sometimes led, by members of both groups of advocates acting through more visible bodies like Justice, the Legal Action Group and others.

But they have failed dismally in at least two areas. They have consistently failed to force the Lord Chancellor to adopt his proper role in administering the provision of legal aid to the public. They have consistently failed to force the Lord Chancellor to adopt his proper role in ensuring that an effective system of justice is provided by the court system. These twin roles, and the powers that are associated with them, come to the Lord Chancellor and his department from different sources: the first from the Legal Aid and Advice Act of 1949 and succeeding statutes, and the latter by historical accident, since he is the senior Law Lord in the country and presides over the Judicial Committee of the House of Lords, which acts as the Supreme Court of the United Kingdom. The roles do not conflict with one another. The better administered the legal-aid system the better served are the courts and vice versa. The Lord Chancellor and his department should be the champions of both. They are not. Their decisions should be based on principle and not on financial stratagem. They are not. The advocate has failed to mobilize public opinion against what is increasingly seen as an abdication by the Lord Chancellor of his true roles to unremitting financial constraints from the Treasury. As a result, the public have become puppets on financial strings pulled by the Treasury and unprotected by those who should be their guardian.

The 1949 Act, together with Acts covering education, health and housing, was one of the legislative lamps by which all citizens were to have the path to new rights, freedoms and opportunities lit for the first time. For centuries it had been recognized by the courts that all citizens were equal before them. But to be equal before them, one has first to be able to get into them. Now they would be able to do so. In their book *A Strategy for Justice: Publicly Funded Legal Services in the 1990s*, the Legal Action Group observe:

In 1949, the Lord Chancellor's Department confidently asserted the purpose of legal aid to be that, 'No one will be financially unable to prosecute a just and reasonable claim or defend a legal right.' By the time of its 1991 eligibility review, its tone had changed: legal aid had become '*a conditional financial support*, provided by the tax-payer, for individuals whose financial circumstances would prevent them from taking or defending proceedings without assistance with their costs'. [The italics are mine.]

The aim of the 1949 Act was to replace a system, if it could be called that, based equally on chance and charity, with one based on civil right. Sir Seton Pollock, then Secretary to the solicitors' Law Society, identified the three basic principles built into the Act:

(i) Irrespective of means there must be *access to all courts* within the jurisdiction and the legal services required to make the right effective . . .
(ii) those availing themselves of such facilities should be required to pay towards the cost of the services received *no more than they can reasonably afford* (if anything), having regard to their actual resources;
(iii) the services provided must be of *the same standard* as apply in respect of those able to pay their own way, including the right to choose the legal adviser. [The italics are mine.]

In some areas, notably in the criminal courts, the grant of this civil right has been effective. With only a few practical limitations it can be claimed that a man accused of a criminal offence has the pick of the legal profession open to him in all the courts exercising criminal jurisdiction all the way up to the House of Lords and without being called on to pay more than he can reasonably afford.

But the Act and its successors (now the Legal Aid Act 1988) have not been equally effective in the civil courts. The original and the later Acts require an assessment to be made of the financial circumstances, income and capital, of any person seeking to bring or defend civil proceedings before a legal-aid certificate is granted. The level of 'eligibility', as it is called, was set in 1949 at such a point that in 1950, the first full year, about 80 per cent of the population qualified for legal aid on income grounds. By 1973 that proportion had shrunk to 40 per cent. It is even lower today. The percentage of certificates issued where the assisted person is not asked to make any contribution of any kind towards the cost of legal representation is now over 83 per cent, indicating that legal aid is effectively now only available to those in receipt of the lowest levels of income. The Acts have no in-built mechanism to guard against inflation. Levels of eligibility are adjusted, up or down, as and when the Lord Chancellor decides to act or is pushed into action by the Treasury. In Holland, which has a system broadly comparable with our own, eligibility levels are linked to statutory rates of maintenance and to wages in such a way that the Ministry of Justice, the supervisory body, cannot tamper with the levels of eligibility or, by protracted inaction, similarly reduce the availability of courts to the population. No attempt has been made to explain why such a simple, sensible procedure cannot be introduced in this country.

In recent years, successive Lord Chancellors have been driven into making speeches which seem to concentrate solely on the need 'to control costs', referring again and again to the 'escalating legal-aid bill'. The speeches have recently been sprinkled with such essay subjects as 'Whilst justice is priceless, it cannot be at any price', and occasionally what appear to be views wholly inimical to the right of the citizen to litigate a just cause; '... where public money is at stake, it may be necessary to try to decide whether the litigation is "absolutely necessary"' (the Lord Chancellor delivering the Royal Society of Arts lecture on 'Access to Justice', 12 July 1992), and 'It is important to ensure that people have access to legal services where they need them, *and* where recourse to the law is the best solution' (the Lord Chancellor in a speech to the Law Society conference, 24 October 1992). This is the language, the dire language, of the proponents of ADR, or 'alternative dispute resolution'. There can be no doubt that there is a powerful and, in some areas, justified move towards mediation, conciliation and arbitration of disputes. In matrimonial disputes, within or without the strict boundaries of a conventionally recognized marriage, the public generally would be likely to support any move towards avoiding the confrontational continuance in a court of the confrontational attitudes developed in a marriage. But this is not because of the costs involved in going to court. It is because it would be a reasonable and just course to take. In fact in many cases skilled mediation, conciliation and arbitration might well prove to be more expensive and less satisfactory. Even the Lord Chancellor, in the same speech, acknowledged that '... agreements reached too much under the surveillance of authority are less effective in terms of durability and party satisfaction'. At once the purity and simplicity of the principles identified by the 1949 Act become submerged in the language of consumerism: 'durability' is a word which may be applied to a pair of shoes, 'party satisfaction' are words which may be applied to Christmas crackers. They are words which should never be applied to people seeking the proper resolution of a problem which it is beyond their own capacities to solve. More important, no government minister should be heard to suggest that a government-appointed body should decide if a member of the public's litigation is absolutely necessary simply because of competing public financial demands.

Of course, the demands on the legal-aid fund are escalating. They will continue to do so. It was, and continues to be, obvious that justified claims of a kind and in a quantity unheard of ten or twenty years ago will increase in any civilized society that recognizes that the inherent right of the public to seek redress of wrongs should be reflected by decisions in the courts in their favour. At the same time expectations rise and must be matched by widening rights to protection and representation. For instance, up to 1970 and the disposal of the case against the barrister referred to on page 40, it was unheard of that a barrister should be sued for professional negligence. In the year 1990–91 over 100 claims against barristers were settled in the claimants' favour by the Bar insurance scheme. In the year 1991–2 over 400 such claims were similarly settled. The number of legal-aid certificates granted for personal injury on the grounds of negligence by doctors or hospital staff has risen over five years from 4,500 to 18,600, a fourfold increase. The number of people seeking *advice*

233

from solicitors, not representation in court, under legal aid (by way of the 'green form' scheme) over the ten-year period 1981–91 has risen from below 150,000 a year to close to 550,000 a year. In 1984 Parliament decided that people arrested on suspicion of having committed a crime were not being properly protected by the police when detained in police stations. It was decided they should be given immediate access to a solicitor. This could only be done under the legal-aid umbrella. The number of claims paid under the scheme to provide this protection has risen from below 200,000 in the first full year to over 650,000 in 1991–2. It now costs over £53 million a year. (It is right to recognize that the payment to solicitors for each visit to a police station under the scheme has fallen by 10 per cent in real terms over the same period.)

Given therefore the obvious and inevitably increasing demands on the provision of services under the legal-aid umbrella, it is equally obvious and inevitable that the bill for providing those services will rise. To complain about it serves no purpose. To claim that it must be 'curtailed' or 'contained' serves no purpose. The fact that the bill has risen as little as it has is entirely because trade associations have been obliged to develop internal complaints procedures and the Lord Chancellor insists upon the term 'courts' excluding all 'tribunals'. The advocate, whose prowess and whose shortcomings in court have been identified in this book, has signally failed to prevent this. This probably does not much matter in the first field, that of self-regulation, save that there has been less outside critical examination of the way in which such bodies work than is desirable. In the second, in the work today undertaken by public tribunals, it matters a very great deal, and in this, if in no other, the advocate bears a substantial responsibility.

In 1979 the Royal Commission on Legal Services reported that the total number of cases heard by tribunals in 1978 was six times the number of contested civil cases disposed of at trial in the High Court and the County Court. Such cases are generally much simpler and shorter than those heard in the traditional courts of law. They involve sums which frequently are trivial by comparison. But as David Tench of the Consumers' Association has correctly observed, small claims do not necessarily mean simple claims. Furthermore, the importance of the issues for the applicants to the tribunals cannot properly be measured by the amount of money at stake or the absence of legal complexity in the case. The vast majority of applicants are those least capable of presenting any case to an adjudicating body, let alone one which involves their own position. Appearing as unrepresented suppliants before such bodies as the supplementary benefit Appeals Tribunal they are thus doubly disadvantaged. They are quite unable to pay for representation. A significant proportion do not even know how to go about getting advice. This has disastrous results. In 1976 half the applicants to the supplementary benefit Appeals Tribunal out of a total of 55,000 were not represented and did not even appear at the hearing. These applicants achieved a 'success rate' of only 6 per cent. Those who were represented, even if absent from the hearing, achieved a rate of 37 per cent. The Commission concluded:

Although the extent and nature of representation is not necessarily typical of all tribunals, these figures indicate that success is related to representation ... It follows that it is desirable that every applicant before *any* tribunal should either be able adequately to present his case in person or to obtain representation. [The italics are mine.]

This recommendation followed a change of heart by the Lord Chancellor's Advisory Committee, a body created at the same time as the introduction of legal aid to assist and advise the Lord Chancellor in its administration. For many years the Committee took the view that to support the presence of lawyer advocates in tribunals would be to encourage inflexibility in the proceedings, because the lawyers would inevitably bring with them the formality associated with court procedures. The seventeenth report rejected the principle of representation for applicants in the appeals tribunals referred to in the previous paragraph on two grounds. Firstly, that the right to representation was exercised in only 0.25 per cent of cases, which is merely to say that the disinherited shall remain so. Secondly, that '... the issues almost invariably contain no matter of law, and informality is a feature of tribunal hearings to which great importance is attached because of the personal and sometimes rather intimate nature of the appellants' circumstances.' The accuracy of the first part of this statement is open to considerable doubt. The second part is simply stating that appellants would prefer to have their personal circumstances aired on the appeal in front of unknown members of a tribunal, when they would shrink from revealing those same circumstances to someone sympathetic to them.

Happily, in 1975 the Advisory Committee changed their mind and advised the Lord Chancellor that legal aid should be extended to all tribunals. Unhappily, the then Lord Chancellor, and since then his successors, have been able substantially to ignore the advice.

Some progress has been made. Advice is available through the green-form scheme from all solicitors who participate in it. Advice, and in some cases representation, is available through Law Centres and Citizens' Advice Bureaux. But the provision of all these services varies from area to area, and from office to office. The very inconsistencies highlight the need for at least a degree of uniformity. Free representation is, by variants in the legal-aid scheme, also available to convicted prisoners appealing to the Prisons' Board of Visitors, and to appellants to the Mental Health Review Tribunals and the Immigration Appeal Tribunal, all areas where special and obvious pressures can be brought to bear. The number of cases is small, less than 10,000 in any year, and the cost minimal. In the vast majority, where there is a sustained need for representation, there is no right to legal aid. The need for it is overwhelming.

In July 1989 a report was published based on research conducted by the Faculty of Law at Queen Mary College, University of London. The research concentrated on four types of tribunals, those hearing social-security appeals, immigration adjudications, industrial tribunals and mental health review tribunals, and included 'the effect of representation on the outcome of tribunal hearings'. The research established that in all four tribunals:

the presence of a representative significantly and independently increases the probability that appellants and applicants will succeed with their case at a tribunal hearing.

With representation, the probability of success was increased in the four tribunals respectively from 30 per cent to 40 per cent, from 20 per cent to 38 per cent, from 30 per cent to 48 per cent and from 20 per cent to 35 per cent. In industrial tribunals where the employer respondent is legally represented and the applicant is unrepresented the applicant succeeds in only 10 per cent of cases. The research reported:

The experience of representatives (lawyers and laypersons) is that unrepresented appellants and applicants are disadvantaged at tribunal hearings because there is an imbalance of power between the parties, because appellants and applicants do not understand the law, are unable to present their cases coherently and are unaware of the need to furnish the tribunal with evidence of the facts that they are asserting. The problem is particularly acute in industrial tribunals where cross-examination presents an impossible hurdle for applicants. Representatives do not believe that tribunals can compensate for these disadvantages. Their beliefs were largely supported by observation.

Industrial tribunals exist to redress injustice in the workplace. They are the only courts available to those who have been discriminated against on the grounds of sex or race. The Manchester industrial tribunal commented on one case involving racial discrimination:

This case highlighted the necessity for applicants in discrimination cases to be properly represented. The only way that an applicant's case can be satisfactorily presented is by a properly briefed advocate. So much of an applicant's case depends on in-depth cross-examination of the respondents' witnesses. Such a cross-examination can in most cases only be conducted by a skilled advocate.

In that case the applicant's representation was financed by the Commission for Racial Equality. They commented:

There must surely be a case for the availability of legal aid, with proper safeguards, in discrimination cases.

The Legal Action Group note that 'the need for representation is underlined by the successful use of the very limited funding from the Commission for Racial Equality and the Equal Opportunities Commission' to provide representation in selected cases: in 1991 in respect of the EOC only in 124 cases.

Industrial tribunals exist to protect employees' statutory rights. They do not have jurisdiction over an employee's contractual rights. These can only be enforced in the County Court or the

High Court, which in turn have no jurisdiction over statutory rights. Legal aid is available to a disadvantaged employee in the County Court and the High Court but not in the tribunal. Frequently, in order properly to protect the rights of a wrongly dismissed employee, it is essential to issue proceedings in both the court and the tribunal. The root of both sets of proceedings is identical – wrongful dismissal – yet representation may only be given in one place, the court and not the tribunal. The anomaly, the stupidity of such a system, the injustice of such a system, is plain. Small wonder that in the Bar's response to the Civil Justice Review in 1991 the Bar said:

> . . . legal aid is the only means by which the ordinary citizen has access to Justice. To deal piecemeal with legal aid can lead to disparity and injustice: it can lead to withdrawal or reduction of legal aid from one sector where it is urgently required because it is perceived that too much has been spent on another sector . . .

and they drew our attention to what they mildly call the 'absurdity' of the present situation as described above.

Statements of this kind by barristers and solicitors, the professional advocates, have fallen on deaf ears. For the public, they have too often seemed simply to reflect the public's existing belief that the lawyer interferes too much already, is too rapacious in his demands for payment and that this is simply another route by which the lawyer can enrich himself at public expense. The advocate has failed to capture the audience he needs to force the Lord Chancellor to correct the injustice of lack of representation. He has also failed to identify clearly the route by which the Lord Chancellor can escape the squeeze on him exerted by the dead hand of the Treasury. There is a route.

Section 11 of the Courts and Legal Services Act 1990 permits the Lord Chancellor to provide that 'there shall be no restriction on the person who may exercise rights of audience' in certain classes of case in the County Court. Until he exercises that power, only barristers and solicitors have the right to act as advocates in all hearings in the County Court. He has done so only in relation to the Small Claims Court, ordering that any person may exercise full rights of the professional advocate provided the client, the party to the proceedings, attends the hearing. This allows a claimant to be accompanied by a friend or a paid layman to advise him, support him, cross-examine for him and address the District Judge for him, and if paid, paid at a fraction of the cost of the professional lawyer.

This small step shows the direction the Lord Chancellor should take, for Part II of the same Act contemplates the granting of rights of audience to a wider body of persons and in all courts and tribunals. The Advisory Committee set up to discharge the major functions under the Acts is required to

have regard to the need for the efficient provision of legal services for persons who face special difficulties in making use of these services, including in particular special difficulties in expressing themselves or in understanding.

The Act permits, in effect, the licensing of bodies capable of representing the interests of the public in the specialist fields covered by tribunal work, bodies whose members are not necessarily academically trained as lawyers, but trained certainly by experience in the fields where they are desperately needed.

If the professional lawyers have priced themselves out of this huge field so that, save in a handful of cases, the public cannot afford to employ them as advocates, and if public money is truly not available to allow the employment of the professional advocate under the Legal Aid Act, then there is no reason now why a specialist body of advocates drawn from the Law Centres, Citizens' Advice Bureaux and Welfare Groups should not be licensed and paid to do the work in the place of the professional advocate. As in the Small Claims Court, such representation can be undertaken at a fraction of the cost of the professional lawyer. Such a course envisages the creation, at least the emergence, of a species of advocate different from those whose activities are described in this book. If the professional advocate does not like the idea, he should be told to lump it. There is a need. He does not, and the system under which he operates does not, supply the need.

The professional advocate is entitled to demand two things only. First, that the 'cab-rank rule' set out in Chapter 2 shall apply to all bodies of advocates licensed under the 1990 Act. Section 17 of the Act permits this to be done. Sub-section 3 reads:

As a general principle, the question whether a person should be granted a right of audience . . . should be determined only by reference to

239

(a) ...

(b) ...

(c) whether ... the rules of conduct [of the body providing the services] make satisfactory provision ... requiring any such member not to withhold those services –

 (i) on the ground that the nature of the case is objectionable to him or to any section of the public;

 (ii) on the ground that the conduct, opinions or beliefs of the prospective client are unacceptable to him or to any section of the public ...

This puts into Parliamentary language the cab-rank rule which the barristers have imposed on themselves. Although Section 17 contemplates a different tier of advocate, it cannot be permitted to introduce a different class of advocate, one which can dispense with the rule. In this field, if in no other, no exceptions can be permitted. It is an essential element in the protection of the interests of the public.

Second, the professional advocate is entitled to demand that this new breed of advocate at least aspires to achieve the same qualities that are identified in this book. The canvas on which they will paint will be smaller than that available to the professional advocate. That is no reason for not choosing the brush to use, the paint to apply with the same care, the same love. The English advocate appearing in the international courts, in particular in the European Court at Luxembourg and the Court of Human Rights at Strasbourg, is recognized to be the finest in the world. This should be the aim of all advocates, no matter how small the cause.